SLAVISTIC PRINTINGS
AND REPRINTINGS

edited by

C. H. VAN SCHOONEVELD

Indiana University

TEXTBOOK SERIES: 6

ANTON ČEXOV AS A MASTER OF STORY-WRITING

Essays in
Modern Soviet Literary Criticism

Translated and Edited by

LEO HULANICKI

and

DAVID SAVIGNAC

with an introduction by Leo Hulanicki

1976

MOUTON

THE HAGUE · PARIS

PG
3458
Z8
A513.

ISBN 90 279 3014 7

Printed in the Netherlands

PREFACE

In preparing this selection of essays on Čexov, the editors have been guided by a twofold purpose.

This book is intended primarily for English speaking readers who are unable to read Russian. We have endeavored to present a selection of Soviet criticism on Čexov hitherto unavailable in English and for the most part out of print in Russian. Many of the selections have been taken from works not specifically devoted to Čexov, but rather to discussions of imagery and style in general. Such material could easily escape the attention even of Russian speakers who have a particular scholarly interest in Čexov.

Our second purpose in selecting these essays has been to present a cross-section of Soviet literary criticism of the past fifteen years, a period marked by a renaissance in the study of literature as verbal art, which became possible after the partial de-Stalinization of Russian cultural life. In choosing these essays, we have been concerned with presenting the views of a wide variety of Soviet critics. These range from "veterans" of criticism as Viktor Šklovskij, a leader of the Formalist movement of the 1920s and 30s; academician V. V. Vinogradov, an eminent linguist and theoretician of artistic language; Abram Derman, a life-long Čexov scholar; Gennadij Pospelov, a representative of the sociological school of the 1920s, to a number of theoreticians active from a more recent date.

We have attempted whenever possible to present these selections without omissions, as they appeared originally. However, in order to avoid repetitions of redundant material, some editing in certain instances has been necessary. In such cases, we have made every effort to insure that neither the substance nor the context of the writer's thought has been altered. Not all of the repetitions could be eliminated since the same Čexov stories were discussed by different writers.

Throughout the book we have used the transliteration system commonly used in scholarly Slavistic studies. (See the key on page 7.) Editors' notes are always in square brackets, sometimes incorporated in the text to facilitate the task of the reader, sometimes as footnotes.

The entire translation - including quotations from Čexov - has been made by the editors. In order to reproduce faithfully the thought of the various writers, we have, in the process of translation, placed emphasis on fidelity to the original rather than on artistic effect in English.

This book is intended to serve faculty and students alike in Slavic, English, and Comparative Literature Departments, as well as the general public interested in Čexov.

It is our pleasant duty to express our debt of gratitude to Miss Jennifer McDowell and Dr. George Grant for reading and criticizing the introductory chapter of our book, and especially to Mrs. Mary Vandervoort for reading through the manuscript and for her many valuable suggestions.

The Editors

KEY TO TRANSLITERATION OF THE CYRILLIC ALPHABET

Cyrillic	Latin	Cyrillic	Latin	Cyrillic	Latin
а	a	Л	l	Ц	c
Б	b	М	m	Ч	č
В	v	Н	n	Ш	š
Г	g	о	o	Щ	šč
Д	d	П	p	Ъ	''
е	e	р	r	Ы	y
Ж	ž	с	s	Ь	'
З	z	Т	t	Э	è
И	i	у	u	Ю	ju
Й	j	Ф	f	Я	ja
К	k	х	x		

KEY TO THE PRONUNCIATION OF THE RUSSIAN TRANSLITERATION USED IN THIS BOOK

a - as in father
b - as in bed
c - ts, as in nuts
č - ch, as in cheap
d - as in dog
e - as in bed
ë - yo, as in yoke
f - as in for
g - as in get
i - ee, as in see
j - y, as in you
k - as in kind
l - as in laugh
m - as in man
n - as in now
p - as in pole
r - as in run
s - as in saw
š - sh, as in show
šč - shch, as in fresh cheese
t - as in top
u - oo, as in boot
v - as in vow
x - h, as in hand
y - as in syllable
z - as in zone
ž - z, as in azure

-ij and -yj may be pronounced as the y in sunny. The ' and the " may be ignored by the non-Russian-speaking reader.

CONTENTS

INTRODUCTION

1. HISTORICAL BACKGROUND

Problems of craftsmanship in artistic literature have again come to
the foreground of Soviet literary criticism. The appearance during
the past fifteen years of many publications devoted to discussions of
literary style, imagery, and structure contrasts sharply with criticism of the preceding quarter century, which was dominated by concern with political ideology. The nature and significance of this new
trend, however, can neither be understood nor evaluated without
tracing its origins to previous developments in which it is deeply
rooted.

A tendency to disregard the specific features of literary art pre-
vailed in Russian literary criticism in the beginning of this century.
As Roman Jakobson stated: "the literary scholars of the period could
be compared to the police, who, when planning to arrest a certain person would - just to be sure - detain everyone and everything in his
apartment as well as all the passers-by in the street." (1) What
Jakobson had in mind was that the study of literature at that time
consisted of many topics of great variety: problems of philosophy
and psychology, discussion of religious, political and social views,
discourses about writer's biographies, etc., which were only peri-
pheral to the problems of literature as art, per se. Stylistic devices were considered as secondary, decorative elements, not as
an inherent part of the artistic verbal fabric. The best example of
this sort of work is the famous monumental History of Nineteenth
Century Russian Literature edited by D. Ovsjaniko-Kulikovskij and
published in 1912.

It is precisely in the search for 'literariness', those specific qualities distinguishing literature as verbal art, that the Formalist trend
in Russian literary criticism emerged in 1914-1916. Formalism intended to establish an objective, empirical discipline, immune as
much as possible to philosophical, social, and political bias. This
new movement grew rapidly, attracted a number of eminent scholars,
established itself in academic institutions and produced a great number of penetrating, thought-provoking publications. Although the
movement was not created in a void and had critically digested and
absorbed numerous contributions of Russian (A. Veselovskij, A.
Potebnja, A. Belyj) as well as German scholars (O. Walzel, E.
Sievers and others), no one can deny its utmost originality. It is
impossible in a brief introduction to do justice to this remarkable

trend, or to delineate even its most important input into literary scholarship in general and to Russian literary criticism in particular.

At the beginning the Formalists tended to concentrate on surface elements: poetic language and sujetal patterns. It was in the study of poetic language that they made their greatest contributions. Their research resulted in an elaborate theory of Russian verse as well as in the penetrating analysis of artistic prose style. The study of sujetal patterns was not so successful. It followed rather a narrow path. Formalists saw in a literary work only a pure form which they interpreted as "not a thing, not a material, but simply a relation of materials". (2) The Formalists liked to reduce the whole body of a novel or short story to a schematic representation which was sometimes expressed by mathematical formulas. The meaningful 'material' - characters, their milieu, the entire psychological and social flesh of the work - was granted only the modest role of supporting the formal construction: supplying the 'motivation' for artistic devices. Thus, for example, Gogol''s "The Overcoat" was presented solely as a combination of interwoven pathetic and satiric fragments which with their contrastive juxtaposition created an effect of the grotesque. (3)

The shortcomings of such an approach were soon recognized by the Formalists themselves and this approach was gradually abandoned. As early as 1924 Ju. Tynjanov admitted the constructive role of the 'material'. (4) The structural significance of all elements participating in the literary work and creating artistic effects was eventually recognized. This marked the gradual transformation of Formalism into Structuralism. In a very few years substantial steps in that direction were taken but were abruptly stopped when political forces destroyed the whole movement in 1929.

In its first thirteen years (1917-1930), the Soviet government did not exercise tight control over literary matters. There was some degree of freedom in the field of literary criticism, which explains why the Formalist-Structuralist movement was able to develop. This period was marked by relatively free discussion and exchange of thought between the Formalists and several Marxian groups. Since K. Marx and F. Engels had little to say regarding literary matters, it was difficult to judge the claims of these groups to be truly Marxian. The most prominent - the Pereverzev group - preached a crude form of economic determinism in literature: they classified Russian writers according to their social origins as members of Marxian economic classes - feudal, bourgeois, petty bourgeois, and proletarian. The literary production of writers was explained in terms of their class origin. The content and even the form of their literary works were, they insisted, derived from class consciousness. The Pereverzev group, however, finally was found to be 'un-Marxian', was labeled vulgar sociologist, and was disbanded by the Soviet government at about the same time as the Formalists were.

The following quarter century (1930-1956) was a period of cultural stagnation. The political atmosphere, reflected by the collectiv-

ization of agriculture, five year plans, and growing population of
concentration camps, was highly unfavorable to the expression of
individual views. In problems of poetics, a uniform point of view,
established and controlled by party organs, was maintained. Little
remained to discuss. Some technical works devoted to versification
and to the style of individual writers still managed to appear, but it
was impossible to express anything fresh and even slightly controversial in matters regarding theoretical principles.

The atmosphere changed radically in 1956, since as an aftermath
of Stalin's death many of his policies were condemned and discon-
tinued. This brought a renaissance in the interest of theoretical problems in literature and other fields of art. A hunger was felt for theoretical research free of close control, a hunger which could finally be
satisfied.

The situation was, however, quite distinct from the 1920s. While
everyone was still required to hold the Communist party view on
literature and no open dissension was permitted, a great variety of
opinions could be voiced as long as they did not contradict the party
doctrine and offered lip service to it. Meticulous control over theoretical views in literary criticism was no longer enforced.

As a result, there was a great proliferation of works in literary
criticism. Some books written, but withheld from publication during
the Stalin years, now appeared. There were animated discussions
in periodicals; for example, an extensive symposium on word and
image was carried on (1960) in the review Voprosy literatury. The
works of some foreign theoreticians even opposed to Marxian doctrine were translated and edited with favorable, although cautious,
comments - for example, works of Roman Ingarden, whose phenom-
enological studies on literature appeared in Russian translation in
1962.

2. THE PRESENT PERIOD

The Formalist-Structuralist movement has, to be sure, a great impact on this last period. The specific qualities of literature qua verbal art now become recognized and accepted. The social, political,
or philosophical import of literary works are examined through an
analysis of devices contributing to their structure.

This is seen even in the work by G. Pospelov (Selection VI), a
former member of the sociologically-minded Pereverzev group, and
that of A. Derman (Selections I and V), an old critic of Čexov, whose
previous works had a rather biographical approach, combined with
a psychological portrayal of the author. It is interesting to note that
Derman's book, written in 1952, was published only in 1959 when the
approach to literary criticism had altered radically. (5) It is also
significant that its title was changed from How Čexov Worked to On
Čexov's Craft.

Structuralist tendencies are equally obvious in other selections.
Viktor Šklovskij (Selection III), a brilliant and controversial critic,

was a former leader of the Formalist school. Notwithstanding his socio-political statements expressing his loyalty to the party doctrine, which are scattered throughout his book, he feels free now to express himself on theoretical matters in well-aimed and sometimes paradoxical remarks. He no longer shares the extreme Formalist point of view which he held in his youth, and is now closer to Structuralism. The late V. V. Vinogradov, an academician and lifelong theoretician of poetic language, was associated with the Formalists in the 1920s, but in contrast to them was always more interested in semantics and in semantic clusters of poetic utterances and therefore was close to Structuralism. In the selection presented in this volume (Selection IX) he discusses the contributing effects of language structures in a literary structure. All the authors of the other selections – Dobin (Selection II), Lakšin (Selection IV), Nazarenko (Selection VII), Golubkov (Selection VIII), and Čičerin (Selection X) are – despite the differences in their age – critics of the new formation and have come into prominence rather recently. They attempt to combine Marxian ideology with the structural approach by demonstrating the dependence of the socio-political import of a literary work on the means of its construction. The structural features of particular stories come to the foreground in this analysis.

Thus, in order to reveal the ideological import of "The Flutterer", "Anna Around the Neck" and "On the Cart" Golubkov (Selection VIII) resorts to the examination of structural parallelism of images and to the verbal means of their creation. In some instances he has recourse to the comparative examination of the earlier and final versions of a story. In his analysis of "The Man in a Case" Nazarenko (Selection VII) scrutinizes artistic devices used as 'microstructures' framing the narrative and expressing the ideological significance of the work. The essence of Šklovskij's (Selection III) analysis of the stories "To Sleep, Sleep . . . !", "The Fat Man and the Thin Man", "The Steppe" and others is based on the study of functional significance of 'details'. Similarly Dobin (Selection II) discusses various categories of 'details' and the mastery with which Čexov used them in his stories. Čičerin (Selection X) links the ideological message of "The Beauties" and "The Betrothed" with some syntactic and lexical features. And finally, Vinogradov, in his detailed examination of the role of the socio-professional language, the general verbal tone and the development in characters' dialogue and its interrelation with the author's narrative, is primarily preoccupied with the functional role of linguistic devices in the whole of a story.

The political influence of the Soviet State is still felt. The Western reader may find it difficult to accept many statements which reveal excessive adherence to current Soviet political doctrine. These can be found in scattered remarks. It sounds naive when Golubkov pities Čexov for not having lived "long enough to be able to work out a clear socio-political philosophy" (p. 135). (6) And it is rather amusing to learn from Pospelov (p. 120) that the narrator's longing sentence from "The House with the Mezzanine" ("Misjus, where are you?") symbolically expresses the expectation of some unusual changes in the future. A somewhat ludicrous aspect of Soviet criticism is also revealed in efforts to defend Čexov against his inclusion into such literary trends as Symbolism and Impressionism (Lakšin, pp. 103-104) which are viewed with suspicion by Soviet authorities.

Much more grave, however, are occasional misinterpretations based on distortion in presenting the facts of a story. Such is the case in Derman's discussion of "The Student". Derman states that in this story all the student's thoughts and feelings are materialistically grounded (p. 30). He argues: "So it was enough to warm his body at the bonfire as well as his soul in his artistic success, in the warm tears of the woman who was touched by his story, as the sensation of happiness overflows his heart" (pp. 30-31). Actually, this interpretation contradicts facts in the story. The spiritual change in the student's soul occurred not at the moment when he was at the warm bonfire, but later when he was cold again. And the impact of the student's story on the woman, as Čexov emphatically stresses, "was not because he was able to tell a story in a touching manner" (p. 31). Both 'materialistic' causes mentioned by Derman are simply his invention.

The reading of the selections is also somewhat handicapped by the lack of an established, universally recognized, terminology. While Golubkov and Pospelov understand sujet as a chain of events, something akin to the plot of the story, Šklovskij sees in it the inner structure of the story, its 'undercurrent' which carries out its artistic import. The terminological opposition of 'detail' and 'particular' elaborated by Dobin is not shared by Šklovskij and Lakšin, who use both terms indiscriminately.

In general, however, the selections which we present reveal a fresh approach to Čexovian stories: good taste in their interpretation and deep insight in the analysis of their artistic meaning.

The scope of our selections extends, however, far beyond the analysis of particular stories. In many instances the critics arrive at broad generalizations characterizing typical traits of Čexovian craft. These are brought about by Čexov's linguistic devices, his attitude toward the reader, and the imagery and structure in his stories. Let us consider some of these topics.

3. LINGUISTIC DEVICES

In the discussions devoted here to linguistic stylistics, there is no linguistic analysis in a strict sense; there is, however, an examination of some selected linguistic elements or their combinations which are deemed to contribute in a particular manner to creating literary artistic effects.

It is refreshing to see Čičerin's opposition (Selection X) to the prevailing Soviet cliché point of view which emphasizes the simplicity and accuracy of Čexov's style. Instead, Čičerin finds in Čexov an indirect manner in depicting objects. He examines some syntactic structures as indices which reveal an author's attitude to the depicted reality. For the discussion he selects adversative conjunctions ('but', 'although') and indefinite expressions ('some sort of', 'a certain', 'something', 'for some reason', 'for some uncertain reason', etc.). He sees a necessary connection between ideological contradictions - life which actually exists versus life which could have existed ideally - and the adversative constructions expressing them. It seems, however, that his generalization is not completely sound. Many adversative constructions in Čexov's stories do not carry any ideological load at all. The indefinite expressions, especially when they are used in impersonal sentences, can be viewed quite differently. P. Bicilli (7) sees in them merely a stylistic device which helps Čexov create a synthetic picture of reality in its perspective as focused upon by an observer. This is done by presenting a passive subject who is dominated by his perceptions.

Golubkov (pp. 164-167) makes a similar attempt to establish a correlation between the form and the meaning. He divides sentences (in the story "On the Cart") into two large categories representing respectively reality and the dream world. The formal description of these categories is ambiguous, and so Golubkov falls into contradictions. He quotes a sentence describing the road ('harsh reality' in this story) as an example of rhythmical harmonious structure which, according to him, should describe only the dream world.

Much more convincing is Vinogradov's discussion of Čexov's style. In general, his thesis can be summed up as follows: the application of linguistic stylistics alone cannot lead to conclusions or discoveries about artistic literature. However, it does serve as necessary background. Its usefulness is revealed especially in discerning some particular systems of language oriented to various social dialect and professional uses, such as bureaucratic language, beggar's language, friendly or intimate language. These particular language systems as well as their combinations and interplay are perceived by the reader in their specificity. Used in literary artistic works they can be regarded as inputs contributing to and functionally dependent upon the literary structure of which they are parts. Vinogradov focuses his research on complicated problems of interconnection between an author's language and the language of his characters and on the interplay of their expressive means according to their particular language systems. His analysis of the three short stories can be considered as an illustration of these general principles.

In the first of his excerpts Vinogradov deals with the socio-professional language of two protagonists and examines the functional contribution of their language to the structure of the story. He provides us with a thorough and subtle analysis of verbal mannerisms typical of each character and carefully examines the contributory role of their individual speech as the story progresses. He notes specific variations and repetitions of the same expressions in the author's and in the characters' speech and emphasizes the significance of these expressions in the plot dynamics. All these points reveal judiciously Čexov's mastery in functional utilization of linguistic elements. In the second excerpt Vinogradov studies the expressive language in a story as construction material building the general tone of the story, and in the third excerpt, he attempts to detect linguistic characteristics of the story which should serve as a preliminary to determining an author's style. In all these excerpts his analysis effectively points out some peculiar elements of Čexov's style.

4. ČEXOV'S ATTITUDE TOWARD THE READER

An author's biography and the influence of events in his life and his views upon his work need not in general be a part of the study of his craft. There is, however, a field in which references to the views of an author appear to be both legitimate and fruitful. This occurs when the documentation characterizing his creative manner is examined as reflected in gradual changes in versions of his works and in his own statements about his craftsmanship. This aspect of Čexov's work is the topic of Derman's selection (Selection I).

Derman presents a consistent well-substantiated review of Čexov's ideas and their application, concerning that aspect of his craft which deals with his relationship to his readers. Derman makes the following points: (1) Čexov's writings are addressed to a cooperative reader, who participates in his work by an active intelligent grasping of its meaning, a reader who rejects clichés and welcomes a new interpretation of life; (2) this reliance on the cooperative reader is particularly evident in those segments of Čexov's works in which he depicts situations which are destined to evoke an emotional response from the reader, pity or anger in connection with the depicted matter. In such instances Čexov exercises great restraint in expressing his own emotions. According to his views and practice, the reader's emotions are stronger when the author remains aloof.

Derman presents few original ideas, since similar points already had been advanced by some British and American critics. As early as 1923 in the first book on Cexov's short stories to appear in English, W. Gerhardi (8) expressed essentially the same view although he did not develop it so emphatically and extensively. He cites the same statements of Čexov that Derman did, among them Čexov's quotation about the role of the jury, which Čexov assigned to the reader, who, according to him, is supposed to resolve the problems stated correctly by the author. Other statements by Čexov which Gerhardi quotes are concerned with the requirement of emotional restraint on the author's part. These were also noted by J.B. Priestley (9) and Somerset Maugham. (10) But compared to earlier discussions Derman's is more elaborate and presents Čexov's manner of cooperation with the reader as a fully developed theory. Particularly notable is his comparative analysis of two versions of the short story "The Fat Man and the Thin Man".

Derman's view is not shared by Golubkov (p. 135) as far as the last period of Čexov's writings is concerned. Golubkov sees a gradual abandonment of Čexov's restraint in expressing his ideas and emotions and finds in his latest works elements of persuasion, of openly taking a position in the social and family conflicts he depicts.

5. IMAGERY

Čexovian devices of imagery occupy an important place in our selections. The main emphasis in them is not, however, on the use of tropes but on the use of ordinary language in its depictive function. The most original and systematic contribution in this respect is Dobin's (Selection II) discussion of detail.

Dobin explains the nature of detail and the range of its application by comparing it with the particular and by commenting on various examples in the context of Čexov's stories. Thus we learn that the major power of detail lies in "recreating a phenomenon in its entirety with one or two strokes" and that the importance and strength of the detail consist in its ability to represent the whole in "the extremely brief element". While "detail is intensive", Dobin says, "the particular is extensive". Detail is individual: the particular is effective only in plurality. Dobin's distinction between the detail and the particular is gratifying. Other critics use the two terms interchangeably.

With admirable insight and great acuity Dobin examines the artistic effects created by Čexov's use of various details. He begins with the detail as a means to recreate the world as perceived by the senses, the world contemplated by an observer; then he considers detail as demonstrating the meaning of an event in its social connections, then as a device forming portraits of main protagonists and secondary personages, and finally as a leitmotif recurring through the length of a story. However, Dobin nowhere gives a satisfactory definition of the detail. In fact he includes into that term so many heterogeneous devices that it would be difficult to find a definition covering all of them. This creates an ambiguity in the use of this term which needs some elucidation.

So far as detail is a device of imagery, it has its roots in the distinction between seeing and recognizing, as set by Viktor Šklovskij. (11) "Things perceived several times", said Šklovskij, "are perceived as recognized: the thing is in front of us, we know it but we do not see it". The goal of art is to give us the awareness of a thing perceived, and not as automatically recognized. Detail can be used as a powerful instrument to achieve this goal. Indeed in most of Dobin's examples (blood on potatoes; pink pigeons flying in the smoke; moonlight sparkling on the broken bottle, etc.) it plays the role of a magic flashlight sharply illuminating specific areas of reality here and now. A synthetic combination of at least two semantic elements (objects, colors, lights) into a new unit produces in our mental vision an illusion of coalescent reality. (12) The meanings of ordinary words conveying their general informational values become fused in a particular image. With the help of detail some parts of reality here and now are perceived as focused upon by an observer.

Some examples which Dobin also calls "details" do not, however, enter into this concept, for example, the phrase "he is a flunkey" ("The Lady with the Little Dog") or the leitmotif of losses ("Roth-schild's Violin"). It is obvious that these devices have nothing to do with depicting the reality here and now. It would be difficult to find a principle under which they would be united in the same group of devices with imagery details. Dobin's interpretation overextends the function of detail. The category of detail becomes too inclusive and therefore shapeless.

6. STRUCTURE

Equally important are observations regarding the structure of Čexov's stories. A distinction is made between two kinds of structure in a literary work: the structure of the tale and the inner structure of a work which conveys the meaning or 'artistic' import (13) of the whole. While the tale's structure resides in linear development which is pri-marily represented by the plot, the inner structure consists in the deep relations of components of the work, in bringing them together in a way that reveals its artistic import. (13)

Among our selections, the most extensive study of tale structure in Čexovian stories is carried on by Derman (Selection V). He sub-divides the discussion into three parts, dealing in turn with the prin-cipal stages of the tale's structure: beginning, development, and denouement.

Derman emphasizes Čexov's evolution using the beginnings of tales which in his latest period brought him to eliminate introductions in his stories. In "Ariadna" and "My Life", which Derman cites as examples, Čexov opens abruptly with the action of the protagonists. To Derman this constitutes a revolutionary step.

Doubtless, brevity was a conscious demand Čexov imposed upon all writers, including himself. But this was not a characteristic of Čexov alone. Here we should disagree with Derman and view such dynamic beginnings rather as evidence of the Puškin-Tolstoj tra-dition. Puškin's abrupt "Guests were arriving at the summer house" fascinated Tolstoj. The latter, even from his inception as a writer, used very matter-of-fact beginnings (see his early works "The Raid" and Childhood). Even Turgenev, far less dynamic, starts his Fathers and Sons directly with action. It would be incorrect to consider ab-rupt beginnings as a specifically Čexovian innovation.

On the other hand, as can be seen in the same stories quoted by Derman, a beginning with an action does not eliminate a lengthy 'ex-position'. (14) Thus, for example, in "Ariadna" the very laconic start in which the narrator-protagonist begins to act is followed by four pages devoted to a description of the narrator, an account of his views and exposition of the main facts which preceded the begin-ning of the story. A similar situation occurs in "My Life", where on the first two pages 'exposition' is intermingled in almost equal proportion with the characters' action.

What really distinguishes Čexov's beginnings in the mature works

of his last period is rather the lack of 'complication' in a usual
sense. In such stories as "Anna Around the Neck" (1895), "On the
Cart" (1897), "The Gooseberries" (1898), "Ionyč" (1898), "The Darling" (1899), "The Betrothed" (1903), the beginning action flows
into the next step without a complicating dramatic element. We see
the sequences of life naturally following each other, rather than the
rising of a conflict.

A much more sound and valuable contribution is Derman's treatment of the middle of a tale. He describes Čexov's ingenious method
of presenting changes in characters' lives over an extended period
of time by presenting certain signposts (as in "Ionyč"). These Čexov
describes by using recurrent details or other noteworthy characteristics; their subsequent changes are correlated with the corresponding changes in the life of the characters.

Although Derman fails to mention it, the recurrence of details and
themes has a much broader application in Čexov. As P. Bicilli, (15)
who was followed by Lakšin (Selection IV), noted, recurrent devices
can also characterize consequences of a sudden change as compared
with the initial situation (for example, the Thin Man's repeated introductions of his family in "The Fat Man and the Thin Man") as well
as the stability of an element which offers a background to other
changes (Dymov's "Please, gentlemen, have a bite to eat" in "The
Flutterer"). Recurrent details can also depict space (three snipes
in "The Steppe") as Šklovskij correctly noted (Selection III, p. 80).

Derman's strong point is his analysis of Čexov's denouements,
especially those of his final period. Here Derman follows A. Gornfel'd (16) in the main, but supplies some additional evidence. Both
critics find originality in Čexov's substituting the surprise endings
typical of his earlier works with endings in which the protagonists
meditate over the very sense of their lives.

Discussions about the inner structure of Čexov's stories are
usually carried on in conjunction with an examination of their tale structure. However, the peculiarities of the latter (lack of 'complication',
spotty development of the tale and lack of proper denouement) often
signify an absence of formal sujetal scheme. This sometimes causes
the inner structure to be sole bearer of the story's organization.
Pospelov (Selection VI) finds the unifying element holding Čexov's
story together in its 'undercurrent'. The latter relies not on the
unity of action but rather on the unity of the main protagonist's
thought.

This is why in Čexov presentations of small facts of life and of
characters' fleeting impressions acquire such great importance.
Vadim Nazarenko (Selection VIII) considers them to be micro-
components of the whole structure. The themes and details dispersed
throughout the entire story are taken from their linguistic context
and linked together by the power of the reader's memory and imagination. These interconnections can be effected even between the most
separate parts of the story. Nazarenko's treatment of Mavra in "The
Man in a Case" illustrates this principle. Nazarenko represents an
imagist branch of Soviet contemporary scholarship as opposed to its

linguistic one.

Undoubtedly the reader will find many other points which are important and need clarification. However it is felt that further extension
of the introduction would make it unwieldy.

Leo Hulanicki

NOTES

(1) Roman Jakobson, Novejšaja russkaja poezia (Prague, 1921),
p. 11.
(2) Viktor Šklovskij, O teorii prozy (Moskva, 1929), p. 226. (First
edition, 1925.)
(3) Boris Ejxenbaum, "Kak sdelana šinel' Gogolja", Poètika
(Petrograd, 1919).
(4) Ju. Tynjanov, Problema stixotvornogo jazyka (Moskva, 1965),
p. 25. (First edition, 1924.)
(5) Derman died in 1952 leaving his book not quite completed. This
certainly also contributed to the delay in its publication.
(6) (The page numbers not preceded by titles refer to the present
book.)
(7) P. Bicilli, Tvorčestvo Čexova (Sofia, 1942), pp. 40-44.
(8) William Gerhardi, Anton Chekhov (N.Y., 1923), p. 80.
(9) John B. Priestley, "Chekhov as Critic", Saturday Review, 1925
(Oct. 17), p. 446.
(10) Somerset Maugham, A Writer's Notebook (1949), p. 144.
(11) V. Šklovskij, "Iskusstvo kak priem", O Teorii Prozy, 2nd ed.
(Moskva, 1929), pp. 10-13. (The article first time appeared in 1917.)
(12) W. Gerhardi commenting on this device called it "a literary way
of conveying the effect of painting" (Anton Chekhov, pp. 142-143).
(13) Suzanne K. Langer, Problems of Art (London, Routledge and
Kegan Paul, 1967), p. 67.
(14) 'Exposition' here is understood as the presentation of the initial
situation -- all information about characters and events preceding the
action in the story which are necessary to understand it.
(15) P. Bicilli, op. cit., pp. 70-72.
(16) A. Gornfel'd, "Čexovskie finaly", Krasnaja Nov', 8-9 (1939).

I

THE ESSENCE OF ČEXOV'S CREATIVE APPROACH (1)

A. DERMAN

1

Čexov's poetics contains a definite center towards which all its most important components gravitate. This center is fashioned consciously by the theoretical beliefs of the writer, and it thus differs in its origin from that which served as the basis of the poetics for the great majority of other writers in Čexov's generation.

Even if we set aside those writers who prudently indulged the tastes of the marketplace and turn to the finest literature of the time, we easily discover that its men of letters, led by the best of intentions, placed their stakes on a 'passive reader', on the weakness of his apathetic receptivity, and on the laziness of his thinking processes, which were not inclined to independent, intense work. Although their themes seldom deviated from commonly accepted 'truth', these writers trusted their reader so little that they ran beside him, not daring to leave him alone with the protagonists of their works, and, carrying a school pointer through the pages of their books, continually prompted the reader on how he should respond. Such writers deprived the reader of his most important function, and at the same time inevitably relinquished discipline in the process of their creative work.

In the realm of art, restraint is not what might be called good manners. It is a necessary condition for the correct life of an artistic work - it consists in the correct distribution of the roles between the creator of the work and the reader, when the former presents honestly prepared material intended for independent work in the mind and feelings of the latter.

When restraint is violated, there is basically a new kind of role distribution: the author of a work assumes a significant part of the functions of his reader. Out of distrust and the fear that the reader will not interpret his work as he intends, or that he will have the wrong reactions or reach the wrong conclusions, the author thinks for him, feels for him, makes conclusions for him, and, in general, reacts for him. In the imagination of the distrustful author, the reader, spectator or listener is a passive being, living spiritually 'in a ready-made world'.

Since he is afraid that the reader might react coldly to a dramatic situation, the author makes it melodramatic. In his attempt to elicit from the reader a delicate or touching expression of sympathy, he 'pedals', and as a result he causes the delicate to appear to be mincing, and that which is touching becomes sugary and sentimental.

If the author lacks trust in the reader's ability to guess from a nuance the character of a hero or a situation - then he enters into 'explanations', which a comprehending reader skims over in boredom . . . .

2

By way of digression, we must keep in mind that the great significance of art is based on the aptitude for creative collaboration; without it, art immediately turns into empty amusement. What would Tatjana Larina [heroine of Puškin's Evgenij Onegin] or Othello have been worth if the reader lacked the ability to see 'them' around himself in their innumerable variations? And what does this vision consist of, if it is not in creative interpretation and assimilation?

From the very beginning of Čexov's literary activity, this ability on the part of the reader was always his preoccupation. Threads stretched out from this point towards the most important and most characteristic aspects of Čexovian poetic, his credo, which can be roughly formulated in the following way:

An artist's literary work consists of a text and a 'subtext', (2) but the latter lives in the former only if the text is created effectively by the writer. To extract the 'subtext' from the text is the exclusive right and duty of the reader.

It is necessary to emphasize that this formula expresses the opinion of a special sort of writer. To illustrate, it is sufficient to recall the creative work of such a titan as Tolstoj, who quite often intruded into the 'subtext', even interrupting the text with moral epigraphs. But as far as Čexov is concerned, one must say that his theory as well as his creative practice clearly expresses the sharp differentiation between text and 'subtext'.

At one time Čexov characterized his contemporary reader as being stagnant and passionless. But, as we shall later see, he did not stop at this; Čexov's battle with the reader's flaws was firmly based on the premise of not usurping the reader's individual right to the 'subtext'.

When Suvorin [A. S. Suvorin (1834-1912), editor-publisher of Novoe vremja, a (politically) conservative magazine with a high literary reputation] reproached him for an overly objective depiction of horse thieves in the story "The Thieves" (originally "The Devils"), Čexov wrote the following in answer:

You criticize me for objectivity, calling it indifference to good and evil, an absence of ideals and ideas and so forth. When I describe horse thieves, you want me to say that stealing horses is bad. But certainly this has long been a well known fact without me. Let a jury try them - my job is simply to show them as they are . . . .
When I write, I rely upon the reader and assume that he himself will add the subjective elements which are absent in the story (XV, 51). (3)

Regarding a story sent to him by Suvorin, Čexov begins his comments in a characteristic way, as if starting from the most important thing:

Get rid of the maid! Her appearance on the scene is not realistic because it is accidental and needs explanation besides; it complicates an already complicated plot, but most important - she dampens enthusiasm. Throw her away! And why make explanations to the public? The public must be frightened and nothing more - it will become interested and once more will start to think . . . . (XV, 296).

To draw the reader into collaboration with the writer: this, clearly, was Čexov's aim.

When Čexov compared his readers to the members of a jury, he was creating something significantly greater than a mere simile. A long time before the exchange of letters concerning "The Thieves" he wrote to the same Suvorin in the form of a generalization:

You are correct in demanding of the artist a conscious relationship to his work, but you confuse two concepts: the solution to the problem and the correct presentation of the problem. Only the second is obligatory for the artist. In Anna Karenina and in Onegin no problem is resolved, yet they satisfy you completely, simply because all the problems in them are correctly posed. A court of law is obliged to present questions correctly, but let the jury decide according to its own preferences (XIV, 208).

3

This most important aspect of Čexov's poetics is emphasized in those instances where the matter is directed to the problem of how an author reacts emotionally to a situation charged with moral content which he himself has depicted. The participation of the author in this reaction was a kind of established tradition, the destruction of which involved both dissatisfaction and rebukes. Čexov was quite often criticized for his indifferent attitude toward the joys, sorrows and moral conduct of his heroes.

However, in most instances he was misunderstood, for, although he refrained from direct censure of his hero or from an expression of sympathy for him, etc., Čexov by no means abdicated a reaction towards good or evil; instead he shifted it entirely onto the reader in lieu of sharing it with him. And when he dealt with works where the habit of a direct author's participation in moral reaction was especially great - with works saturated with strong dramatic or joyful feelings - Čexov was extremely conscious of refraining from such a reaction, finding in these feelings special reasons for greater restraint. Moreover, while as a rule he did not explain to the reader his use of a given depictive device, he did make an exception to clarify his restraint in describing strong feelings, and he found a special form for doing this in one of his earliest stories - "Enemies" (1887).

Dr. Kirillov's only son had just died at the age of six. At that very moment Abogin, a neighboring landowner, came to summon the doctor to his wife, who had suddenly fallen ill. Kirillov resolutely refuses, but Abogin begs him to come.

> Abogin's voice quavered from emotion. There was considerably more cogency in this quavering and in the tone of his voice than there was in his words. Abogin was sincere, but it is remarkable that every sentence which he uttered came out stilted, heartless and inappropriately flowery . . . . He himself sensed this, and, fearing that he might not be understood, tried with all his might to make his voice soft and gentle and get his way, if not by words, then at least by the sincerity in his tone of voice.

At this point Čexov unexpectedly takes the reader away from the situation being depicted and adds - directly from himself - a significant generalization:

> In general, words, however beautiful and deep they may be, affect only those who are unconcerned; they cannot always satisfy those who are either happy or sad. This is why silence most often is the highest expression of joy or sorrow; lovers understand each other best when they are silent, and a fervid, passionate speech spoken at the graveside affects only the bystanders, whereas it seems cold and insignificant to the widow and children (VI, 31-32).

4

Čexov's motivations in advising writers not to infringe upon the reader's 'monopoly' on the 'subtext' are also very significant.

As an example consider an excerpt from a letter of his to M. V. Kiseleva [a writer of children's stories and a friend of Čexov], whose literary experiments Čexov strongly encouraged:

> . . . one of these days you will receive an invitation to submit by January a hunting story, a short one, of course, full of poetry and beauty of all sorts. You have observed hunting with hounds more than once, you have seen people from the Pskov area, etc., and it will not be hard for you to create something suitable. For example, you might be able to write a sketch, "Ivan Gavrilov" or "The Wounded Elk" - in the latter story, if you haven't forgotten, the hunters wound an elk, she has a human look in her eyes, and no one ventures to finish her off. This is not a bad sujet, but it is a dangerous one insofar as it is difficult to protect oneself from sentimentality; you have to write it in an unembellished style, without words of pity, and begin it thus: "On such-and-such a date some hunters wounded a young elk in the Daragonovskij forest . . ."

But if you shed a few tears, you will remove the severity from the
sujet (XIV, 446-447).

Here are a few more lines quite typical of this. The writer T. L.
Ščepkina-Kupernik [a writer and translator, a close friend of the
Čexov family (1874-1953)] reminisces:

> I recall that one day, apropos of one of my stories, he said to me,
> "Everything is fine, artistic. But look what you said here, for
> example: 'She, poor girl that she was, was prepared to thank fate
> for the trial which had been sent to her.' But it should be that the
> reader himself who, having read that she thanks fate for the trial,
> would say: 'Poor girl' . . . Likewise you say: 'It was touching to
> see this scene' (where the seamstress nurses the sick girl). But
> the reader himself should say: 'What a touching scene . . .' In
> general: love your heroes, but never say so out loud." (4)

Čexov's attitude toward any given aspect of artistic mastery was not
static and often underwent strong changes in the course of years, but
till the end of his life he remained true to restraint dependent on the
creative cooperation of the reader.

Among Čexov's many remarks on this subject, the comments in
his letters to Maksim Gor'kij are particularly interesting. Aside
from the fact that they pertain to the very last period of Čexov's creative activity, reflecting thus the entire rich experience of his work,
there also lies in these letters the mark of deep responsibility, which
is easily understood. Čexov addresses himself here to a writer, on
whom, captivated by his giftedness, he placed great hopes, and who,
with a sort of truly violent persistence, at the same time demanded
of Čexov the most merciless criticism. Let us not forget, however,
that he was still barely more than a novice writer! "You are still
young and have not yet settled" (5) - Čexov reminded him in a letter.
All this together extremely sharpened Anton Pavlovič's [Čexov's]
feeling of responsibility and compelled him to have a special open-
ness, and at the same time, exactingness. Čexov himself recognized
this. "Be a kind man and comrade", he asks his young colleague,
"don't be annoyed that I read you admonitions in my letters like an
archpriest", (6) to which the 'student' replies with unconcealed delight: "I am extremely pleased that in your letters to me you 'read
admonitions' like an archpriest - I have already told you that this is
very good. You treat me better than all other 'fellow workers of the
pen' - that is a fact." (7)

Already in his second letter to Gor'kij, in response to Aleksej
Maksimovič's [Gor'kij's] demand that he point out his faults, Čexov
writes:

> I will begin by saying that you lack restraint. You are like a spec-
> tator in a theater who expresses his delight so unrestrainedly that
> he keeps both himself and others for listening. This lack of re-
> straint is particularly felt in the descriptions of nature with which

you interrupt dialogues; when one reads these descriptions, one wishes they were more compact, shorter, say, in two or three lines. Frequent recollections of sweet bliss, whispers, velvetness, and so forth, give these descriptions a certain verbosity, monotony - and they dampen one's enthusiasm, almost fatigue one. Lack of restraint also is felt in the depiction of women ("Malva", "On the Rafts") and in love scenes. This is not scope, it is not breadth of the brush - but it is simply lack of restraint. (8)

"Not to hinder listening" - in a direct sense, this means not to pedal, not to forestall or push the reader's natural reaction, but to believe in the reader's ability to understand an image correctly. Čexov does not even make an exception in a particular case of a reader's social emotion. On the contrary, in his letters to Gor'kij, Čexov points out that in his reasoning on this subject, he proceeds from the idea of a full-fledged, competent reader. "In your 'Kirilka' ", he writes, "the figure of the district head of the Zemstvo spoils everything, although the general tone is sustained well. Don't ever depict local heads of the Zemstvo. There is nothing easier than depicting an unsympathetic authority, the reader loves it, but it is a very unpleasant, a most ungifted reader." (9)

Nothing is easier than to expose the practical fallacy of the above advice not to depict an 'unsympathetic authority'. It is quite sufficient to point to the inconsistency of Anton Pavlovič himself, who in his "The Peasants" had recently presented a cursory but merciless portrayal of an 'unsympathetic authority' in the person of the district police officer. But what interests us now is that aspect of Čexov's advice which concerns the reader, not the writer. Why, in Čexov's opinion, do portrayals of an unsympathetic authority fit the taste of an unpleasant, ungifted reader?

The answer is that the portrayal of an authority other than 'unsympathetic' was almost never found, and therefore the reader's perception of such portrayals was almost mechanical, without mental effort, emotionless. And if the reader likes this, if he likes such a portrayal, then that reader is like a music lover who prefers to hear familiar melodies which do not demand fresh, intense attention for their appreciation.

5

The application of this principle of restraint, which flows from a trust in the reader's active receptivity, reveals itself with particular clarity in Čexov's creative practice when we consider two versions of a single work published at different times. We will limit ourselves to two instances which at first glance are not only unconnected, but directly contrasting. In one version Čexov found it necessary to dot the 'i''s more clearly, and most characteristic here is the subtle 'dosage', that is, the limitation of the author's 'addition'. In the sec-

ond instance it is the opposite: Čexov removed a large dot which he
had previously placed above an 'i'.

According to the reliable evidence of the author's brother, Ivan
Pavlovič, Čexov considered the small sketch "The Student" to be one
of his best stories. Let us recall the content of the story.

Velikopolskij, a student in a theological university, is returning
home from snipe hunting chilled to the bone from the wind which
had suddenly turned cold, and hungry from having fasted strictly all
day - it was Good Friday.

> Shaking from the cold, the student was thinking of how the very
> same sort of wind blew also in the time of Rjurik [semi-legendary
> founder of the Russian state], of Ivan the Terrible and of Peter the
> Great, and that under their reigns there had been the same terrible
> poverty and hunger. There were in those times the same thatched
> roofs full of holes, ignorance, weariness, the same wilderness
> surrounding, darkness, a feeling of oppression - all these horrors
> existed, do exist and shall continue to exist, and even a thousand
> years will pass, but life will not be any better (VIII, 345-346).

The student comes closer to a fire where two peasant women with
whom he is acquainted are warming themselves, and, completely
under the power of his cheerless thoughts about this oppressive, eternal, evil poverty and darkness, he strikes up a conversation with them.
On the day before they had heard in church a reading from the gospels
about the sufferings of Christ, about Peter's denial of Christ. Aware
of this, in his conversation with them the student unconsciously
mingles his cheerless thoughts with the dramatic gospel legend, pour-
ing his anxiety into the story of Peter's denial, giving it a touching
lyrical coloration. When he tells how Peter began to weep after his
denial, he adds his own thoughts: "I can imagine: a very quiet, very
dark garden, and in the silence one can barely hear the muffled sob-
bing, . . ." and then one of the women, an old woman who was also,
to be sure, cold and hungry, began to weep.

The student leaves the bonfire and continues on, but his thoughts
take yet another turn.

> 'If she began to weep', he reflects, 'that means that everything
> which had happened with Peter on that terrible night has some rel-
> evance for her . . .'. If the old woman began to weep then it was
> not because he was able to tell a story in a touching manner. . . .
> And joy suddenly welled in his soul, and he even stopped for a mo-
> ment to take a breath. 'The past', he thought, 'is linked with the
> present by an unbroken chain of events, flowing one from another.'
> And it seemed to him that he saw both ends of this chain; he touched
> one end and the other end moved. When he was ferried across the
> river and then, going up the hill, was looking at his native village
> and then to the west, where the cold, crimson sunset glowed in a
> narrow band, he was thinking that truth and beauty, which guided
> human life there in the garden and in the chief priest's courtyard,

have continued uninterrupted up to the present day and evidently
always constituted the most important thing in human life and on
earth in general. And the feeling of youth, health, strength - he
was only 22 years old - and the inexpressibly sweet expectation
of happiness, an unknown, mysterious happiness, gradually overpowered him and life seemed to him to be delightful, miraculous
and full of high significance (VIII, 348).

The story ends with these words.

Let us ask ourselves what this story is about. What is its subject
matter?

Youth is the subject matter! It is a story about how youth is sweet,
fresh and poetic, and how it is naive and credulous.

There are two emotional states of the student Velikopolskij:

first - "ignorance, weariness, . . . wilderness surrounding, darkness, a feeling of oppression - all these horrors existed, do exist,
and shall continue to exist, and even a thousand years will pass, but
life will not be any better."

second - "truth and beauty, which guided human life there in the
garden and in the chief priest's courtyard, have continued uninterrupted up to the present day. . . . Life seemed to him to be delightful, miraculous, and full of high significance."

Our imagination is unable to conceive of a more contradictory train
of thought than that represented in Velikopolskij's two emotional
states. Surely some very strong incentive is needed for a thought to
rush from one pole to another as this one does.

This motivation is pointed out quite clearly by the author:

Now the student thought about Vasilisa: if she began to weep, it
means that everything which took place with Peter on that terrible
night has some sort of relevance for her. . . . If the old woman
began to weep, then it was not because he was able to tell a story
in a touching manner . . . (VIII, 348).

Here is the strong stimulus which quickly transforms the student's
emotional state: Vasilisa's tears!

In all of Čexov it is difficult to find another work where each word,
each thought and sensation of the hero, would be so materialistically
grounded and so convincingly motivated by physiological and psychological preconditions!

Velikopolskij is the son of a sexton and a student in a theological
university; the episode takes place on Good Friday, with all of its
dramatic ritual of the 'Lord's Passion' - here is a series of clearly
defined moments of an ordinary religious practice, which create a
predisposition towards a mystical inclination of thought in the student.
He is hungry, cold - these are physiological preconditions for a de-
spondent mood. But he is young, healthy, strong, easily excited; his
presentiment and expectation of happiness are his natural condition
(Čexov reminds us that he was only 22 years old) asking the reader's
indulgence towards the naivete of the hero. So it was enough to warm

his body at the bonfire, as well as his soul in his artistic success -
in the warm tears of the woman who was touched by his story - as
the sensation of happiness overflows his heart, and this happiness
changes in a moment from a dark and cheerless philosophy into one
that is bright and full of the joy of life.

Such a harmonic combination of delicacy and ease of design on
one hand and severe deliberation and firmness on the other is not
found so often even in Čexov. Nevertheless, when the story appeared
in print, there were those who ascribed a religious tendency to its
author; in some cases the character of these opinions permits one
to posit not so much a deliberate distortion of the writer's intention
as an honest error of misinterpretation.

It must be kept in mind that Čexov paid close attention to criticism,
and felt it necessary to dot the 'i' in the given instance, to exclude
the possibility of a reader's honest error and incorrect interpretation of the author's intention.

He did it in the following way. First, in the original edition, the
story's title was "In the Evening", which was typical of Čexov's
titles. He always tried to give them an ambiguous character (Ivanov,
Three Sisters, "On the Cart", "Three Years", etc.). Čexov gave the
story a new title: "The Student". This was already a very light accent:
the center of gravity was shifted to the factor of the hero's age, as if
addressing the reader's attention to it.

However, the additions which Čexov made are even more explicit.
One of them stands out in an extremely telling place - where the
student interprets the old woman's tears. Instead of "If the old woman
began to weep, then it is not because he was able to tell a story", in
the new edition we read, "If the old woman began to weep, then it is
not because he was able to tell a story in a touching manner, but because Peter was close to her, and because with all her being, she
was concerned in what happened in Peter's soul."

Here the 'pointing finger' is seen a bit more clearly both in regard
to deliberate poignancy of the student's story about Peter and in the
naivete of the student himself, who ascribed to the woman thoughts
which had entered his own head only at that very moment.

This 'pressure', very clear in character, was of such a nature
that it made the naivete of the student's syllogisms even more naive,
and made the gentle ironic contrast between youthful thoughtlessness
and severe reality even more obvious. At the same time it is an extremely light, airy strengthening of the tone, which does not at all
destroy the generally reticent atmosphere of the story.

Now let us look at a second instance - where Čexov took the dot
from an 'i'. His famous story "The Fat Man and the Thin Man" was
printed in 1883 in Oskolki. Three years later, in reworking it for
inclusion in his anthology Motley Stories, Čexov drastically changed
the whole first version, putting the finale into its present shape. For
the sake of clarity we will present both variants in parallel.

Two old school chums meet and recognize each other, and exchange
initial, joyful greetings. Then the Fat Man asks the Thin Man how he
is getting along, and the latter answers:

32

1883 Edition

"... We get along somehow. I
served in the department of
'Prefaces and Misprints' and
am being transferred here as a
secretary in the same institution.... I'll be working here.
They say the boss is a real
beast; Well, the hell with him.
I'll get along with him somehow.
He has the same surname as
you. Well, how about you? I
guess you're already a State
Councillor? Right?"

"So.... So it's you, it seems,
that has been appointed as my
secretary?" the Fat Man said
in a deep voice, puffing himself
out like a turkey cock. "You are
late, kind sir, in appearing at
work.... Yes, late...."

"Y-y-you? It's you?... I,
Your Excellency...."

The Thin Man suddenly paled,
but soon his face was distorted
all over with a broad smile....
He himself shrivelled, bent
down, grew narrow.... His
suitcases, packages and cartons
shrivelled, became wrinkled....
His wife's long chin became
even longer; Nafanail moved to
the front and instinctively, by
reflex, buttoned up all the buttons on his jacket....

"I, Your Excellency.... Very
delighted! A friend, one might
say, of my youth, and suddenly
you have become such a magnate.
Hee - hee!"

"It is not a very good idea to
be late."

"Excuse me, sir, I could not

1886 Edition

"... We get along somehow. I
worked, you know, in a department, and now am being transferred here as a supervisor in
the same institution.... I'll be
working here. Well, how about
you? I guess you're already a
State Councillor? Right?"

"No, my friend, try a bit
higher", said the Fat Man, "I've
already reached Privy Councillor
.... I have two decorations."

The Thin Man suddenly paled,
turned stony, but soon his face
was distorted all over with a
broad smile; it seemed as if
sparks rained down from his
face and eyes. He himself shrivelled, bent down, grew narrow
.... His suitcases, packages
and cartons shrivelled, became
wrinkled.... his wife's long
chin became even longer; Nafanail moved to the front and buttoned up all the buttons on his
jacket....

"I, Your Excellency.... Very
delighted! A friend, one might
say, of my youth, and suddenly
you have become such an important man. Hee - hee!"

"Come now, let's not have
this", the Fat Man said with a
wry face. "Why that tone of
voice? We were friends in childhood; why worry ourselves about
rank here!"

"But surely - How can you,

be here on time because my wife was sick... Luiza here... a Lutheran...."

"I hope so, kind sir", said the Fat Man, extending his hand to the Thin Man. "Goodbye.... I expect to see you at work tomorrow...."

The Thin Man squeezed three fingers as a handshake, bowed down with his whole body and giggled. His wife smiled.... Nafanail clicked his heels and dropped his cap. All three were pleasantly stunned.

sir..." giggled the Thin Man, shrivelling even smaller. "The kind attention of your excellency ... is a kind of elixir.... This, your excellency, is my son Nafanail... my wife, Luiza, a Lutheran, in a way...."

The Fat Man was about to retort, but there was such excessive awe, sweetness and deferential distance on the face of the Thin Man that the Fat Man felt sick to his stomach. He turned away from the Thin Man and offered his hand in parting.

The Thin Man squeezed three fingers as a handshake, and bowed down with his whole body and giggled like a Chinaman. "Hee-hee-hee." His wife smiled. Nafanail clicked his heels and dropped his cap. All three were pleasantly stunned.

What was it that caused such a sharp reworking of the finale? It was a readdressing of the sketch. In the initial edition the author addressed himself specifically to that sort of reader whom he later called "unpleasant and ungifted", who prefers familiar situations, hackneyed conditions, familiar heroes in familiar, well-worn places in literature: a privy councillor 'puts down' a collegiate assessor, etc. From such a reader an author does not expect either labored thought or a fresh feeling of perception. But in the second edition the sketch is designed for the thinking reader who has already succeeded in mastering social and moral axioms and who does not stand in need of constant reminders that two plus two equal four; it is for the reader who is able to sense that however nasty a privy councillor may be who would rudely and arrogantly slight his school chum because the latter is merely a collegiate assessor, it is more sickening and more terrible that the collegiate assessor himself would not consider himself a human being in front of the privy councillor even though the latter conducted himself quite well and did not emphasize his superiority.

6

We will now turn our attention from those instances where Čexov reveals his techniques and his principles by making revisions of an initial version to a typical Čexovian device which is not complicated by additions.

It is in one of the closing chapters of the short novel "The Peasants". The grip of hopelessness tightens more and more firmly about the family of Nikolaj Čikildeev, a waiter from the Slavjanskij Bazar, a Moscow hotel. After he fell sick, he was thrown out unwanted onto the street, and came with his family to his native village. Here he is a burden to his relatives, who are also crushed by bitter poverty. Čexov depicts the gloomy existence of the family by means of bare traits:

> The day passed. The long autumn evening set in. In the hut they wound silk. . . . They got the silk from a nearby factory and the whole family earned very little from it - some twenty kopecks a week. . . . The only light was from a single small lamp - it burned dimly and smokily. . . . Old Osip told in a leisurely manner about how they lived before the Emancipation [the Emancipation of the serfs occurred in 1861]. . . . How the bad peasants were flogged with birch rods or were exiled to the family estate near Tver and the good ones were rewarded. . . . A short bald old man, General Žukov's cook, entered. . . . He sat down, listened a bit and also began to recollect and tell various stories. Nikolaj, sitting on the oven (10) with his legs dangling, listened and kept asking questions about dishes which they prepared in the time of the masters. . . .
> "Did they make cutlets a la maréchal in those days?" Nikolaj asked. "No."
> Nikolaj shook his head reproachfully and said, "Ah, what miserable cooks you were!"
> . . . They always slept badly in the hut; there was something nagging and persistent to keep each of them from sleeping; the old man had a pain in his back, the old woman had her worries and her own ill nature, Marja had fear, and the children were hungry and had the itch. Now, too, their sleep was troubled; they turned from side to side, talked in their sleep, got up for a drink of water. Fekla suddenly howled loudly in a harsh voice, but immediately controlled herself and from time to time sobbed, gradually more softly and muffled until she finally grew quiet. . . .
> Nikolaj, who did not sleep all night, got down from the oven. He took out his tail coat from his little green trunk, put it on, and, going to the window, stroked the sleeves, held the coat by the tails, and smiled. Then he carefully took it off, put it in the trunk, and lay down again (IX, 209-212).

Why have we said that this device is typical of Čexov?

First, because it is 'constructed' from very simple 'material'; second, because it has an unusually 'innocuous' appearance. This entire scene with the dress coat is, at a quick glance, some sort of passing episode or perhaps something even more - an ordinary sketch illustrating a milieu. Third, we have called this a typical Čexovian device because it is dependent upon the creative cooperation of an active reader who, in Čexov's words, will add the 'elements lacking' and will feel how complicated and tragic this deceptively simple episode with the tail coat is. And finally, fourth, it is typical of Čexov because it is amazingly fresh and original.

Čexov detects a 'ray of light' in the consciousness of one of his heroes and it is precisely the one who is the most doomed, who has come to the final limit of a dark existence saturated with suffering.

This 'ray of light' will also bear the chief weight here: the waiter's dress coat, a traditional, classical symbol of a man's deprivation of his human dignity, the symbol of an oppressed despised existence – is a holy relic for Nikolaj Čikildeev, a memory of heavenly bliss!

This device is typical and characteristic for Čexov specifically because it is completely conditioned by his central principle: to trust in the reader. Only a reader of that sort could be approached with a device in which there was just one step from the sublime to the ridiculous, from a dark tragedy – if one understands it – to a vulgar farce – if one does not perceive its content.

The 'preparation' made for the proper interpretation of the episode involving the dress coat was also characteristic of Čexov: we have in mind the conversation in the hut about food, and Nikolaj's rejoinder about cutlets a la maréchal: "Ah, what miserable cooks you were!" The feeling of superiority which rings through this proud exclamation begins imperceptibly to bring the reader into that spiritual world where a waiter's tail coat is an emblem of happiness.

Čexov's attitude towards the reader was demanding, but it would be a very serious error to interpret it as the haughty sort preached by propagandists of 'art for the few', 'art for the elite' – that is, by the representatives of the aristocratic tendency in art. It is exactly the opposite! Čexov was an implacable foe of all that refined, polished, purposely exquisite, unnatural and whimsical art, that art which comes from an 'ivory tower' isolated from real life. But within the category of art which was hostile and foreign to him, he also included that oversimplified, impoverished art which haughtily condescends to the limited understanding of the mass reader – a term which signified an inferior reader. Čexov, remember, felt that such "a reader, if he is not educated, nonetheless desires and tries to be educated; he is serious, thoughtful and by no means stupid".

7

There is the valid question of whether Čexov deluded himself when he demanded the reader's creative cooperation to such a significant scale. Did there not remain much in his works which was obscure to the reader in this system of 'hints' with such limited 'aid' on the part of the author?

First, it must be noted that Čexov had occasion to receive confirmations of his trust in the reader: letters, where the reader correctly interpreted the author's hints. Thus, for example, regarding the episode of Čikildeev's tail coat, the writer received a remarkable letter from Južin, a dramatist and well known Moscow actor. In it he wrote:

> Your "The Peasants" is the greatest work in the whole world in
> many years – at least for a Russian. . . . Your talent in "The
> Peasants" is remarkably high and whole-hearted. . . . And every-
> where one finds the incomparable tragedy of truth, the irresist-
> ible force of a spontaneous Shakespearean sketch; it is as if you
> were not a writer, but nature itself. Do you understand what I
> am trying to say? In "The Peasants" I feel what kind of weather
> there was on a given day, where the sun was in the sky, what the
> slope of the river bank was. I see everything without the aid of a
> description, and I see the dress coat of the waiter who has re-
> turned 'to the people' – I see it with all its seams, just as I see
> the unalterable destruction of all of Čikildeev's hopes for life in
> the chambers of the Slavjanskij Bazar. I never cry: but when he
> put on and then put away his tail coat, I could not read any further
> (IX, 582).

In the above letter from Južin, Čexov received approval for his device of a 'hint' in its concretely episodical expression. In a letter
which he received about his story "My Life" similar approval of the
device in its general form was expressed. It was a letter from the
writer A. Lugovoj-Tixonov, literary editor of Niva magazine. This
was in the fall of 1896, when Čexov's story "My Life" was printed
in the monthly supplements to the magazine. When he received the
second half of the manuscript of the story, Lugovoj wrote:

> The beginning of the second part seemed first a bit strange to me
> because of its failure to state fully many actions and psychological
> motives; the absence of the engineer at his daughter's wedding
> seems strange – not so much his physical absence at that moment,
> but it seems that his very existence was forgotten – but all this
> serves only to strengthen the impressions of those strokes by which
> the attitudes of the father towards his daughter are depicted on the
> subsequent pages. The whole preliminary work of tinting and group-
> ing is completed in the reader's mind itself, and when you put on
> the final patch of light, it stands out even brighter because the
> reader awaits it with intense attention. I do not know whether the
> reader will have such an impression, but this sort of understate-
> ment always impresses me the best. I think that every sort of
> reader likes it too. Dalmatov (11) always says: "The audience
> always likes to be clever."

Because of his clarity and temperance, Čexov was a man of rare
awareness. Letters such as Južin's – and particularly Lugovoj's –
were, one would suspect, precious documents for him, but one could
guarantee that in no way were they able to eliminate the problem which
always confronts an authentic writer and particularly a writer who is
also a reformer: does the general reader comprehend the most important thing which the writer has offered in his work?

Nowadays a writer receives a direct answer to this in the form of those thousands of letters which the readers send to him. In former times letters of this kind were not at all numerous. Nevertheless, Čexov did receive an answer, but in a different form: it was in the great success of his books among readers, in the unusual and hitherto unprecedented demand for them, and in the avid interest in his work. Could this have been the case if the restraint of his devices made his works incomprehensible and inaccessible to the general reader?

Čexov's attitude toward the writer was even more demanding than towards the reader: he made demands concerning the quality of the writer's creation. When one reads the advice scattered about in his letters to writers, the references to his own and others' blunders, especially when one studies attentively the structure of his works and in particular those alterations which he made before republishing them, then among the variety of these elements a general dominant idea is clearly seen - the precept which stood immutable before Čexov: to depict life without fail in all its complexity, with no allowance for the danger that the reader "would not understand", but always to depict it with simple means. To depict the complex in a simple way, with loss neither to the complexity nor to the simplicity of its depiction - this is what 'Čexovian' means.

NOTES

(1) [From: A. Derman, O masterstve Čexova (Moskva, Sovetskij pisatel', 1959). Chapter II, pp. 21-22; 23-25; 27-29; 30-45.]
(2) [By subtext is meant inner structure (of the work) intended by the author to express the import of the work.]
(3) [Numerals in parentheses in this essay refer to the volume and page number in Čexov's Polnoe sobranie sočinenij i pisem (Moskva, Goslitizdat, 1944-1951).]
(4) A.P. Čexov v vospominanijax sovremennikov (Moskva, Goslitizdat, 1947), pp. 218-219.
(5) M. Gor'kij and A. Čexov, Perepiska, stat'i i vyskazyvanija (Moskva, Izdatel'stvo Akademii nauk, 1937), p. 46.
(6) Ibid., p. 51.
(7) Ibid., p. 52.
(8) Ibid., p. 12.
(9) Ibid., p. 16.
(10) [In Russian peasant homes, the oven was a fairly large brick and mortar structure. The back part of the oven was warm, not hot, and was large enough to sleep on. The aged, the infirm, and small children were given preference for this select spot.]
(11) A famous Petersburg actor of the time.

II

THE NATURE OF DETAIL (1)

E.S. DOBIN

1

When Kačalov [V.I. Kačalov (Šverubovič) (1875-1948) – one of the
most talented actors of the Moscow Art Theater] was rehearsing
the role of Trigorin in The Seagull, Čexov invited him to talk about
the part. Kačalov awaited the meeting nervously.

> "You see", began Anton Pavlovič, "the fishing poles should be,
> you know, home made, crooked. He makes them himself with a
> pen knife. The cigar is good . . . well, maybe it isn't really good,
> but it comes wrapped in silver paper in any case. . . ." He
> paused, thought a moment, and said, "But most important are the
> fishing poles." Then he fell silent. (2)

Kačalov was bewildered. He had expected something completely different. He "began to pester him about how to handle this or that part
in the role". Čexov answered evasively, probably not without a hidden smile. "Hmmm . . . well, I really don't know. How to handle
it? As well as possible."
    When Kačalov persisted in asking, Čexov showed him how Trigorin
would drink vodka with Maša. He stood up, straightened his vest,
and groaned clumsily twice, "You see, that is the way I would do
it", and in explanation he added, "When you sit for a long time, you
always want to do it that way."
    Kačalov could elicit no more information.
    Perhaps one would attach small significance to this episode had
there not taken place a similar conversation with Stanislavskij regarding the very same role. Stanislavskij's interpretation did not
quite satisfy Čexov.
    "Your acting is excellent, but it is not my character. I did not
write that."
    Stanislavskij became alarmed: in what way had he sinned against
the truth of the image? The answer which followed seemed strange
and incomprehensible. "He has checkered pants and his shoes are
full of holes." (3) Only after six years, during the second staging
of The Seagull, did Stanislavskij understand the significant meaning
which Čexov placed in insignificant trifles, which at first glance appear unimportant or even completely meaningless.
    For Čexov these were not trifles but carefully thought out, exact
details which were right on target. Čexov had this in mind when he

summoned Kačalov to talk and hinted about the home-made fishing
pole and the ordinary cigars wrapped in ostentatious foil. He was
dissatisfied that Stanislavskij played Trigorin as a dandy who would
dress for swimming in white pants and elegant shoes instead of common checkered pants and shabby footwear.

When Stanislavskij searched more deeply into the play he solved
Čexov's 'puzzling charade'. "The point was not simply the checkered
pants or the shabby shoes or the cigars. After Nina Zarečnaja reads
over some of the sweet but pointless short stories of Trigorin, she
falls in love - not with him, but rather with her girlish daydreams.
It is precisely here that the tragedy of the wounded seagull lies; in
this there is the mockery and crudeness of life." (4)

Stanislavskij discovered an equally important idea in Čexov's comment about an actor who played Astrov (5) "as a degenerate landowner in greased shoes and peasant shirt", which was the current
stage cliché in depicting provincial landowners.

"Čexov was indignant: 'You just can't do it that way. Listen. I
specifically wrote that he wears elegant ties. Elegant ones!' " (6)

By that time Stanislavskij already knew how to look closely at a
Čexovian detail which might appear to be thrown in for no good
reason. He unerringly read the thought lying behind a particularly
incisive observation.

"Here the point of the matter was not in the tie, but in the main
idea of the play. Astrov, a naturally talented person, and the poetically gentle Uncle Vanja decay and languish in a remote place,
whereas the dullard of a professor is in the bliss of Saint Petersburg
and rules Russia with people not much different from himself. Such
is the hidden meaning of the stage direction about the tie." (7)

Even the supersensitive Stanislavskij did not immediately understand the hidden significance of a Čexovian detail. What Čexov
cloaked in a detail was new and unexpected. The load which detail
had to carry was unusual and, at first, insufficiently understood.
It was a psychological, dramatic, and social load.

In his use of detail Čexov followed the path marked out by Gogol',
Dickens, Tolstoj, and many others. To a great degree, however, he
enlarged the artistic possibilities inherent in it. In a Čexovian detail
one finds not only an extraordinary expressiveness and relief, but
also an enormous thought capacity, an ability to evoke a wide circle
of associations. Čexov usually answered the questions of Moscow
Art Theater actors concerning images of his plays by simply stating,
"Everything is written right there." Everything! In spite of the fact
that besides the speeches, he used only the bare language of stage
directions.

Detail played an incomparably greater and more important role
in Čexov's system of imagery than in that of his famous predecessors. In many respects it determined the method of his artistic
thought. A study of Čexov is perhaps the most suitable way to examine the very nature of detail.

2

We will begin with a description, with a vivid reproduction of the world which is visible and observable by the five senses.

When he was still young, Čexov persuaded his older brother Aleksandr, a writer of fiction, to refrain from such descriptions of nature as, "the setting sun, bathing in the waves of a darkened sea, flooded with crimson gold . . ." or "the swallows, flying above the surface of the water, chirped merrily".

Čexov strongly recommended that one eliminate such platitudes. He objected not simply to banality. Čexov admired Turgenev's description of nature - it would be rather surprising if he had not. "But . . . I feel that we are already growing out of descriptions of this type and that something different is needed." (8) Čexov sought a new approach, a new principle of description.

"But finally evening comes", we read in Turgenev's Hunting Sketches.

The sunset flares up into a conflagration reaching up to the zenith. The sun sets. The air nearby is somehow especially translucent, like glass; far away the gentle mist is descending, warm to the sight; a vermilion glow falls, with the dew upon the clearings so recently splashed with the streams of liquid gold; long shadows started to spread from trees, from bushes, from high haystacks. . . . The sun has set; a star has kindled and trembles in the fiery sea of the sunset. . . . Now it grows pale; the sky turns blue; separate shadows vanish; the air is filling with haze. (9)

A wonderful landscape, filled with charm. What did Čexov renounce, from what did he depart? He renounced the long-shot, to use a cinematographic term; he renounced viewing from a distance.

"You will get a moonlit night if you write that on the mill dam a piece of glass from a broken bottle sparkled like a bright small star and the black shadow of a dog or wolf rolled like a ball, etc." (10) This advice to his brother found its way into The Seagull as characteristic of the devices proper to the writer Trigorin. In the play, Čexov contrived to compress the 'super-laconic' description even more. He discarded the simile of the 'bright star'. He made the object more precise: instead of "a piece of glass from a broken bottle" - "the neck of a bottle". Details are compacted more tightly; it is not the shadow of a dog (or of a wolf) that is connected with the dam, but the shadow of a water wheel.

New paths of expressivity are found in the closeup and in the extremely limited selection of items.

"Descriptions of nature must always be short." (11)

"Brevity is the sister of talent." (12)

"Shorten it, man, shorten it." (13)

Čexov's letters are full of similar aphorisms. Usually the letters express dissatisfaction with his writings. Only once do we find a proud statement: "I have the ability to speak briefly on long subjects." (14)

These words express an entire work philosophy. The esthetic worth of detail is in part proclaimed in them. The charm of detail is found in the magic power of <u>recreating a phenomenon in its entirety with one or two strokes</u>. The neck of a broken bottle, the shadow of the water wheel - "and the picture of a moonlit night is ready".

This economy of means is perceived, not as limitation, not as a lack, not as poverty, but as just the opposite, as wealth. The apparent but fascinating sensation of fullness and completeness of a phenomenon, an object, or a picture drawn with one stroke is the source of esthetic delight. Comparing it with the usual contemplation of beauty and of the expressiveness of the surrounding world, we are convinced that only art gives such joy.

Nikolaj Čikildeev's "legs became numb and his gait changed so that once, walking along a corridor, he stumbled and fell <u>with the tray of ham and peas</u>" ("The Peasants"). The detail is rather fleeting, yet it is an exact stroke, revealing the event as though it had happened before the reader's eyes. Such is the primary, basic function of a detail: "to present a picture by using a petty particular", as Čexov himself said.

The matter, however, lies not just in the observable whole. A phenomenon is coordinated with its surroundings in many ways. The imprint of the surroundings lies on the object. The characteristics of people and their paths of life are reflected and interrelated.

"Ham and peas" does not simply reconstruct the restaurant surroundings which were part of Nikolaj Čikildeev's life. We all know with what agility waiters carry trays piled with courses, skillfully maneuvering between merry-makers, dancers, and drunks. When a waiter falls with a tray in his hands (and with just one course), it is a sign of complete infirmity, the end of his career.

This detail also contains a hidden contrast between the established routine and the misfortune which gave the final blow to the poor waiter. The banality of "ham and peas" emphasizes the sudden drama. They shall continue, as before, to carry ham and peas through the aisles of the <u>Slavjanskij Bazar</u>, but Nikolaj Čikildeev shall no longer be there.

All of this Čexov puts into a single detail.

"The sparkle of the neck of a broken bottle and the shadow from the mill wheel" is a <u>contemplated</u> world, a fraction of that on which a concentrated ray of attention falls. "Ham and peas" is more characteristic of the new thing which Čexov brought into the realm of artistic details: it is a detail as a fragment of <u>that which is actually happening</u>.

In "The House with the Mezzanine" the estate is described: "During a thunderstorm the whole house trembled and, it seemed, cracked into pieces, and it was a bit frightening, especially at night, when <u>all ten large windows were suddenly illuminated by lightning</u>."

From the picture of the village fire in "The Peasants" it is evident how a detail 'tightens' the mainspring of the story. In the first lines, in the <u>long-shot</u>, the tone is narrative, restrained, even peaceful in outward appearance: ". . . on the thatch roof of one of the last huts stood a pillar of fire seven feet high which swirled and strewed sparks on all sides, just like a splashing fountain. And suddenly the whole roof went up in bright flames and the crackling of fire was heard."

When, at a <u>normal viewing distance</u>, Čexov turns to people, a dramatic note appears and is strengthened: ". . . all those who ran from below were out of breath and could not talk because of their trembling. They jostled one another, fell down and, not adjusted to the bright light, saw poorly and did not recognize one another."

The highest point, the culmination, depends on the detail: "It was dreadful. It was especially dreadful that <u>doves were flying in the smoke over the flames</u>." And further, "Ol'ga, bathed in light, was choking" and was looking "with horror on the <u>red sheep</u> and at the <u>pink doves</u> which flew in the smoke".

The more the field of vision narrows and the more the eye approaches detail, the stronger the tension becomes. The reflected light contributes to this. Direct sight is found only at the beginning of the scene. Then, ". . . the light of the moon was obscured and soon the whole village was enveloped by a red, flickering light; black shadows moved along the ground and there was a smell of burning". And in the end - red sheep and pink doves.

'Reflectiveness' separates the object from the other facets of a phenomenon, from the conglomerate of its multiple particulars. Detail becomes all the more distinguished, 'compressed', both in visible, material existence and in emotional depth.

In Čexov's later prose, detail appears more and more often as the striking point of an event, as the focus of the drama.

An investigating magistrate and a district doctor come to the post-mortem of the body of a suicide ("On Official Duty"). "On the floor, right next to the table legs, lay a long, motionless body, covered in white. In the dim light of a little lamp, beside the white covering, <u>nearly new rubber galoshes</u> were clearly seen."

Even recently the owner of the galoshes had not been thinking about death. Now he abruptly ended his life, ". . . and everything was bad and sinister here: the dark walls and the silence and these galoshes and the inertness of the dead body".

The galoshes are mentioned before the dead body. They strike the eye. The picture would not be so melancholic were it not for this absurdly insulting petty everyday item. There is another detail which is sinister because it is so commonplace. The suicide "ended his life somewhat strangely, behind a samovar, <u>after having laid out snacks on the table</u>". We learn very little about the suicide in the remainder of the story, but the details communicate sharply the absurdity and horror of what has happened.

In the story "The Murder", this form of imagery is used with even more dramatic effectiveness.

Sickly Matvej argues endlessly with his rich first cousin Jakov Ivanovič and his sister Aglaja, exposing their sanctimonious, abnor-

44

mal religious observances. On a fast day he asks Aglaja to give him
some vegetable oil. At first she refuses, but nonetheless places the
bottle of oil on the table in front of him, not because she has pity on
her sick brother, but "with a smile full of malicious joy, evidently
happy that he was such a sinner". Matvej mixes the oil into the potatoes. Jakov Ivanovič, embittered because they have distracted him
from doing a penance of endless bows to the ground and the singing
of prayers, hurls himself at his cousin.

" 'But I say that you may not use any oil!' Jakov shouted still
louder, turning red all over. He suddenly seized the cup, raised it
above his head, and with all his strength hurled it to the floor so that
splinters flew." He roughly drags Matvej from behind the table.
Matvej, startled, resists and accidentally tears Jakov Ivanovič's
collar.

The murder takes place suddenly, in a moment. How is it described? Aglaja "shrieked, seized the bottle with the Lenten oil and
with all her strength hit her hated cousin directly on the top of his
head". Matvej staggered. "Jakov, breathing heavily, excited and
feeling pleasure because when the bottle struck Matvej's head, it
cackled as if it were alive", points with his finger to Aglaja for a
flat iron sitting nearby.

The murder itself is not shown. "Only when blood poured over
Jakov's hands . . . and when the ironing board fell noisily and Matvej, in turn, slumped over it, did Jakov's anger cease and then he
understood what had happened." The horror of what he has done lies
heavily upon him. "But nothing was so frightful for Jakov as blood-
stained potatoes; he was afraid of stepping on them."

Instead of the murder scene, we see only bloodstains on potatoes.
The reflected detail, one point, one stroke, acts no less strongly
than a minutely described picture.

The accessories of the scene are sparingly selected: a cup with
potatoes, a bottle of oil, an ironing board, and a flat iron. (15) All
these things (and only these) take part in the action. The first blow
is struck with the focal point of the argument - a bottle of oil. The
pleasure felt by Jakov Ivanovič "because when the bottle struck Matvej's head, it cackled as if it were alive" serves as a stimulus to
the crime. The flat iron is the murder weapon. Matvej falls dead
on the ironing board. On the potatoes is the sinister gleam of the
crime. Each object is used up, every 'gun' is fired. (16) The quarrel arose over potatoes and oil. The potatoes contain an unforget-
table imprint of the murder.

3

Čexov learned the art of the salient, concentrated detail first of all
from Lev Tolstoj. We will recall Karenin's ears, the locks of hair
on Anna Karenina's neck, the short moustached lip of the wife of
Andrej Bolkonskij, Princess Mar'ja's radiant eyes, Captain Tušin's
small pipe, the meaningful creases on the forehead of the diplomat

Bilibin, and so forth.

Contemporaries clearly sensed the novelty of the Tolstoj view of the image, the isolation of a bright detail replacing the familiar descriptions full of particulars which sometimes reached the point of scrupulosity (as in the case of Gončarov). Tolstoj likes to repeat a newly discovered detail, to return to it. In Čexov a detail appears, as a rule, but once.

Characters often appear in Čexov for just one instant, sometimes not even taking part in the main action. They are presented with one small characteristic, but this solitary stroke is so emphatic and it so exactly captures the person, that it becomes a portrait.

Regarding the elderly wife of his excellency ("Anna Around the Neck"), "the lower part of her face was so disproportionately large that it seemed as if she had a large stone in her mouth".

The student in the white, unbuttoned uniform jacket was the first to climb up onto the roof of the burning hut ("The Peasants"). He "shouted with a shrill, hoarse voice and in such a tone, as if putting out fires were a common thing for him".

At the end of "The New Dacha" mention is made of the new owner of the dacha, "He wears a cockade on his cap, he talks and coughs like a very important official, although he is only in the rank of collegiate secretary, and when peasants bow to him, he does not respond to them."

Sometimes a portrait is given with a single remark. A young merchant, a donor, comes to a bishop (in the story of the same name). " 'May God grant it', he said, leaving. 'Absolutely without fail! According to the circumstances, Right Reverend. . . . I hope it would.' " Through the meaningless weaving of bureaucratic yet solemn, obsequious words there arises the appearance of a dark, puffed-up merchant, and together with it an aura of servility and of grovelling which stifles the sick, good, helpless old man - the bishop.

Sometimes a single word is sufficient.

" 'It's caddishness' ", says Šelestov, the father of Manjusja, appearing at the beginning of a story ("The Teacher of Literature"), " 'caddishness, and nothing else. Yes, it's caddishness.' " These same words appear again at the end of the story after a lapse of a long period of time. " 'It's caddishness' ", he says, "and I'll tell him that right to his face: 'It's caddishness, kind sir!' "

The repetition here is necessary. The obsession of a conservative sputtering venomously against "today's young people", among whom are "few gentlemen", is emphasized. Šelestov himself is, of course, a 'gentleman' from head to toe. Together with the stupidly repeated "caddishness", the polite suffix "-s" (17) and "kind sir" produce a specially refined impression: "Yes sir, caddishness, sir"; "It's caddishness, kind sir!"

Sometimes intonation expresses that which is most important.

The commissioner of rural police wrings old debts out of peasants. " 'I am asking you (18) . . . . It's you I'm asking, why don't you pay up your arrears? You keep not paying and I have to answer for you!' "

"The commissioner jotted down something and said to Osip, <u>in a calm, even tone of voice - as if he was asking for some water</u>: 'Get out!' " ("The Peasants").

The commissioner is neither a beast nor a bloodsucker. He simply is carrying out the duties of his office efficiently and dispassionately. He is not depicted grotesquely. "When he sat down in his cheap carriage and coughed, then even by the expression of his long skinny back it was evident that he no longer remembered Osip nor the elder nor Žukovo's arrears, but rather that he was thinking about something personal." The commissioner was very ill and might reasonably expect compassion, but neither sympathy nor compassion was forthcoming. The terribly profound workaday heartlessness, the common and legalized relationship to the peasant as if to something completely low, is expressed here by the intentional ungrammatical use of a word and an indifferent intonation.

The remarkable socio-historical typicalness of the commissioner, old Šelestov, and the civil servant is quite obvious, as are the many hundreds of fleeting, silhouetted images, drawn with one stroke of the pen.

The features of a man are revealed by a small trait, but in it we find class-caste traits, the sharp contradictions of life and the character of the time.

4

The particularly important role which detail plays in Čexov's view of the world becomes quite clear when we turn our attention not to episodical characters (where a large part of the brevity is predetermined), but to the main protagonists.

What is said about Misjus' ("The House with the Mezzanine")? Remarkably little (even if one does not compare it, say, to the broad, lengthy descriptions of Gončarov's heroes); considerably less than is said about her noisy and self-confident sister Lida. Misjus' has thin hands and large eyes. She talks little, and, it seems, about whatever crosses her mind - which might be completely uninteresting: the soot in the servant hall caught fire, a worker caught a large fish in the pond. It is just as if it were intentionally brought out that she has no distinguishing traits. However, one feature is clear on the otherwise deliberately featureless background. Misjus' reads avidly and continuously. "Upon arising in the morning, she immediately took up a book. . . . She read all day, looking into the book avidly, and only because her gaze sometimes became tired, stunned, and her face turned pale could one discern how much this reading wearied her brain."

Lida with her straightforward, absolute principles is described by distinct, sharply drawn features. Misjus' is outlined in cautious halftones. Čexov, it seems, feared excessive delineating. Nothing at all is said about what Misjus' reads, what she thinks about what she has read, or what she says about books.

But then a detail appears and the image of the girl is brightened
from within. "We were picking mushrooms and talking, and <u>when
she asked about something, she stepped a little ahead to see my
face</u>."

How this gesture opens a crack into the soul of Misjus' - timid,
pure, untarnished! How much it says about her emotional state at
that particular moment. Heartfelt trust in the artist (who tells the
story) seized the girl's soul. The light breezes of the first love
were passing by, still unclear to Misjus' herself. A sparing detail
pierces into the very depths of her character.

"Ženja (Misjus') walked beside me and tried not to look at the
sky - <u>so that she wouldn't see the falling stars, which for some
reason frightened her</u>." At first glance this seems like an unnecess-
ary detail; in any case it is not absolutely essential. Later one sees
how indispensable it was. Ženja bows to the authority of her domi-
neering elder sister who does not allow contradiction. But her new-
born feeling is so strong that she dares to sneak out at night for a
walk with the artist. He covers up her cold shoulders with his overcoat and, unable to restrain himself, showers her with kisses.

" 'Till tomorrow!' she whispered, and, <u>as if afraid to disturb the
silence of the night, she gently embraced me</u>."

These two unusually exact details fully reveal the vulnerability,
the frailty of the young being. If these details were not given, the
emotional drama enacted after Ženja has told Lida about her love
for the artist would remain unexplained. Everything takes place behind the scenes. We learn only the result: at the insistence of her
elder sister, Ženja renounces love and happiness. She leaves without seeing the artist again or saying goodbye. Although he does not
describe how Ženja yielded or what she went through, Čexov lets
us know <u>why</u> it happened. The details reveal it.

Even when images are fully drawn, a detail often serves Čexov
as the final, concluding stroke, delineating a character once and
for all.

Anna Sergeevna, the 'lady with the little dog', is completely bound
up in her narrow little world - first with her hateful family, fenced
off from any large interests, and then in her anguished, unresolvable
relations with Gurov. It seems she is completely disinterested in
what goes on about her. She does not even know where her husband
works.

She says, "My husband is, perhaps, a good, honest man - <u>but you
see, he's a flunkey</u>!"

This one word makes it evident that in certain personality traits -
and rather high ones at that - Anna Sergeevna surpasses the people
of her circle. She even surpasses Gurov, the pleasant gentleman
from Moscow. Certainly at one time Gurov felt like slipping away
from this heavy, tiresome affair with a married woman to the quiet
comfort of a well-to-do existence.

The magnetic force, the mental charm of 'the lady with the little
dog', exists not only in the force of her love and devotion, but is
also found in her pure moral feeling, in the unyielding intuitive

understanding of what is noble and what is base - in spite of the fact that it is expressed neither in action nor in her field of interests nor in intellectual endeavor.

Čexov modestly avoids a detailed description of Anna Sergeevna's mental worth, but the word dropped by her in passing speaks of her mental nonconformity. 'The lady with the little dog' is free from the biased life views of a privileged milieu in which everyone depends on a yet more privileged person who stands higher on the official ladder.

If we were to eliminate these words, "He is a flunkey", then the story would be deprived of something very important and significant. One of the most shining feminine images in world literature would grow dull.

In Čexov one occasionally encounters small scenes which, it seems, were thought up for the sake of adding sharp, distinctive details.

Anja's old husband ("Anna Around the Neck") goes with her to the theater every now and then.

> When they were passing by the buffet, Anna would very much have liked something sweet; she was fond of chocolate and apple pastry, but she had no money, and she was too shy to ask her husband. He would take a pear, squeeze it with his fingers, and ask hesitantly, "How much?"
> "25 kopeks."
> "Really!" he would say, and put the pear back; but since it was awkward to leave the buffet without buying anything he would then ask for soda water and drink the whole bottle alone and tears welled up in his eyes, and Anja hated him at such times.

Life in the village becomes totally unbearable for Nikolaj Čikildeev - his whole life a hardworking waiter - because of the poverty, the greediness of the grandmother, the malicious reproaches of Fekla, and the savageness of morals and manners. At night "he took out his tail coat from his little green trunk, put it on, and, going to the window, stroked the sleeves, held the coat by the tails, and smiled. Then he carefully took it off, put it in the trunk, and lay down again." A waiter's dress coat in the halo of a bright dream! This detail sharply delineates the abyss of a peasant's sorrow, the misfortune of Nikolaj Čikildeev.

The nature of detail in such small scenes appears with particular distinction if one imagines them displayed visually, as on a cinema screen. Doctor Starcev "had yet another diversion, into which he was imperceptibly drawn, little by little, that was - in the evenings to pull out of his pockets paper banknotes procured by his practice . . . yellow and green, smelling of perfume and vinegar and incense and blubber oil. . . ."

The disastrous metamorphosis of a man is presented with the brevity of genius: a young doctor with spiritual interests and yearnings has become a grasping, heartless moneygrubber. Čexov completely avoids extensive psychological descriptions. A spiritual fall is indicated by a single sharp, rough stroke of a brush, by a detail which strikes mercilessly hard.

In "The Teacher of Literature" the metamorphosis is reversed: it is painful but beneficial. The story begins with a happy, carefree horseback ride. Flowers are fragrant, music is being played in the city gardens, the shadows of poplars and acacia are comfortable, and "it was evident that all those strollers hurrying into the garden to hear the music enjoyed looking at the cavalcade".

At the side of the gymnasium teacher Nikitin was a girl of eighteen with whom he had fallen in love. There were no obstacles along the path to happiness, not even the slightest. At the first declaration of love the proposal is accepted. The wedding ceremony in the church was joyful and solemn. The dowry was rich. Upon arrival from the church, Nikitin is in a state of bliss and sprawls on a Turkish divan. "I felt so tender, comfortable, and cozy, as never before in my life."

Manjusja (Maša or Manja) builds her little nest and the family happiness is unclouded. It appears especially precious when Nikitin recalls his past orphanhood, poverty, unhappy childhood, and sad youth. " 'I am endlessly happy with you, my joy', says Nikitin to Maša, playing with her fingers or unbraiding and again braiding her hair."

But the moment arrives when the teacher of literature is suddenly sickened by the comfort, satiation, and prosperity. He thinks a while about how "apart from the soft light of the icon lamp beaming on the quiet family happiness, apart from this little world in which he and this cat lived so quietly and sweetly, there was indeed yet another world. Suddenly he passionately longed for that other world, he longed to work in a factory or in a large workshop, to speak from a rostrum, to write, be published, make a stir, get tired, and suffer."

This happens after his first tiff with his wife. Not an argument, not a clash, but a tiff. Nothing had changed in their relationship. Nobody had encroached on the family well-being. Maša had only censured Captain Poljanskij for having accepted a transfer to another town. He had behaved badly in regards to her older sister Varja.

"Why badly?" asked Nikitin, . . . "As far as I know, he did not propose or make any promises. "
"Then why did he come so often to her house? If one doesn't want to get married, then one shouldn't come."

What happened? Almost nothing. Could Nikitin make any serious reproach? Almost none. However, "a heavy anger, like a cold weight, sank in his heart and he wanted to make some rude remark to Manja and even to jump and hit her".

To hit Manjusja?! Manjusja, the builder of "an unusually pleasant life which reminded him of pastoral idylls". For what?

"So that means", he asked, controlling himself, "if I visited your
house often, then I certainly had to get married to you?"
"Of course. You yourself understand that perfectly well."
"Nice."
And a minute or so later he repeated, "Nice."

A landslide, a catastrophe has taken place. "Peace is lost, probably
forever, and happiness for him is no longer possible." But not as a
result of adultery (as in the story "The Wife") or of some serious
clash. The catastrophe was prepared little by little, and the path to
it is marked exclusively by light, subtle details.

Nikitin "observed carefully how his sensible and practical Manja
built her nest". Three cows were bought. There were in the cellar
many jugs full of milk and small pots of sour cream which Manjusja
kept for butter. "Sometimes by way of a joke, Nikitin asked her for
a glass of milk; she was disturbed, since this was disorder." When
Manjusja found in the cupboard an overlooked piece of sausage or
cheese as hard as a rock, she would say with an important air, "The
kitchen help can have this to eat." Such a tiny piece is fit only for a
mousetrap, notes Nikitin, but Manjusja heatedly proves to him that
"it is all the same to servants".

This is the only implied criticism of Manjusja, and even here it
is lit by a rosy, idyllic light. When Manjusja refuses Nikitin a glass
of milk, he "laughed and took her into his arms and said, 'Well, well,
I was just joking, my precious, just joking!' " After the argument
about the dried up piece of sausage, "he agreed with her and embraced her in delight".

But that light is too rosy, too idyllic. Manjusja is too rosy and
appetizing. At the time of their first tiff Nikitin "glanced at her neck,
her full shoulders and bosom, and recalled the word which the briga-
dier general had once said in church: 'rose' ". Details which are not
sharply worded at all or striking to the eye uncover the character of
Manjusja - 'rose'. A rosy, appetizing, hopelessly narrow being, who
with the years shall become even more economical, miserly, and
limited.

The saturation of Čexovian details which are sprinkled and scattered here and there is striking. They project a satisfied beatific
stupor which envelops Nikitin, as well as the impetus to a rift, to
new vision.

When he was falling in love, Nikitin liked everything at the
Šelestovs, even the word "caddishness", which the foolish old man
liked to repeat. But reading Gogol' or Puškin aloud in class "tires
the teacher of literature", who has become torpid from family happiness. He looks at his watch and says, "with a sigh, as if admiring
the writer, 'How good!' "

Before the conversation about the 'mean trick' of officer Poljanskij, Manjusja "was, by all evidence, sleeping with great pleasure".
Beside her lay a purring white cat. Manja awoke and eagerly drank
a glass of water.

" 'I had my fill of marmalade', she said, and smiled."

And Nikitin begins "to feel irritated at the white cat which stretched out and curved its back". This is an irritation against himself for having grown soft amidst pots of sour cream and jugs of milk.

These light brush strokes are implicit and are charged with important meaning.

5

The sparkle of the neck of a broken bottle plus the shadow of the water wheel present the picture of a moonlit night. Let us place next to it another Čexovian picture of a moonlit night:

> The only light was from a small lamp - it was burning dimly and smokily. When somebody stood in front of the lamp and a large shadow fell over the window, bright moonlight could be seen ("The Peasants").

The first picture presents a phenomenon by itself. In the second there is both a picture of a moonlit night and a melancholy image of peasant poverty. The bright moonlight emphasizes the darkness of the peasant hut and the meager, sad light of a kerosene lamp.

In the story "Three Years", a husband tries to make up with his young wife who doesn't love him. He had insulted her, but now he passionately seeks forgiveness; he kisses and hugs her. The reconciliation does not take place. "And like a bird she bent beneath her the leg which he had kissed." In a sharply caught detail there is a vivid expressiveness and the psychological situation at the given moment and a life drama. Such details present character, conflict and action in their living integrity.

A detail can embody something lying outside itself. "Here old birches stood on both sides of the road. They were as sad and unhappy as their owner Vlasič, and were scraggy and lanky as he." A yellow acacia was "also scraggy and lanky" ("Neighbors").

In "The Peasants", "The grandmother dashed out from the hut with a long stick and then for about half an hour screeched near her cabbages, which were as flabby and scraggy as she was."

Before us is another aspect of detail: the characteristics of one phenomenon shed light on another. Detail reminds and accompanies, enlightens and gives an appraisal.

The gymnasium teacher Belikov "went out in galoshes and with an umbrella even in fine weather and he always wore a warm quilted coat. His umbrella was in a case, and his watch was in a case of grey suede, and when he took out his pen knife to sharpen a pencil, the knife was in a little case; and his face, it seemed, was also in a case, since he always hid it in his collar . . . And when he sat down in a cab he always ordered the driver to put up the top."

The circle of generalization becomes wider. Greek and Latin, which Belikov teaches, "were for him, in fact, the galoshes and umbrella in which he hid from real life". Further: "And Belikov also tried to hide his thoughts in a case." Only circulars and articles in which something was prohibited were clear for him. "And he always found a certain element of ambiguity in a permission and in a sanction."

The story ends: "And indeed the life we lead in the city, in stuffiness, in the crush, the useless papers we write, the vint (a Russian card game) we play - isn't that a case? And when we pass our whole life among loafers, pettifoggers, stupid idle women, and speak and listen to all sorts of rubbish - isn't that a case?"

This philosophical, social, historical, and psychological generalization became so broad that when you say "man in a case", you do not always recall the image of Belikov himself. But it would not have arisen if it were not so clearly true to the life of the teacher of dead languages, or if the artist had not found such a brightly perceived, capacious and all-embracing detail.

The town Ukleevka, as one learns in the beginning of the story "In the Ravine", was famous for the fact that at a wake a sexton sat down at a jar of caviar and no power could tear him away from it until he ate the whole lot. An emaciated, greedy sexton is portrayed. An event is described. But most important, we are presented an image of life so stupefied and deprived of rational thought that, in the course of many years, it was possible to say of a large and populous town only that a sexton once ate a jar of caviar at a funeral.

There is still another type of detail - the leitmotif.

When Marfa, the wife of the coffin maker Jakov, is dying ("Rothschild's Violin"), he measures her and makes a coffin. When it is finished, he writes in his notebook: "For Marfa Ivanova, one coffin, two rubles forty kopeks." He keeps track of losses in the notebook. His wife's coffin is a loss.

Jakov earns additional money by playing the violin. If anybody in the city has a wedding without music, or if the tinsmith Šaxkes, the head of the local wedding orchestra, does not invite him to play, then that is a loss. "The police inspector was sick for two years and was withering away, and Jakov patiently awaited his death, but the police inspector went to the district capital for treatment and there he died. " An obvious loss, "at least about ten rubles, since an expensive coffin with silk brocade would have been required". On Sundays and holidays it is a sin to work. A loss! Monday - a bad day. Also a loss!

Jakov Ivanov makes a note of all these losses. When he adds them up for a year, the total amounts to over 1000 rubles. If only he had put that thousand in the bank, he would have come up with forty rubles interest. Another loss!

True, when they buried Marfa, Jakov "read the psalter himself so as not to pay a sexton, and he did not have to pay for the grave since he was the godfather of the cemetery guard's child. Four peasants carried the coffin to the cemetery, not for money but out of respect for the deceased. Behind the coffin walked old women, beggars, a pair of jurodivy [jurodivy - 'fool in Christ', characterized by eccentric behavior, reputed to have a gift of prophecy], and the oncoming people crossed themselves piously. . . . Jakov was very pleased that everything was done so honorably, seemly, cheaply, and without offense to anybody."

For the most part there was however just loss upon loss. For example, he could have taken up river fishing and sold the fish. "He might have rowed, in the past, a boat from estate to estate and played the violin, and everybody would have paid. He might have run barges, raised geese, and sold the dressed geese and down in Moscow. He might possibly have gotten 10 rubles a year from the down alone. But he had missed his opportunities, he did nothing at all. Such losses! Ah, such losses!" Moreover, he could have done all three at once: fished, run barges, and raised geese. He could have acquired quite a large amount of capital. But he did nothing, his life passed, and looking back he sees that "there is nothing but losses - and such terrible ones at that - enough to make one shiver".

Losses overshadowed everything. Before her death, Marfa reminds him that many years ago, a blond haired infant had been born to them but later had died. "You and I then used to sit by the stream and sing songs . . . under the willow." But the coffin maker recalls nothing, neither the little baby nor the willow.

Only later does he remember the baby and the green willow, quiet and sad. When he falls ill and believes he is dying, a horrible thought enters his mind: "There will be only profit from death; one does not need to eat or drink or pay taxes. . . ." This is bitter and insulting: from death a man gets profit, and from life a loss. Jakov was constantly counting up losses. He forbade Marfa to drink tea "because even without that the expenses were high, and so she drank only hot water". The most terrible, irreparable loss consisted in the fact that a life was controlled by a constant dread of losses.

Jakov suddenly begins to understand that losses were not at all where he saw them earlier. "And why couldn't a man live in such a way that there would be no waste and losses? . . . Why did Jakov quarrel all his life, growl, get into fights, offend his wife, and, one asks, why did he frighten and insult the Jew yesterday? Why do people in general keep each other from living in peace? What losses come from that! What terrible losses! If hatred and malice did not exist, people could profit so greatly from one another."

The initial detail naturally, easily, and strongly turns into a comprehensive social and moral thought. Here the nature of the detail is different from that of the "sparkle from the neck of a broken bottle". We enter into the sphere of allegory, of transferred thought. Details which are metaphors serve as the fulcrum of the artist's most important idea. "A Case", "the recording of losses" run all through a work and become its spirit and thought.

As is well known, Tolstoj's style is almost devoid of metaphors. But when he has recourse to a detail-metaphor - and this happens rarely - then it is remembered forever. Such is the memorable 'oak' of Andrej Bolkonskij - personifying the sudden change in the hero's character.

An observation, which became a detail-metaphor, definitely suggested the idea behind "Xadži-Murat". "A bush hangs onto the edge of a dusty, gray road", Tolstoj wrote in his diary on July 19, 1896, "another is broken and splashed with black dirt, the stem hanging down and dirtied; <u>the third shoot sticks out sideways, also black from dust, but nevertheless alive and showing red in the middle. It recalled Xadži-Murat to me.</u> I would like to put it down on paper. He defends life until the very end, and, alone in the whole field, he somehow still successfully defended it" (Emphasis Tolstoj's).

6

It is not an accident that Engels' famous definition of realism is threefold: "Realism implies, besides truthfulness of details, an accuracy of transmitting typical characters in typical situations." (19) "Detail" is placed side by side with 'characters' and 'situations'.

Tolstoj says that the effectiveness of art (its "contagion", in his terminology) "is reached only then and to the degree that the artist finds those extremely brief elements out of which a work of art takes shape". (20)

<u>Only then and to that degree</u>! It could be that Tolstoj exaggerates the meaning of "extremely brief elements"! It would seem rather that the force of art lies in the opposite, in the huge generalization of uncoordinated phenomena, in typification. Actually, both of these 'contradictory' theses are true. They do not exclude one another; rather, it is in their dialectical unity that the specific character of art is revealed.

The "extremely brief elements" are not at all reduced to the fact that an artist vigilantly observes and records the particulars, the smallest traits, the slightest variations of the spirit, the shape of character. The sense and force of a detail lie in the fact that in <u>the "extremely brief" is included the whole</u>, which at times is very large. The esthetic effect is connected with the simultaneousness and inseparability of both poles of perception.

Detail is a miniature model of the 'substance' of art. Within each individual character is a type. In the chain of isolated incidents there is time, history. In a specific collision are the contradictions of society. In single fates are the laws of an epoch. Neither 'characters' nor 'situations' are possible nor conceivable in art outside of "extremely brief elements". Such is the nature of art.

Both elements in art - broad pictures which generalize reality ("typical characters in typical surroundings") and details - are inseparable and interconnected.

7

We usually use the terms 'detail' [Russian <u>detal</u>'] and 'particular' [Russian <u>podrobnost</u>'] as synonyms. Čexov, the virtuoso of detail, having uncovered its new, richest possibilities, rose up against particulars.

"You have heaped up a whole mountain of particulars, and this
mountain has hidden the sun." (21)

"In the foreground of the picture are many particulars. . . . It
is necessary to sacrifice them for the sake of the whole. . . . Particulars, even those which are very interesting, weary the attention."
(22)

"A mass of particulars, which are piling up." (23)

"Particulars spread out all over like spilled oil." (24)

The novels of Pisemskij are "tiring because of the particulars".
(25)

All of the above are taken from a single volume of Čexov's letters.
We will note that Čexov uses the plural - 'particulars' - and emphasizes this plurality; many particulars, a mass of particulars, a
mountain of particulars. In this, evidently, is the essence of the
distinction. A particular exercises its influence in the plural. Detail
gravitates toward the singular. It replaces a series of particulars.

Detail is intensive. Particular is extensive.

By his side stood a man about forty years old, broad shouldered,
broad cheeked, with a low forehead, narrow Tartar eyes, a short,
flat nose, a square chin, and black, shiny hair, as stiff as bristles.
. . . He was dressed in a sort of shabby frock coat with smooth
copper buttons; an old black silk kerchief was wrapped around his
thick neck.

Two lines later another person is described.

This was a somewhat short, stocky man of about thirty, pock-
marked and curly haired, with a blunt, stub nose, alive, brown
little eyes, and a little scanty beard. . . . He wore a new, thin
peasant coat of gray broadcloth with a velveteen collar which
sharply contrasted with the edge of his scarlet shirt buttoned up
tightly around the throat ("The Singers" from Turgenev's Hunting
Sketches).

The contrast between portraits of this sort and the laconic description of the little girl in "The Peasants", "tow-headed, unwashed and
indifferent", is quite evident; in "The Peasants" the step from exter-
nality to the conditions of life and to emotional makeup is extremely
rapid, and the very mode of life is strongly grasped.

However, it is incorrect to say that Čexov's statements deny the
role of particulars. Both details and particulars in equal measure
pertain to the sphere of the "extremely brief elements" to which
Tolstoj assigned a decisive meaning in art. The category of "detail"
included by Engels in his popular formula of realism embraces both
details and particulars; the difference is only in the level of laconism
and density in the norm of selection and in the measure of brevity.

Čexov objects to an abundance of particulars and to their excess-
iveness. He writes to Gor'kij, "It is clear when I write 'a man sat
on the grass'; it . . . is clear and does not hold one's attention. On

the other hand, it is unclear and burdensome if I write, 'a tall, nar-
row-chested man of medium height with a chestnut beard sat on the
green grass which had already been trampled down by those who
walked on it; he sat silently, timidly, and fearfully glanced about.'
This is not immediately graspable, but literature must be absorbed
immediately, in a second." (26)

Of course there are no universal quantitative criteria equally bind-
ing for all, nor can there be. Čexov found new ways of intensifying
images in their semantic connections, new artistic resources in
associations and rapprochement of objects and phenomena. Hence,
the new, elevated intellectual and artistic charge in detail.

The 'Čexovian' placed a distinct imprint on contemporary prose.
However, the tendency of the greatest contemporary prose writers
to laconic detail does not by any account mean that the stylistics of
particulars has outlived its time or become outmoded.

Without particulars a literary work is unthinkable; and they are
found even in Čexov's works.

On the first page of "The Peasants" there is a description of a
village hut. "It was dark, crowded and dirty there." Nikolaj
Čikildeev and his wife and daughter "were looking with bemusement
at the huge dirty oven which occupied almost half the hut. The oven
was dark from soot and flies. And the flies! The ovens sagged to
one side, the logs were set crookedly in the walls and it seemed
that the hut would collapse at any moment. In the front corner near
the icons labels from bottles and scraps of newspaper were pasted
up - in place of pictures." The transition from 'long-shot' to 'close-
up' is characteristic.

Čexov set particulars in motion in his own way. Ol'ga Ivanovna
"produced a beautiful crowded arrangement near the piano and fur-
niture out of Japanese parasols, easels, multicolored rags, daggers,
busts, photographs. . . . In the dining room she papered the walls
with cheap popular prints, hung up sickles and bast shoes [shoes
made out of soft wood fiber] , put a scythe and a rake in the corner,
and so the dining room was in Russian style. To make the bedroom
more cavelike, she draped the ceiling and walls with dark broadcloth, hung a Venetian lantern above the beds, and next to the door
she placed a figure with a halbert" ("The Flutterer").

It is a description of rare thoroughness for Čexov.

It is, however, immediately evident that the aim of the artist was
not the completeness of the surroundings. The description is
composed meticulously. The chain of particulars is <u>intentionally</u>
long. The character and makeup of the 'flutterer' is found in the
conglomeration of things, knick-knacks, and trifles ("rags", "busts").
Everything is done for show. It is an exhibition, an attempt to be
original, a painstaking desire to show off. Every object was supposed to create an effect, to startle. But behind the external refine-
ment there is banality, emptiness, an absence of inner delicacy.

The 'chapel' of Jakov Ivanovič and Aglaja ("The Murder") is described in the following way:

. . . in the front corner stood an icon case with ancient family icons in gilded mountings, and both walls right and left were covered with icons in the old and new school, in icon cases and without them. On the table, covered to the floor with a tablecloth, stood an icon of the Annunciation, and close to it were a cypress cross and a censer; wax candles were burning. Next to the table was a lectern.

Just as in "The Flutterer" the thought behind the description is not to present a picture of day-to-day living. Objects were arranged in such a great number, they were made visible to a high degree because they had become of main importance in life. Jakov Ivanovič and Aglaja worship not God, but candles, censers, the lectern, incense, icons - those objects which pertain to church ritual. The objects press heavily. That is why the description is made heavy. A long enumeration is necessary.

In both "The Flutterer" and "The Murder" the heaviness of particulars expresses the strength of the objects which overpowered people. Ritual has overcome belief. Pseudo-refined taste masks the callousness, the egotism of the 'flutterer'.

The arrangement of particulars, their correlation, all depends on the artistic task. The landowner Belokurov ("The House with the Mezzanine") is described in the following manner ". . . he used to get up very early; he walked in a long-waisted peasant coat, drank beer in the evenings and constantly complained to me that he found sympathy nowhere". The lack of coordination of the particulars is striking. Yet this very lack of coordination fixes the character of the personage.

NOTES

(1) [From: E.S. Dobin, Geroj. Sjužet. Detal' (Leningrad, Sovetskij pisatel', 1962), pp. 345-372.]
(2) V.I. Kačalov, "Vospominanija", Čexov v vospominanijax sovremennikov (Moskva, 1954).
(3) K.S. Stanislavskij, "A.P. Čexov v Moskovskom Xudožestvennom Teatre", Čexov v vospominanijax sovremennikov (Moskva, 1954).
(5) [Actually Stanislavskij is speaking about Uncle Vanja, main character of the play of the same name.]
(6) Cf. note 3.
(7) Cf. note 3.
(8) A.P. Čexov, Polnoe sobranie sočinenij i pisem (Moskva, 1949), vol. 16, p. 32.
(9) [From: "The Forest and the Steppe", epilogue of Turgenev's Hunting Sketches.]
(10) Polnoe sobranie sočinenij i pisem, vol. 13, p. 215.
(11) Ibid.
(12) Ibid., vol. 14, p.342.
(13) Ibid., vol. 16, p. 62.

58

(14) Ibid., vol. 14, p. 239.

(15) At the beginning of the scene are several words: "... between the oven and the table, at which Matvej sat, was stretched an ironing board; on it stood a cold iron".

(16) [An allusion to the statement made by Čexov to S. Ščukin, a priest (1873-1931). See Chapter V, p. 108 of the present book.]

(17) [There is no exact equivalent for this in English; basically it represents an overly exaggerated politeness.]

(18) [The word 'you' is in an incorrect grammatical form in the Russian text. Dobin alludes to this below.]

(19) K. Marks and F. Engel's Ob iskusstve (Moskva-Leningrad, 1937), p. 163.

(20) L.N. Tolstoj, Polnoe sobranie sočinenij, (Moskva, 1951), vol. 30, p. 128.

(21) A.P. Čexov, Op. cit., vol. 16, p. 214.

(22) Ibid., vol. 16, p. 184.

(23) Ibid., vol. 16, p. 395.

(24) Ibid., vol. 16, p. 219.

(25) Ibid., vol. 16, p. 60.

(26) Ibid., vol. 18, p. 221.

III

A.P. ČEXOV (1)

VIKTOR ŠKLOVSKIJ

Writers usually begin by imitating: they reach out to old heights, not knowing that their paths lead through new terrain.

In his works as a child, Lermontov to a certain extent rewrote Puškin's poems; Gogol' began with a poem; Dostoevskij wanted to write dramas along the themes of Schiller; and even Tolstoj did not escape the path of Sterne.

Čexov began very quietly, imitating no one although often parodying well-known writers.

He received his literary passport in the "Letter Box" of an editorial office, which corresponded inattentively with young authors, sometimes condescending to print their works, at other times returning their manuscripts with brutal mockery.

When he had already won renown, Čexov remained the friend of his old neighbors in small magazines, who envied him as one of their own, not understanding that he differed from them.

Meanwhile he had done a most difficult thing: he found something new in that which is commonplace.

He strove to avoid the old sujet conflicts which had been used in literature for centuries.

He found a new manner of building structures through description, method of juxtaposition, and in the difference in the formation of commonplace occurrences.

He noticed contradictions in the character of man, and so became a very severe judge of man, for there are no small and commonplace people - all should be great. A high court is present in any story by Čexov.

A century imitates Čexov, it is true, a century which is yet to be completed and which still has not noted his exacting demands.

[Lev] Tolstoj recognized Čexov's worth.

To Čexov it seemed that in Tolstoj's eyes all writers were equal, and so Tolstoj was equally condescending towards all of them.

However, Tolstoj's diaries reveal that he understood Čexov had a new method of revealing the human soul, and that he, Tolstoj, wished to use this method in his favorite work - "Xadži Murat".

Tolstoj saw the Čexovian method of description as suitable for what is great and heroic.

Čexov died at the very beginning of his rise.

When Tolstoj was ill, he once asked Čexov to kiss him. As Čexov bent over, the old man pressed his young friend to his hairy lips, and then, loosening his grip on Anton Pavlovič slightly, he smiled and said, "But I don't care for your dramas. As bad as Shakespeare is, he is still better than you."

I am writing down the above conversation from memory, as Gor'kij told it to me. I know that other records exist, probably also not verbatim. Mischievous in his recuperation, Tolstoj made a comparison between two giants - Shakespeare and Čexov - those with whom he was not in agreement.

1. FEATURES OF ČEXOVIAN NOVELLAS

I.A. Bunin wrote the following anecdote about Čexov in his memoirs:

> One writer was complaining, "I am embarrassed to tears over how weakly, how poorly I began to write!" "Ah, you don't say!" Čexov exclaimed, "But that is wonderful - to begin poorly. Understand, that if everything comes out right for the novice writer, he has had it; write him off as a loss."
> And he began to argue heatedly that only <u>clever</u> people mature early and rapidly, that is, only those who are essentially unoriginal. Such people lack any real talent because cleverness is the ability to adapt. Cleverness lives easily, but talent is tormented, seeking self-expression. (2)

This is not true of all writers. Lermontov began to write early and achieved unusual success and mastery at an early date, although it did not come easily.

Čexov had his difficulties when he began to write: he himself created and refined his own skill. He could not always overcome the taste of the reader, and when he said that he had to squeeze the slave out of himself drop by drop, he was not talking only about day-to-day life.

He threw away what he squeezed out.

Čexonte [Čexov's first pseudonym. He used it when he began to write.] was a talented journalist, but Čexov included few works of his first period in his collected works.

The writer sieves and throws useless ore onto the dump, retaining the pure gold.

To break up such dumps and again salt them with gold and to publish the works enthusiastically in large printings is somewhat unwise.

Of course, even in the earliest of Čexov's publications there are successful records of nuances which were not noticed before, but these were only paths to success. One cannot bring all readers to supper via the back door.

A writer's success should not be obscured by his half successes.

One must present Čexov as distinct from Čexonte - that is, respect the creator who succeeded in rejecting traditional plots, naturalistic views of life, and feeble imitation.

Čexov despised writers who understand and love life as it is described in other novels; it is as if they eat predigested food.

As a youth he wrote parodies on almost every type of contemporary translated literature. He did it not unlike the people in Captain Hatteras' icebound steamship, (3) who shattered the ice surrounding their ship in order to sail to hitherto unreached places.

Čexov built his sujets, while exposing the contradictions within the topic-sujet itself; he had a good command of the plot, as is evident in a parody such as "The Swedish Match". But he had to build a new sujet upon discovering the very essence of a topic. . . .

2. AN ANALYSIS OF SOME SITUATIONS AND CONFLICTS IN THE TALES OF ČEXOV

One must differentiate between the sequence of events of an artistic work and its sujet structure.

Only by paying careful attention to this can we evaluate the alleged absence of denouement in Čexov.

Čexov's moral solutions are original. In his stories the point is not in the absence of a final scene: this is also found in ancient literature - what is important is that his heroes' fates and their sufferings remain not so much incompleted as unavenged, unexpiated.

The broadening of the methods of sujet construction continued in Čexov's time. "Daily routine" enters into the writer's art in a much greater and broader degree: a piece cut out of life is made meaningful through the structure. Historically it was the sketch [očerk] which could have helped to reevaluate the experience of great literature.

In the sketch the subject matter is not usually examined in its own temporal development, but, so to speak, is presented in its simultaneity.

Let us take Čexov's sketch "In Trubnaja Square in Moscow". It is a description of a Moscow market in which animals were sold. This sketch was first printed in 1883. In a letter to Lejkin [N. A. Lejkin (1841-1906), writer and publisher of Oskolki, a humor magazine, in which Čexov worked under the name Čexonte], Čexov himself called the story a "gentle little scene".

Lejkin, who also wrote sketches, based his little scenes on accentuated peculiarities of everyday language, on the emphasis of its strangeness and illogicality.

Čexov wrote a little scene of a completely different sort; it is a description which contains its own contradiction as a kind of hidden conflict - those visiting the market gently love animals and torture them.

The whole work breaks up into a series of small scenes which are somewhat like portraits of people and animals. The scenes have no solution, but the end contains an evaluation, which also serves as a denouement.

This story was not published by Lejkin because it appeared to Lejkin to have a "purely ethnographic character".

For Čexov: cognition of the subject matter was the sujet.

For Lejkin: the sujet was equal to an anecdote. It was not so much Lejkin's sketches, but rather older essays, coming from the age of Belinskij [V. G. Belinskij - eminent Russian literary theoretician and critic of the 1830s and 40s], from the early Turgenev, which gave Čexov the basis for a new construction of an artistic work.

As Čexov presents it, life is contradictory and blind. The people of "In Trubnaja Square" do not see themselves. They torture animals, they torment each other, but in fact the market place is the brightest spot in their lives.

Čexov begins the general description of the market place from its sadly zoological features.

He says that the people there below are like lobsters in a basket.
. . .

The utilization of a series of events differs among writers.

A number of sketches depicting the life of cabmen existed. A cabman changes fares, his life seems to consist of disconnected, vaguely discernable sensations, over whose sequence he has no control.

In 1886 the young Čexov, under the pseudonym of A. Čexonte, published "Anguish" in the Peterburgskaja Gazeta in the section "Flying Notes".

The story begins with an epigraph - which Čexov rarely uses.

The epigraph is taken from the psalms: "To whom shall I tell my sorrow? . . ."

The epigraph prepares the reader from the beginning for the acceptance of something unusual. A collision takes place between the theme (the cabman) and the tone of the epigraph.

The landscape, which in a common sketch is usually presented extensively, is given briefly in this work - through details.

Twilight begins, then comes evening darkness; street lamps grow somewhat brighter. The cabman's work begins to quicken. The course of events is constructed on his search for fares.

Such is the general situation in the story.

Its conflict consists of the fact that the cabman, Iona, has lost his son and wishes to express his grief to someone, but there is no one to listen.

The cabman is interested in his fares as people who might hear him out.

Iona transports people, complains about his fate, but the people are not concerned.

A sort of revue takes place: fares enter and leave the poor cabman's sledge. Čexov's story gives pictures of human insensitivity to the deep grief of a father who has lost his son.

As a result, the cabman expresses his sorrow to his horse.

The denouement here is the lack of a denouement, the endless grief, the lack of an answer, the absence of an end. The conflict does not obtain a solution in events; it is suspended in the concluding conversation as if in tragic parody.

The cabman goes to his mare; she is eating hay. The old man tells his sorrow to his horse.

"The little horse munches, listens and breathes on her master's hands. . . . Iona is carried away and tells her everything. . . ."

The lack of an ending, the lack of denouement in events becomes a structural denouement. The length of the final conversation with the horse, the attempt of the cabman to make her understand the matter, shows the separation of the man from his fellows.

The landscape of "Anguish" is monotonous. It is night and snowing. The monotony of the snow emphasizes the grief of the cabman.

He notices the weather because he grieves so. The denouement takes place in a secluded stable. It is the cabman's home, and the horse is his only society.

Let us take the situation presented in the story "Van'ka".

The situation: a boy has been apprenticed to a shoemaker. The shoemaker and his family oppress the boy.

A conflict arises: the boy wants to resolve the situation - he complains to his grandfather, but he is so helpless that he does not even know how to write an address. The address which he writes on the envelope - "To Grandfather in the village" - is the denouement, and it emphasizes the hopelessness of his situation.

The hopelessness is emphasized by the day on which Van'ka writes the letter - Christmas Eve. Christmas stories in the 19th Century tradition were always written with happy, reconciling endings, as if realizing the words of the Christmas canon - "Peace on earth, good will to men."

The time of action of "Van'ka" is Christmas Eve. The story was printed in Peterburgskaja Gazeta, Nr. 354 (December 25, 1886), that is, in the Christmas issue. The sharp deviation from the genre increased the tragedy of the ending.

On that blessed evening Van'ka Žukov, apprenticed to a shoemaker, writes a letter to his grandfather, telling him about the life of a little boy apprenticed to an artisan.

He narrates in fragments, thinking about his village.

The village is presented as idyllic, and at the same time its poverty shows through.

Van'ka writes: "Grandfather, dear, when the Master has a Christmas tree with sweets, take a gilded nut for me and hide it in the little green chest."

This unfulfilled dream about a single gilded nut which they might, perhaps, put aside for the boy, shows the poverty of the world to which the boy wishes to return.

That they let Van'ka write the letter and did not interrupt - this already is happiness. He runs off, without putting on his winter coat, to post a letter without an address.

They told him ". . . that letters are dropped in mail boxes and from the boxes they are taken throughout the whole land in mail troikas with drunken coachmen and loud bells".

Van'ka drops his precious letter into the slot of a mail box.

It is a cry for help.

The cry is imbued with solemnity, it is removed from daily life by mentioning a song and bells, but it is directed to nobody.

It solves nothing.

Van'ka sleeps. He has a dream - Grandfather receives the letter, he reads it, and a dog sits next to him.

So ends the saddest Christmas story in the world.

3. ON THE USE OF DETAILS AND ON THE DETAILS IN ČEXOV'S STORY "TO SLEEP, SLEEP . . !"

On February 16/28, 1857, [Lev] Tolstoj wrote in his "Notebooks": "Andersen's tale about the robe. It is a matter of literature and word - to explain to everyone so that they believe a child." (4) This note is about a fairy tale, "The King's New Robe".

The tale is centered around some swindlers who pretended to weave a cloth which all could see except fools and people who did not fit their positions. All the courtiers and the king himself saw the cloth. They made a robe from the nonexistent fabric. The king dressed up (naked), walked about the streets without a stitch on, and the courtiers went behind him, bearing the train of the non-existent robe. A small child cried out that the king was naked, and everybody repeated the child's words. All saw that the king was, in fact, naked. From the general commotion the king understood this too; but the parade continued, the naked man walked on, and behind him followed the courtiers, bearing the nonexistent train.

In order to write such a tale, it was necessary to think up a specific situation and then create its conflict: a person who was per-suaded that everyone saw him as clothed suddenly turns out to be naked before them all.

Andersen's story about the king's new robe develops step by step. They weave the nonexistent cloth from nonexistent thread; they cut it, sew it, fit it, show it, put it on the king, then discuss the cut of the nonexistent robe. The stages of the sewing are incontrovertible proof that the king is stupid, timid, and will be naked.

The nonexistence of the object - along with the mercenary affir-mation that it does exist - is deepened by the irony.

In Andersen's tale the truth of the child's shout is substantiated.

Usually so-called proofs are indirect in art and the so-called content cannot be extracted from the artistic form - it cannot be poured out of it.

The content lies in a labrynth of meaningful links and only through them can it be proven by the artist himself; indeed it does not even always prove exactly that which the artist intended.

The king of the old world is naked. Certain men bear a nonexistent train and walk in front of the people to their own destruction, which many already foresee.

Therefore one must not assume that first you create a knife - an idea - then you put the knife into a scabbard - a form. The power of artistic form resides in the power of cohesion: every situation is prepared and the most extreme conclusions drawn from it become probable and even inescapable.

In Čexov's stories, the depictive aspect of an artistic detail is usually built in series which do not repeat their component elements but develop them. This is the way in which evening is made in the story "Anguish". The passage of time is presented by sticky snow covering the cabman as he awaits his fares. Time passes, snow falls. The description keeps recurring, developing, and strengthening its meaning with each new appearance.

The sequence of events in the story "To Sleep, Sleep . . . !" is as follows: Varja, a little girl, is taken into the home of a shoemaker as a nursemaid. She also helps in the kitchen, runs errands, waits on the table, and cleans up. The baby is sick and cries at night. The girl does not get a minute of sleep. Sleep controls her, its lack poisons her. The events present this explicitly: driven to despair, Varja strangles the baby which she has been rocking.

This is real but improbable. It is possible but not proved. The inavoidability, the tragedy of the crime is not proven; to do so is impossible with a mere enumeration of the girl's duties. The sequence of events does not bring the reader into Varja's situation.

The story is built on the following systems of links.

The urge for sleep, which controls the girl's consciousness, is sovereign - she is somewhat delirious.

The surroundings, the interior here replaces the landscape and plays its role. The surroundings are psychologized; they slowly change under the influence of the deathly weariness of the girl tormented by sleeplessness.

The intensification of the meaning of details is the method of objectivizing this tiredness.

The delirium follows two lines: she sees a room lit up by a little icon-lamp; there appear to her simultaneously a hut and her father on the dirty floor dying from a hernia. She sees the past; she sees her own ruin in the death of her father, and at the same time she is aware of her surroundings.

Let us select one detail from this situation and show it in seven repetitions.

First comes the introduction to the story:

Night. The nurse, Varja, a thirteen-year-old girl, rocks a cradle in which a baby is lying. She is humming almost inaudibly:
    Hushaby, lullaby,
    I'll sing a little song . . .
A little green votive lamp glows in front of the icon; a clothesline is stretched from corner to corner across the room; on it diapers large black trousers are hanging on it. The votive lamp casts a large green splotch on the ceiling, and the diapers and trousers throw long shadows on the oven, the cradle, and on Var'ka [Varja] . . . when the lamp begins to flicker, the splotch and the shadows come alive and start to move, as if blown by the wind. It is stuffy. It smells of cabbage soup and shoemaker's wares.

The situation is clear. We know who is acting and where it takes

place. The smell of shoemaker's wares gives the impression of a
shoemaker's apartment. The surroundings: a green votive lamp, a
clothesline, the movements of a shadow - are given in the beginning
realistically. Then comes a description of night; everyone except
Varja is allowed to sleep.

The surroundings are again restated, but this time more briefly
since the particulars have been given earlier.

Now they are presented in action.

> The votive lamp flickers. The green splotch and the shadows begin
> to move, they creep into Var'ka's half opened, motionless eyes,
> and merge into foggy dreams in her half-asleep mind.

A page and a half is spent in describing her delirium about her
father's death. Varja falls asleep, the master appears; ghostly
reality is restored.

> He gives her a painful pull on the ear and she shakes her head,
> rocks the cradle and sings her song. The green splotch and the
> shadows of the trousers and diapers move back and forth, they
> flicker to her and soon seize her mind once more.

The mistress feeds the baby. A fourth description follows:

> Var'ka takes the baby, puts him in the cradle and begins rocking
> him again. The green splotch and the shadows little by little dis-
> appear and there is really nothing more to go into her head and
> cloud her brain. But she wants to sleep as before - she wants to
> so terribly!

Morning comes. Var'ka's workday begins and her duties are enu-
merated. Evening approaches. A fifth description follows:

> The cricket chirps in the oven; the green splotch on the ceiling
> and the shadows from the trousers and diapers again creep into
> Var'ka's half-opened eyes, they flicker and cloud her head.
> "Hushaby, lullaby", she murmers, "I'll sing a little song . . . "

The recollection is restored - delirium about her father's death.
Var'ka sees her relatives, understands everything, but she is in a
state of half-sleep and cannot understand what keeps her from living.
A sixth description follows:

> Finally, exhausted, she strains all her strength and sight, looks
> up at the flickering green splotch and, listening to the cry, dis-
> covers the enemy who keeps her from living.
> The enemy is the baby.
> She laughs. It seems astonishing to her: how could it happen that
> she was unable to understand such a trifle? The green splotch,
> the shadows, and the cricket seem to laugh and wonder, too.

We see a girl driven out of her mind, seized by a false idea:

> She is delighted and tickled by the thought that now she will be
> delivered from the baby who is chaining her arms and legs. Kill
> the baby, then sleep, sleep, sleep. . . .

The denouement is woven into the seventh description of the surroundings, as if crowning it by this terrible conclusion:

> Laughing, winking, and threatening the green splotch with her
> fingers, Var'ka sneaks up to the cradle and bends over the baby.
> Having strangled it, she immediately lies down on the floor,
> laughs from joy that she may now sleep, and in a minute she
> already is sleeping as deeply as the dead . . . .

The denouement is based not on the insanity of Var'ka, but on the
insanity of the social order.

4. ON DETAIL AS AN ELEMENT OF A NEW SUJET

General esthetic laws to some degree are constant but the inter-
dependence of parts and their relationship is so different that we
should speak about new literary phenomena as in a fresh light, not
forgetting their connection with the past.

We have to understand that the 'complication', that is, the development of the situation, is created in various epochs with the most
different means. The situation can be told by the author beforehand,
as Gogol' does in "The Old-World Landowners" - or it can be suddenly disclosed in a sequence of details, as Čexov does in the story
"To Sleep, Sleep . . . !"

The meaning of the so-called artistic detail is different for various
times and various genres.

Puškin's prose is dry - it speaks about the main thing. Gogol''s
prose is enriched by the analysis of particulars and by their collision.
Čexovian details are chosen more sparingly than Gogol''s, and their
sequence is more strict; they have their own logic of development
and somehow stand in the same row with the developments of the
sequence of events.

Gogol', both in the stories of the Mirgorod cycle and in "The Old
World Landowners" [actually, part of the Mirgorod cycle], reveals
the insignificance of conflict and through the insignificance of conflict shows the emptiness of existence.

Therefore, when a conflict is resolved, for example, when both
the old world landowners die, the story continues and the analysis
continues and is deepened.

This was true also in "The Story of How Ivan Ivanovič Quarrelled
with Ivan Nikiforovič" [another story from the Mirgorod cycle] . The
story ends with a very famous phrase: "It is dreary in this world,
gentlemen." This is the denouement, a resumé of the absurdity of

life.

Conflicts in Čexov's stories are resolved not through events, but structurally.

The system of details summarizes the life situations of the heroes, expressing not the accidentalness but rather the unjustness of everyday phenomena.

5. ON THE MEANING OF OPPOSING DETAILS

Čexov did not need a conventional plot such as an intrigue.

Some of his novellas are based on a very simple contrast which presents a clear-cut situation and later develops into a sequence of collisions inherent to that situation.

In the story "The Fat Man and the Thin Man" the focus is on recognition.

Old friends meet. The social position of each has changed. The collision consists in stages of recognition.

But here a man recognizes not his own kind among strangers, but a stranger amid his own kind: a school comrade has become an important official - a V.I.P.

The denouement comes about when the lower ranking civil servant is happy not over the success of his friend but at his inaccessibility, and does not even attempt to continue the friendship.

The usual type of collision - for example, the bitterness of the separation of friends, the despondency of a Falstaff who has lost in the king a friend and prince, a comrade in various adventures - is removed.

The collision of a poor man who discovers the inaccessibility of his old friend is removed.

Čexov's collegiate assessor enjoys not the grandeur of his friend, but rank in general, incarnate in his old friend.

It is the final sinking of the story of the Eternal Titular Councillor, about whom so much has been written, always pitying him. Besides, the Thin Man himself had already received the following rank two years previously.

Those people who were still Akakij Akak'evičes [hero of Gogol''s "The Overcoat"] at the end of the 19th century no longer evoke pity.

The place of action is presented immediately, with a single reference; the situation is also presented at once:

"Two friends met in Nikolaj railroad station[railway connecting St. Petersburg and Moscow]. One was fat, the other was thin."

In their characteristics are found only those features which set the heroes apart: "The Fat Man had just eaten at the station, and his greasy lips were shiny like ripe cherries. He smelled of sherry and fleurs d'oranges. The Thin Man had just stepped off the train and was loaded down with suitcases, packages, and cartons. He smelled of ham and coffee grounds."

The Fat Man appears alone. Behind the Thin Man is his family - which is his world, his social opinion, and the chorus of his tragedy.

A little thin woman with a long chin looked out from behind his back. This was his wife, and the tall high school student with the squinting eye was his son.

A meeting takes place. It has a friendly character. The ending of the scene will then be used in a restated form in the denouement.

"Porfirij!" shouts the Fat Man upon seeing the Thin Man. "Is that you? Old buddy! Long time no see!"

"For heaven's sake!" the Thin one exclaims. "Miša! My childhood friend! Where'd you pop up from?"

The friends kissed three times and stared at each other with tear filled eyes. Both were pleasantly stunned.

The Thin Man immediately begins to talk about himself and of his own; for him there is no one in the world besides them. His world is so empty that the fact that his wife is a Lutheran somehow separates and even to a certain extent raises him above other thin men who do not have even that distinction.

The characteristics of the wife are repeated constantly, without change. Those of his son Nafanail - more exactly, his pose - are repeated with changes which show a change of his conduct from in-attentiveness to grovelling.

"Dear old chap!" began the Thin Man after the kisses - "I didn't expect this at all! What a surprise! Well, look right at me! The same handsome fellow you were! Same dandy and lady's man as before! My God! Well, what's with you? Rich? Married? I'm married, as you see. This is my wife, Luiza, née Wanzenbach . . . a Lutheran . . . And this is my son, Nafanail, a student in junior high. This is my childhood friend, Nafanail! We were in high school together!"

Nafanail thought a bit and took off his hat.

The Thin Man happily recalls the story of his friendship with the Fat Man. When he was in school, the Thin Man was quiet and ob-sequious.

"We were in high school together!" the Thin Man continued. "Re-member how they used to tease you? They called you Herostrates because you burned a hole in a schoolbook with a cigarette and they called me Ephialtes because I liked to play the informer. Ho-Ho! . . . We were such kids! Don't be bashful, Nafanail. Come up closer to him. . . And this is my wife, née Wanzenbach . . . a Lutheran."

Nafanail thought a bit and went behind his father's back.

The Thin Man tells all about himself: his wife gives music lessons, he makes cigarette cases; he then asks a question from which arises the conflict.

"Excellent cigarette cases! I sell them for a ruble apiece. If someone takes ten or more - well, I give him a discount. We get along
somehow. I worked, you know, in a department, and now am being
transferred here as a supervisor in the same institution . . . I'll
be working here. Well, how about you? I guess you're already a
State Councillor? Right?"

This rank had already been the ideal of the Thin Man and, perhaps,
if his friend had reached this rank, he still would have kissed him
upon departure. But a recognition takes place.

"No, my friend, try a bit higher", said the Fat Man, "I've already
reached Privy Councillor . . . I have two decorations."

The Thin Man changes; not only does he change, but his possessions
change too, as does his family.

The Thin Man suddenly paled, turned stony, but soon his face was
distorted all over with a broad smile; it seemed as if sparks rained
down from his face and eyes. He himself shrivelled, bent down,
grew narrow . . . His suitcases, packages, and cartons shrivelled,
became wrinkled . . . His wife's long chin became even longer;
Nafanail moved to the front and buttoned up all the buttons on his
jacket. . . .

The Fat Man tries to limit the obsequiousness. He is completely unsuccessful.
The servility is without ulterior motives; it is senseless.

"But surely - How can you, Sir" giggled the Thin Man, shrivelling
even smaller. "The kind attention of your excellency . . . is a
kind of elixir . . . This, your excellency, is my son Nafanail . . .
my wife, Luiza, a Lutheran in a way . . . ."

Informal speech disappears - the vocabulary becomes syrupy and
elevated. Now as a result of the new circumstances everything previously said is no longer valid. He must present his family again to
the very same person - but this time as to a superior. The world of
the Thin Man is changed by the new light of servility.

The Fat Man was about to object, but there was such excessive
awe, sweetness and deferential distance on the face of the Thin
Man. [The Fat Man] turned away from the Thin Man and offered
his hand in parting.
The Thin Man squeezed three fingers as a handshake, and bowed
down with his whole body and giggled like a Chinaman: "Hee-hee-
hee." His wife smiled. Nafanail clicked his heels and dropped his
cap.

This is the fourth description of the Thin Man's family.

The denouement is constructed on the repetition of the sentence. When the friends met, "Both were pleasantly stunned." Now it is said of the Thin Man's family: "All three were pleasantly stunned."

The description of the Thin Man's family is presented several times and always with the same details, which are transformed and restated. In the final instance the family is mentioned as a unity.

While elaborating collisions which arise from the simplest situations, Čexov does not rush to the end of his stories. Recurrences, while seeming to coincide completely, sharply delineate elements which are not repeated and shed light on the collision in its entirety.

There is no psychologization in this novella, except for mentioning that the Fat Man almost felt nauseated.

In this novella - as in "The Chameleon" - psychologization is left out, and expression of personages' mental differences is given through distorted dialogues - which include unexpected utterances which seem completely lacking in motivation.

Čexov evolved such a solution from the technique of journalistic 'small scenes', but created new methods of revealing the absurdity of the commonplace through the displacement of particular elements of reality. False reality refutes itself, since its manifestations are emphasized.

6. A FEW WORDS ABOUT METONYMY

The analysis of various types of contradictions is the basis of art. We have shown here the obvious contradictions in a novella.

Through juxtaposition-contrast, an artist reaches the essence of an object. Contradictions and links of contradictions lie at the base of parallelism, of metaphor; they exist hidden in a motif and are strengthened in the sujet - in which an object is recognized through its realization in action.

The essence of the interactions of people is revealed by sharp-witted contraposition. The divergence, the sensing of differences which constitute the main part of the scene in the station, points to something even more: the meaning of social inequality.

We will now look at another example, the development of a simple situation into a novella.

In A. Afanas'ev's Russian Folk Tales there is a record of a 'folk anecdote', which I shall give in paraphrase. A gentleman comes to a peasant. The peasant has forgotten the gentleman's surname, but he recalls that it is connected with birds. A bird name. They begin to go through the names of birds, and as a result, it turns out that the surname is Willow. (5)

They ask him: "You said it was a bird name, didn't you?" The peasant retorts by saying everyone knows that birds perch in willow trees.

The whole thing takes up nine lines. It is in Volume III, number 467.

One can say that in a certain way the anecdote is based on metonymy. Cicero defined metonymy as a trope in which "instead of an exact correspondence of word to an object, another word with the same meaning is substituted, adopted from the object found in very close connection with the given object". (6)

Other rhetoricians define metonymy as a renaming which borrows the name of related and closely connected objects.

In general, in metonymy we choose one word in place of another, using some kind of material dependence between the two concepts.

When a Roman orator called his fellow citizens Quirites, he singled them out as spear bearers, as full fledged citizens. When, during a mutiny of soldiers, the ringleader called his soldiers Quirites, he used this word not because soldiers were always armed, but because this metonymic designation characterized first of all a citizen - the kind that would defend his fatherland.

Metonymic connection is based on the properties of thought: words which designate objects and phenomena form distinctive thought groups.

Remembering is similar to the search for metonymic connections; metonymy is not a recollection, but the use of one property of language in order to impart coloring to ideas.

One word can replace another on the basis of their mutual relationship.

The metonymies of Isakovskij [M. Isakovskij - a contemporary Soviet poet. Many of his poems became the lyrics of popular songs.] are bold and interesting.

Sometimes he simply points out the place in his songs where a hero and his actions should appear, giving to it features of 'related' surrounding, and he obtains an emotional construction which reaches everybody in the song.

"A Solitary Accordion" without a description of the accordionist gives a feeling of love which is neither settled nor past.

Another song is about a love letter which contains neither words nor single letters. There are only dots . . .

But by their relatedness, by their tight connection with hundreds of carefully considered, tender letters and thousands of unspoken words of love, they act as if they were spoken and realized.

This is the boldest method of metonymic operation for the purpose of creating emotion.

More often than not, metonymy uses a juxtaposition of mutually interrelated features.

V. Pudovkin, assembling spring in the film Mother, attempted to evoke in the viewer an image of spring, uniting frames which depict birds, melting water, and laughing children.

He told me that in the Chinese writing system, the character signifying 'bird' consists of a combination of the signs for 'tree' and 'voice'.

I do not mean to imply that this is how it actually exists in the Chinese writing system, rather that this is how the producer understood it to be.

It is as if a bird is the voice of a tree. The mutual connection can create an effective trope.

But the folk anecdote parodies the path of remembering by mutual connection, presenting the process of recollection as a change in a series of mistakes. This particular anecdote is, so to speak, 'more formal' than a Čexovian story.

The very system of remembering is parodied; the shortcomings of the method of remembering by analogy are examined.

The folk anecdote is converted into Čexov's novella "A Horse Name". The writer first stresses the necessity of recalling a name, but at the same time he parodies this necessity.

A general has a toothache. A steward advises him to cure it with a charm. A man who lives in Saratov is able to charm things away. An accumulation of particulars about this man begins: this accumulation masks both the inanity of the prayer against the toothache and the inanity of the telegram about the prayer.

"About ten years ago, your Excellency", he said, "in our district a certain Jakov Vasil'ič worked in the excise office. He worked charms on teeth, and did a first-rate job. He would come, go over to a window, mumble, spit - and the toothache vanished! He had some sort of gift of power . . ."
"And where is he now?"
"After they fired him from the excise office, he went to Saratov to live with his mother-in-law. Now he lives off teeth. When somebody has a toothache, he goes to him and he helps. He treats the local people in his own home, but treats those who live in other cities by telegraph. Send him a dispatch, your Excellency, and explain the matter to him . . . 'Alexej', servant of God, has a toothache; I request that you cure it.' Send money for the cure by mail."

The General agrees to send a telegram.

The address is needed. They remember the first and middle names immediately. Then begins a search for the surname. In the first round they think of twelve surnames.

". . . Couldn't it be Colt? No, it's not Colt. I remember that it is some sort of horse name, but exactly which . . . escapes me."

Then they begin to recall in a metonymic fashion every property of horses and all kinds of gear. More than thirty different surnames come up altogether.

The denouement comes when the horse name is finally found, but is no longer useful to anyone: the tooth was extracted and the pain has gone away.

The steward comes mumbling.

"Bay . . . Saddle . . . Strap . . . Steed . . ."
"Ivan Evseič!" the doctor said, turning to him, "could I buy from you about six bushels of oats? Our peasants sell me oats, but they're of low quality."
Ivan Evseič stared stupidly at the doctor . . .

"Your excellency, I've recalled it!" he shouted happily with a strange voice, flying into the general's study. "I've remembered it, thanks to the doctor. Oates! Oates is the name of the excise man! Oates, Your Excellency. Send a dispatch to Oates!"
"The hell with it!" said the general with contempt and raised two figs to his mouth. "I don't need your horse name any more. The hell with it!"

'Oates' as a horse name is a pure metonymy.

If in the folk anecdote about the 'bird' name, the surname turned out to be Willow because birds sit on willows, then in Čexov's story a horse name turns out to be Oates - because horses eat oats.

But in the anecdote the surname was not needed from the very start - we find simply a sorting out of retraced tracks of words on the basis of related words.

In the novella the name is in a way needed from the start, and becomes obviously unneeded once they have extracted the tooth.

Speaking in literary terms, in the anecdote a situation is given, but in Čexov's novella a situation is unfolded in a series of sequential stages - a series of developing collisions.

Wit is transformed, it grows into analysis; the pulsation of life is seen through it. The pulse of the Russian person of that time was weak.

7. FLUIDITY AND DUALITY IN ČEXOV'S DENOUEMENTS

The situations which Čexov selects for his stories are such that they create the sort of collision in which the unexpected in man is revealed at the same time as the true. Čexov's heroes seem to reveal their lives unwittingly. In "A Tripping Tongue" a young woman has arrived from the Crimea. She chatters to her husband and does not allow him to stop her, saying "Be quiet, be quiet and be quiet." In spite of herself, she talks about her love affairs with Crimean-Tartar guides. She unmasks herself, because for her a moral transgression is normal; she simply lacks morality.

Another Čexov story is about prostitutes. The prostitute has her own professional name and professional psychology, but at the same time she has a true human psychology which is revealed in a specific situation.

Bilibin, a friend of Čexov, once offered the writer the following theme: "To depict a respectable man - but one forgotten by fortune - who has gone to a friend to ask for a loan. Doesn't it seem that there is nothing shameful here? But his tongue will not move and he starts to talk about something entirely different, and finally leaves without having made the request." (7)

Čexov accepted this theme and wrote "A Gentleman Friend" - a story about a prostitute.

From Bilibin's suggestion the writer used only the essential fact - awkwardness in asking for a loan. The story begins in the following way:

> The most charming Wanda, or, as she was named in her passport,
> the honorable citizeness Nastasja Kanavkina, was discharged from
> the hospital and found herself in a predicament which she had
> never before experienced: she was without a roof and without a
> kopeck in her pocket.

The whole situation is related drily and briefly – objects are named
directly and plainly. The meaning of details is explained and emphasized.

Without her professional dress the woman feels almost naked: "It
seemed to her that not only people, but even horses and dogs were
staring at her and laughing at her simple dress. She could only think
about that dress . . ."

The woman decides to ask a 'gentleman friend' for money – she
will hurry to the dentist Finkel' and demand 25 rubles. But, dressed
in her common dress, Nastasja is modest. She enters, sees herself
in the big mirror on the stairs, without a high hat, without a stylish
blouse, and without bronze-colored shoes. In her thoughts she no
longer calls herself Wanda, but Nastasja Kanavkina. The dentist does
not recognize her; she whispers that she has a toothache. The dentist
extracts a healthy tooth and reminds her of the fee. She gives him
her last ruble.

The novella ends in the following way:

> When she came to the street, she felt even more shame than be-
> fore, but she was no longer ashamed of her poverty. She no longer
> noticed that she lacked a high hat and a stylish blouse. She was
> walking along the street spitting out blood every so often and each
> bit of red spittle spoke about her life, her hard and bad life, of
> those insults which she had borne and would continue to bear
> tomorrow, next week, next year – all her life, until the day she
> died . . .
> "Oh, how terrible!" she whispered, "God, how terrible!"
> However, on the next day she was already at the "Renaissance"
> and was dancing there. She wore a huge new red hat, a new stylish
> blouse, and bronze-colored shoes. And a young merchant from
> Kazan' treated her to supper.

Descriptions in this story are compressed to the limit. Not only is
the dentist the woman's client, but she is his client when she comes
for an appointment. He neither sees nor recognizes her. The narrative is built on the duality of a person's perception of himself, on
the difference between Wanda and Nastja[Nastasja] as defined by a
dress, on the difference between Finkel' the dentist and a 'gentleman
friend'.

Shame comes to a human being when he sees himself as simply a
human being.

As we have seen, Nastja's return to her old life and wage earning is bound up with her dressing of a form - a uniform. This uniform consists of "a huge red hat, a new stylish blouse, and bronze-colored shoes". The uniform was mentioned when Wanda saw herself in the mirror.

The denouements in Čexov's novellas are internally unexpected. They are like discoveries which are made by the writer for himself; these discoveries reject the ordinary denouement and make the hero's character fluid.

At the end a new interpretation of the hero and of the collision which he survives is realized. The collision now stands refuted.

Čexov worked on the story "The Gooseberries" for a long time. There are notes referring to this novella in three separate notebooks.

The narration embraces entire decades in the life of an official who dreamed about going to the countryside. He manages to buy a 'small estate'.

The man is first called simply "X", but the title of the story - "The Gooseberries" - already exists. He wants to buy an estate, marry, and eat home-grown vegetables.

He is a modest and intimidated person.

He works for many years and saves his money like a miser. He finally buys a small estate through a broker.

He bought it and is dissatisfied. He buys a gooseberry bush. It seems to him that all he lacks for his dream to come true is a gooseberry bush.

Two or three years later, when he is dying from stomach cancer, they serve him gooseberries. He says: " 'So this is all life has given me after all.' "

"And in the next room his big-bosomed niece, a loud person, was already managing the household."

In another place the following was jotted down: "(The gooseberries were tart. How stupid, said the civil servant, and died.)" (8)

The story was made as an analysis of one of life's disappointments. In the course of work on the story, the situation remains the same, but the collision changes.

Not every person is able to become disenchanted. More often than not a person changes in the roots of his character specifically because he has seemingly achieved something. Happiness itself is criminal when it is compromising.

There are notes in Čexov's notebooks about the change in the man's ideas and tastes as he seeks the "gooseberries".

It turns out that one must not fear 'unhappiness' but rather self-satisfaction from having achieved an insignificant success.

In the third notebook is a short note: "(Berry: family life has its discomforts. Balcony, it would be good to have tea)."

Later there is another note: "(Berry: from satiation begins liberal moderation)" . . . "(False pride developed, and even our surname C.-G. seemed sonorous and magnificent to him.)"

Later: " (Moderate liberalism: a dog needs freedom, but it is still necessary to keep it on a leash.)" (9)

All these stupidities are directly connected with the idea that the man is satisfied and happy.

There is a separate note: "Someone with a little mallet should stand behind the door of a happy man and he should pound with it constantly to give a reminder that there are unhappy people and that unhappiness certainly comes after brief happiness." (10)

The work continued, and everything became more clear: the point is not that there are other forms of unhappiness or that unhappiness will come. The point is in the very character of a small happiness.

In the final version, the official's brother tells the story.

The collision of the actual story is that the man is satisfied with his sour 'gooseberries'.

"A little mallet" raps now, bringing this to mind.

The official is satisfied with everything.

In the draft of the story he renounced family life.

Now he weds an old, homely widow and almost starves her to death: "And, of course, my brother never thought for one minute that he was guilty of her death. Money, like vodka, makes a man act strangely."

The newly-acquired estate stank. It was situated next to a brick and glue factory.

But the civil servant is satisfied. He changed and went over to the camp of the satisfied. He already belongs to the gentry, and all this came from his happiness.

Nicolaj Ivanyč, who at one time in the District Treasury Office was afraid even to have a personal opinion, now uttered only truisms and in such a tone as if he was a minister: "Education is necessary, but it is a bit too premature for the masses." "Corporal punishment is generally harmful, but under certain circumstances it is useful and irreplaceable."

A thin man thinks that he is fat.

"I know the common people and know how to deal with them", he says. "The common folk love me. All I have to do is move my little finger and they do for me everything I wish."

And, take note, all this was said with a kind intelligent smile. He repeated twenty times: "We, the gentry", "I as a member of the gentry"; evidently he no longer remembered that our grandfather was a peasant and that our father was a soldier. Even our surname – Čimša-Gimalajskij – in actuality an absurd name, now seemed to him to be sonorous, eminent and very pleasant.

He is also satisfied with the gooseberries. He exclaims in delight: "How delicious!"

He ate them greedily and kept repeating: "Ah, how delicious! Try them!"

The gooseberries were hard and sour, but the official felt happy.

Happiness is the tragedy of the denouement. It is tragic that there are "many satisfied, happy people! What an overwhelming force!"

These people are happy! If they are not happy, then they themselves begin to be astonished: you see, they have desired little.

Woe to those who are satisfied, for they are banal. They have closed their doors, they have closed their eyes in an attempt to forget the past and the future.

Woe to them, for their own and their children's teeth shall be set on edge from sour gooseberries. Their children shall forget them and shall seek their own petty amusements.

Their destruction is near, and there shall be no one to weep over their graves: they shall plant gooseberries or strawberries on them.

8. "THE STEPPE"

That which is habitual but no longer exists can be considered to be still in existence. It was not only the swindling tailors who pulled off a trick by dressing the king in the nonexistent robe. The customary relationship to a king prevented people from seeing him as naked. The threat that only an unworthy person would fail to see the king's robe is an inhibition based on tradition.

But writers themselves often carry the train of a nonexistent robe.

The heroes of Dickens' novels, separated lovers and virtuous old men, ought to prove by their existence that the king is indeed dressed and that his robe has only accidental defects.

Tolstoj and Čexov were undressers; their artistic method directed them towards undressing and revealing the essence of phenomena. They were born of the approaching revolution and were marked by it.

Čexov tries to prove that man must be trained for great demands.

He ought to be greedy for life, but not for himself.

He ought not to repudiate happiness nor build it on the unhappiness of the weak.

Tolstoj, in a story, argued that a man needs only seven feet of earth.

Čexov wrote in his first notebook:

"A man needs only seven feet of earth.

"Not a man, but a corpse. A man needs the whole world" (11)

Mastery of the world is a great task.

About thirty years ago I had the occasion to observe how a column of an international sports car rally got lost in the steppe outside of Rostov.

They searched for the road.

Night. The steppe is so broad that in moonlight one can see the curvature of the earth.

In the light of the headlights there is an improbably wide road bestrewn with silver straw under electric lights.

The moon rises.

The Milky Way, densely dotted with silver stars, cuts across the light green sky.

This was not the main road of the land of giants. Čexov described the old steppe road in "The Steppe" in the following way:

Something unusually broad, sweeping, and heroic stretched across the steppe instead of a road; it was a grey belt, well-travelled and covered with dust like all roads, but it was over two hundred feet wide. It bewildered Egoruška by its vastness and led him to fantastic thoughts. Who travels on it? Who needs such a big space? It is strange and incomprehensible. As a matter of fact, one could imagine that gigantic, broad-stepping people like Il'ja Muromec and Solovej Razbojnik [hero and villain respectively in certain Russian folk epics] had not disappeared from Russia and that knightly steeds had not yet become extinct. Gazing at the road, Egoruška envisioned a group of about six high chariots racing side by side like those which he had seen in illustrations in the Bible; each chariot was drawn by six wild, frenzied horses and raised clouds of dust to the skies with its high wheels and the people who drove the horses were the type that can be seen in night dreams or grow up in fantastic thoughts.

At the end of the past century, little of this steppe had been cultivated, although peasants had been thinking about it for centuries.

Only birds, flocks of sheep, trains of carts and merchants gave life to the steppe.

There were no more ox-cart drivers who had created the heroic road through centuries of use.

Instead a carriage travels across the steppe – the same sort that Čičikov [hero of Gogol''s Dead Souls] rode in. On it he had planned to visit the district of Kherson, a place so uninhabited that it could be populated by 'dead souls', mortgaged in the government bank, and uncontrolled by anyone.

Now the carriage showed its age and the journey seemed to be more real: wool has become more expensive and prices change.

People travel in carriages to earn money in wool. Times have changed – the merchant Ivan Kuz'mičov shaves, wears glasses and a straw hat; he looks like a civil servant. He trades in wool. Smelling of dry cornflowers, Father Steristofor, a broadly smiling old priest, in a grey canvas tunic girt with a colorful belt, also goes to trade in wool, and smiles "so broadly it seems that his smile even reaches the brim of his hat. . . ."

There, beyond the steppe, steamships with cargoes of wool sail the Black Sea to foreign ports. The ports are crowded and alive with trains, houses, bridges, and churches.

People in the steppe are like flies in a cathedral: they circle about but do not fill it. The steppe is huge and empty.

How can one express the emptiness of the steppe? How can one describe its quiet monotony without heaping it up with "fragments of landscape"? (12)

How can one describe the steppe without ascribing to it something false, how can one show its vastness in human terms?

In the early morning the business people are going to the steppe;
they have just had a bit to drink and have eaten well. Egoruška, a
boy of nine years, goes with them: they are going to drop him off
at a school.

They have dressed the boy well for the road. He even has a little
coat.

Now: "Because of the speed of travel his red shirt billowed up like
a bubble on his back and his new coachman's hat with the peacock
feather slipped down to the back of his head from time to time."

The hateful carriage carries him from his home and from the cemetery where his father and grandmother sleep day and night.

"Until her death she was alive and brought bagels sprinkled
with poppy seed from the market, but now she is sleeping, sleeping
. . ."

The little boy in the red shirt goes out into the vast steppe like a
float. We shall follow him as we would a striped float, which moves
towards the depths of sky blue waters.

The steppe will be revealed by the boy who, like a little red star,
passes through an endless green plain.

It is so empty that you could recognize a bird if it flew by twice.

At a stream in the steppe Egoruška saw three snipes fly out from
the sedge with a cry.

An hour later he noted: "The same three snipes flew above the
reed-grass, and in their cries you could hear their alarm and vex-
ation on being driven away from the stream."

Even birds are rare on the steppe. They are described in detail.

A bustard flew up. It caught a ray of sun and flashed like a fisher-
man's spoon-bait.

A landrail flew with the wind, never against it. Its feathers were
ruffled.

Calm rooks walk on the dry earth. Thunder rumbled behind the
hills, but the storm had not yet arrived.

How can one select the features of the steppe, how can one render
them?

The carriage still moves a bit too fast. The vastness of the steppe
is yet to be shown, movement must be slowed, business preoccu-
pations must still be shown, as too the neglect of that which is human,
of the merchant, as well as of the flippant, seemingly good old trading
priest.

The carriage moves, overtaking the merchant Varlamov, and the
grown-ups put the boy on the carts so as to increase their speed. Now
the steppe unfolds more slowly; carts move, drivers walk behind
them - ruined by new times, people who have lost their past.

Each of them has his own life; Vasja the driver, who has unusually
keen sight, looks far into the distance with his beady grey eyes and
is delighted: thanks to his sharp vision Vasja has another world -
one of his very own, very nice, inaccessible to others. Vasja helps
Čexov translate yet one more sight of the steppe into reality; he is,
as it were, the artist's telephoto lens. At the same time, Vasja is
one of the failures.

Only Dymov is bored, but in a cheerful and powerful way, not finding either a task or a rival equal to himself.

He swung his shoulders, put his arms akimbo, spoke and laughed louder than anyone else and looked as if he were going to lift up something terribly heavy with one hand and so astonish the whole world. His crazy mocking glance glided along the road, the train of carts and the sky; it settled nowhere, and it seemed as if it would look for someone to kill for no good reason and for something to laugh at.

This is the man of the future. Gor'kij will observe them even more attentively and will understand what they foreshadow.

9. WHAT DO THEY FORESHADOW?

The adults drove away. The boy was cast into huge spaces - it is unknown who needs such space.

Night approaches. The sky is above the abandoned boy. On the steppe the sky is in no way separated from the earth and it is huge.

Egoruška looks at the stars. The theme of death and grandmother appears again. The description is successful because the previously presented description of the graveyard with sleeping relatives is now recalled in the solitude of the steppe. The good people who could have helped are dead.

The boy is alone.

The stars which have been looking down from the heavens for thousands of years, the incomprehensible sky itself and the haze, are all indifferent to man's short life: when you stand eye to eye with them and strive to fathom their meaning, they oppress you with their silence; one recalls the solitude which awaits us all in the grave, and the essence of life seems desperate, terrible . . . . Egoruška thought about his grandmother, who now sleeps in the cemetery beneath the cherry trees . . . He imagined his grandmother in her cramped, dark coffin, forsaken by all, helpless.

The few words about the grandmother spoken at the beginning serve to somehow reveal the complete abandonment of Egoruška, who recalls the dead, not the living.

The length of the action of an image established once and the diversity of its effect in the work are far greater than we would generally assume.

The recollection of the graveyard marked in passing helps to show the new consciousness of the boy.

The consciousness is the relationship to the world: the realization of existence in it. The stars here help the writer to show the significance of this particular event.

The writer comprehends the world in its breadth which is incomprehensible to others, although he speaks, as it were, only about the boy's trip in the cart.

The story is striking in its structure. It alone could be created in such a way; it even seems that it is not created, but observed: the author's intention never shows through.

But we see the steppe because we follow the boy, whom the adults have abandoned as a useless object.

A storm overtakes the train of carts. The people walking near the carts seem to be giants. In the brief flashes of lightning the carts seem immobile, the drivers motionless.

Egoruška finds a place to spend the night: "He inspected his hat, straightened the peacock feather on it, and recalled how he had gone with his mother to buy that hat . . ."

Egoruška inspected his coat. At home it had been an extraordinary phenomenon.

Being a new and expensive thing, it was hung not in the hall but in the bedroom with mother's dresses; they allowed him to wear it only on holidays. Looking at it, Egoruška felt sorry for it - he recalled that both he and his overcoat were cast out to the winds of fate, never to return home, and he sobbed so hard that he nearly fell off his kizjak [dried manure mixed with straw, used in the steppe as fuel; it served as bed for the boy].

The fate of objects expresses the fate of man.

Thus, in the seeming absence of a conflict, an object steadily develops by showing the contradiction of changing elements.

For the moment Egoruška's adventure ends happily: he reached his uncle, Father Xristofor rubbed him with oil and vinegar, and in the morning he was well.

But a huge, vicious world has already been shown. The ends of human fates are already in sight.

In the steppe everything is now in motion; everything has turned over. Solomon, the innkeeper's brother, burnt up money in the oven to prove his defiance of something or other. The drivers are unhappy and recall the past as a happy time. The Countess, who is looking for Varlamov, the rich man, to sell him something more, is not settled.

Thanks to such an exhibition of men's fates, the future of the countryside is already analyzed. The story flows, anticipating the future.

There is much scope. What sort of presentiment lies behind all this?

The story seems at first glance to show a landscape, but it is a story about people who are somehow disturbed by the space; they cannot overcome it.

After Čexov finished the story, he wrote the following to A.N. Pleščeev [a Russian poet, prose writer, and critic (1825-1893)]:

As far as Egoruška is concerned, I will continue his story, but

not now. Silly Father Xristofor has already died. Countess
Dranickaja (Bronickaja) lives very poorly. Varlamov continues
to make his rounds. You write that you like Dymov as material
. . . Such mischievous natures as Dymov's are made by life not
for dissidence, nor for vagrancy, nor for a settled life, but directly for revolution . . . There will never be a revolution in
Russia, and Dymov will finish either as an alcoholic or else in
jail. He is a superfluous person. (13)

The steppe road, narrowing, became overgrown with grass. They
were already bringing the railroad through but still some spaces
remained not taken over by people. People are large, like Dymov,
but they are somewhat unneeded.

In a letter to D.V. Grigorovič [a well-known Russian writer and
friend of Dostoevskij; he was one of the first to discover Čexov's
great talent and assisted in his literary career] (dated February 5,
1888), Čexov wrote: "In my 'Steppe' I lead a nine-year-old boy
through all eight chapters; when, in the future, he gets to Petersburg or Moscow, he will wind up a bad person - no doubt about it."

Egoruška is fated to die by suicide. Here there is much: ". . .
his early puberty, his passionate thirst for life and justice, his
dreams of a reality as broad as the steppe and of activity, his rest-
less analysis, the poverty of his knowledge coupled with the broad
flight of his thought . . ." (14)

The artist still does not see with his frightened glance the inavoidability of the new mastery of the world by new people.

"The Steppe" is constructed on broad panoramas, but this is not
simply a landscape - it is a place which is still unchanged, empty,
and at the same time doomed to change: this is, so to speak, a landscape which is breaking up.

Varlamov makes his rounds on the steppe, and all the people are
changed by his rounds. They make their rounds together with him,
and in this their interrelation is changed.

The drivers following behind their carts are ruined and unhappy
people.

These will become Gor'kij's people: people expelled from life.

Only Egoruška alone sees the steppe to its end. His steppe has artistic verisimilitude; to him, a child, Čexov gave sight; but other
people's sight is cut off, it is bound up by Varlamov's rounds.

10. ON THE CONTRADICTORINESS AND FLUIDITY OF ČEXOV'S
    HEROES

Čexov reveals that people do not achieve their full potential.

In his depiction of life, Čexov first sharpens and shows anew its
vicious stupidity, then he reveals the contradictoriness of his heroes
and, by it, the contradictoriness, the self-denying character of life
itself.

What might have been a naturalistic depiction becomes the preparation for a tragedy.

Man is presented both as he is and as he could and ought to be.

The notes begin with a statement of daily life.

The sujet of "Rothschild's Violin" is written down in the second notebook: once upon a time there lived a coarse man with a gloomy profession - he made coffins.

"(A coffin for Ol'ga. The coffin maker's wife is dying; he makes a coffin. She will die in about three days, but he hurries the work on the coffin because the next day and the following days are holidays, e.g., Easter . . .

"(On the third day she is still not dead; people come to buy a coffin. Because of the uncertainty, he sells her coffin; she dies. He scolds her as they prepare her for the last rites. When she dies, he writes down the coffin as an expense. He had measured her when she was still alive. She: Remember, thirty years ago a blond haired infant was born to us? We sat by the stream. After his wife's death he went to the stream; a willow had grown significantly in thirty years.)" (15)

The denouement so far is that the man went anyway to look at the willow: the growth of the tree signifies that life has passed. The coffin maker so far is just a coffin maker - he is not a musician. 'Losses' are concentrated around the coffin and are transformed by art into losses borne by mankind.

When the story is realised, Jakov Ivanovič, the coffin maker, receives an identity, a characteristic. He is a powerful, heavy and pitiless individual.

> Jakov made good, solid coffins. For peasants and landowners alike he made them his own size and never once made a mistake, for there was no one taller or stronger than he anywhere, even in the prison, in spite of the fact that he was already seventy years old. For the nobility and women, however, he made them to size and for this he used an iron yardstick. He filled orders for children's coffins with great reluctance, making them scornfully, without measurements. And whenever he received money for this sort of work, he would say: "I must admit that I don't like to be bothered with trifles."

He is a fiddler and plays Russian tunes well. He plays in a Jewish orchestra but hates the members of the orchestra, especially the flutist who sits to the left of him. Playing is torture.

> . . . it was hot and stuffy, the air smelled of garlic, the violin screeched, the contrabass wheezed in his right ear, and the flute wailed in his left ear. The flute was played by an emaciated, red-haired Jew with a whole network of red and blue veins on his face, with the same surname as Rothschild, the famous, wealthy, man. And this damned Jew managed to play even the merriest tunes sadly. Without any apparent reason Jakov was little-by-little filled with hatred and scorn toward Jews, and especially towards

Rothschild; he began to find fault with him and abuse him with un-
couth words and was once even about to strike him, and Rothschild
was insulted and muttered, looking at him fiercely:
"If I did not respect you for talent, I would already be throwing
you in my window a long time ago." (16)

Rothschild is really a poor musician and a mediocre, weak individual. But at the same time Čexov, the son of a Taganrog [a small
city in the South of Russia] shopkeeper and an acquaintance of Suvorin, shows the features of the origins of daily anti-Semitism.
Čexov himself "squeezed the slave out of himself drop by drop".
He connects the anti-Semitism of Bronza, the coffin maker, with
his unrealized life and daily trifles.
The life of the mighty Bronza - unbeknownst to himself - silently
rolls down to a big, spacious grave, to a wide coffin. First his wife
dies.
The coffin maker's wife dies happily yet timidly, in fear of her
husband. Her return to youthfulness, her animation are realistically
motivated by her fever.

"Jakov!" Marfa called out unexpectedly, "I am dying!"
He glanced at his wife. Her face was pink from fever, unusually
clear and happy. Bronza was now confused, for he was accustomed to seeing her face pale, timid, and unhappy. It seemed as
if she were now indeed dying and that she was happy that now,
finally, she was leaving that hut, the coffins, and Jakov - forever
. . . She glanced at the ceiling and twitched her lips, and her expression was joyful, as if she saw death, her deliverer, and whispered with him.

The entire description of her death is built on the realization of de-
ficiency, on the bareness of life - expressed for Jakov's wife in her
terror of her husband and for him in his melancholy dread of losses.
He had to make a coffin.

He took his iron yardstick, went over to the old woman and
measured her. Then she lay down, and he crossed himself and
began to make the coffin.
When the work was done, Bronza put on his glasses and wrote in
his notebook:
"For Marfa Ivanova, one coffin, two rubles forty kopecks."
He sighed. All the while, the old woman lay silent, with closed
eyes. But in the evening, when it grew dark, she suddenly called
the old man.
"Do you remember, Jakov?" she asked, looking at him happily,
"do you remember - fifty years ago God gave us a blond haired
infant? You and I used to sit by the stream and sing songs under
the willow." And, smiling bitterly, she added, "The little girl
died."
Jakov strained his memory, but could not recall anything -

neither the little baby nor the willow.
"You are dreaming it", he said.

It seemed as if there were no life at all; it all was an illusion. It
was written down as a loss.
　Pity for the dead woman appears, connected with the thought about
how Marfa treated her husband and his violin:

> Every day she had heated the oven, cooked and baked, fetched
> water, chopped firewood, slept with him in one bed, and when he
> came home drunk from weddings she always respectfully hung his
> violin on the wall and put him to bed, all the time silent, with a
> timid, solicitous expression.

Rothschild comes to summon the solitary Jakov Bronza to the orchestra; Bronza attacks Rothschild with his fists and then goes for a
stroll.

> And there was the old willow with the huge hollow in it and crows'
> nests on it . . . Then suddenly into the memory of Jakov, as if
> alive, came a little baby with blond hair and the willow that Marfa
> spoke about. Yes, that is the very same willow - green, silent,
> sad . . . How it has grown old, the poor thing!

The coffin maker looked about:

> On that bank where the flooded meadow is now there stood then a
> great birch forest and far away there on that bald hill which can
> be seen blue on the horizon there stood then an old, old pine for-
> est. Barges used to course the river. Now everything is plain and
> level, and only one birch remains on the opposite bank, young and
> slender like a young lady, and there are only ducks and geese on
> the stream - you would never think that there were ever barges
> there.

Life returns to the musician through his repentance not for himself,
but for mankind. People live wrong; they destroy themselves and
the land.
　People saved neither the river nor the forest; one could live in
another way, more advantageously and freely, sparing oneself and
the land.

> . . . Life passed without profit, without any pleasure, it vanished
> for no purpose - not even for a sniff of tobacco; nothing lay ahead,
> and if you look back - there is nothing but losses - and such ter-
> rible ones at that - enough to make one shiver.

The theme of losses ceases to be a tally of day-to-day failures. It
is a matter of spiritual loss.
　The theme of coffins recedes. The meaning of that which is human

begins to surface in Bronza.

At night ". . . some sort of ugly faces moved up from all sides and muttered about losses. He tossed and turned and got up from the bed five times to play a bit on the violin."

We see Bronza as he could have been: a great musician expressing the anguish of mankind over the disorder of the world.

He does not regret his life - it has been unreal; he is sad for his violin.

One can't take the violin to the grave. It will be left an orphan, and the same thing will happen to it as happened to the birch and pine forest. Everything in this world has vanished and shall vanish! Jakov left the house and sat down at the threshold, clutching the fiddle to his chest. Thinking of his worthless, lost life, he began to play, not knowing quite what, but it flowed pitifully and movingly and tears flowed over his cheeks. And the deeper he thought, the sadder the fiddle sang.

Rothschild timidly comes to call Bronza to play at a large wedding. Bronza plays a melody, for the fulfillment of which it would have been necessary to transform the land and redesign the sky.

It was necessary to redo everything so that human souls would not be recorded as a loss.

Rothschild listened carefully, standing by his side with his arms folded. The frightened, puzzled look on his face slowly became one of pain and long suffering; he rolled up his eyes as if experiencing a tormented ecstasy, and uttered: "Vahhh! . . ." And tears slowly flowed down his cheeks and dripped onto his green jacket.

The green Jewish coat, which Čexov described with one adjective, was a black wedding coat which had turned green from age. Poverty had changed its black color - all the color was a loss.

Having willed his violin to the flutist, Bronza dies. The flutist becomes a violinist and, recalling the playing of the dying coffin maker, he plays ". . . something so sorrowful and dreary that the listeners cry, and he rolls up his eyes just before the end and says: 'Vahhh! . . .' This new song was so popular in the city that merchants and officials vie with one another in calling Rothschild over, and they make him play it as often as ten times in a row."

But it is only the shadow of the lost melody.

Bronza is an unfulfilled person who only once felt grief not for himself but for his whole past unfulfilled life.

Rothschild is a good, understanding, gifted, and powerless Salieri [a protagonist of Puškin's short tragedy "Mozart and Salieri", in which Salieri is a talented but second rate creator].

The title "Rothschild's Violin" expresses the cohesion of several themes.

Here is the repudiation of petty anger and of anti-Semitism. At the same time Bronza's violin, which ought to have told about the necessity of replanting forests, of filling rivers with water - now, having fallen into the hands of the flutist, a poor soul, succeeds only in making merchants and officials weep and roll up their eyes.

In the seeming lack of conflict, the structure of the novella, bringing characteristics of actuality into new cohesions, shows the unusual in the habitual and in the unusual is the main, the most important element: the pulsation of the essence of the pre-Revolutionary era.

Although he is downtrodden and coarsened, Bronza is a powerful man. Only in music does he overcome his terror of poverty and discover indignation in himself at the absurdity of the whole system of life, realizing himself as Dymov shall in the Revolution.

The musicality of the later Čexov is connected with the broadening of the capacity of his work and with new methods in his analysis.

Čexov's short novel "In the Ravine" tells a simple story, but together with the crime of the merchant family which almost destroys itself by its unbridled greed, a broadened world is presented.

Those personages who would be insignificant and outside of the sujet in an old novel become strong in conjunction with the unfolding of the story, and the conflict of the sujet is solved especially in them.

Lipa, a poor girl given in marriage, the wife of a detective who was sent to prison for counterfeiting, the mother of the baby scalded to death by Aksinja, grows into the figure of a person who induces the writer to see the world in a new way.

The landscape of the eighth chapter of the novel is built around her.

The woman walks from the hospital with the dead baby in her arms; in her path is not merely despair but also a new vision: she meets an elderly migrant who pities her. The landscape advances anew, no longer an evening landscape, but one of night: above the people is the sky with its stars, birds still make sounds and keep each other from sleeping; a landrail cries nearby. Lipa talks with the old man.

" 'Are you holy men?' she asked the old man.

" 'No. We are from Firsanovo.' "

The oppressed one finds a friend and understanding amid her own people. She is not only oppressed, but behind her stands the solution of problems raised by the writer; her enemies shall be conquered; she has friends: vengeance and forgiveness.

The old man speaks: "A bird is not given four wings, but only two, for he is able to fly with just two. So also it is not given to man to know everything, but only a half or a quarter. As much as he needs to know in order to survive - that much only he knows."

The fact of the matter is that man has already wings of a different nature. The old man, comforting Lipa, speaks of Russia, of Altay, of the Amur, and the world expands, and universal sorrow absorbs Lipa's particular sorrow and her dead baby Nikifor, whom evil and still more powerful people have destroyed.

NOTES

(1) [From Viktor Šklovskij, Povesti o proze. Razmyšlenija i razbory (Moskva, Xudožestvennaja literatura, 1966). Vol. 2, pp. 333-335; 336-370.]
(2) I.A. Bunin, Sobranie sočinenij v 5ti tomax (Moskva, Pravda, 1956), vol. 5, p. 279.
(3) [The reference here is to Jules Verne's popular novel, The Adventures of Captain Hatteras, in which there is a trip to the North Pole.]
(4) L.N. Tolstoj, Polnoe sobranie sočinenij (Moskva, 1928-1958), vol. 47, p. 202.
(5) [We have given English equivalents for Russian surnames so that this and the following discussion become clear. Thus Verbitskij is rendered by 'Willow'.]
(6) I am quoting from: O.M. Frejdenberg (gen. ed.), Antičnye teorii jazyka i stylja (Moskva-Leningrad, Ogiz, 1936), p. 218.
(7) A.P. Čexov, Sobranie sočinenij v 12ti tomax (Moskva, Goslitizdat, 1961), vol. IV, p. 543.
(8) A.P. Čexov, Polnoe sobranie sočinenij i pisem (Moskva, Goslitizdat, 1944-1951), vol. 12, pp. 224, 226.
(9) Ibid., vol. 12, pp. 291-292.
(10) Ibid., vol. 12, p. 231.
(11) Ibid., vol. 12, p. 241.
(12) Ibid., vol. 17, p. 168. A letter to Avilova dated Nov. 3, 1897.
(13) Ibid., vol. 14, p. 37.
(14) Ibid., vol. 14, p. 33.
(15) Ibid., vol. 12, pp. 285-286.
(16) [This reflects incorrect Russian, as it was spoken by many Jews.]

IV

AN INCOMPARABLE ARTIST (1)

V. LAKŠIN

It is a well known fact that Čexov's admiration of Tolstoj's artistic genius never diminished. However, one of the writer's contemporaries wrote the following:

> A friend once saw the works of Tolstoj in Čexov's home; Čexov had covered an entire story with pencil marks and insertions. "What are you doing here?" he asked Čexov. "I have been correcting Tolstoj's story." (Unfortunately, I do not recall which one it was.) "I wanted to show how I would have written it . . ." (2)

To N. Ežov, who narrated this episode, Čexov's correcting Tolstoj seemed to be an example of inexplicable impudence and evidence of Čexov's extreme presumptuousness. We evaluate it differently. Čexov's attempt at creative competition with Tolstoj on the margins of his book is yet further confirmation of how clearly Čexov acknowledged the novelty and correctness of his own discoveries in the artistry of words. He felt that he not only could not, but even must not write 'like Tolstoj', and that his understanding of the times and his views on life dictated different artistic goals. Even if these goals are more modest and more limited than Tolstoj's, even if that epic breadth and sweep is not found in them, they still reflect new features of life and point out new landmarks in realistic literature.

And Čexov was right. Tolstoj himself, who often argued with Čexov over the ideological side of his creative work, nevertheless called him an 'incomparable artist'. From the point of view of mastery of form, Tolstoj recognized Čexov's indisputable superiority over Turgenev, Dostoevskij, and, "eliminating all false modesty", over himself. Gor'kij found that Čexov reached the apex of artistic simplicity in his stories and that no other writer could rival him in this. Korolenko called Čexov's realism superrealism. Through the voices of its greatest representatives, Russian literature at the turn of the century proclaimed Čexov's prose style to be the greatest achievement of nineteenth century realism.

In a conversation with a journalist by the name of A. Zenger, Tolstoj stated that Čexov had created "forms of writing that are, in my opinion, completely new to the whole world", and that this was due to his unusual sincerity. In fact, discoveries and mastery in form never come to a writer from without, as some sort of supplement to his artistic thought. The sources of originality in form are always rooted in innovation of content, that is, in the originality

of the author's creative view. To express sincerely and deeply a
new content of life and a new view on things means to discover new
forms. Čexov's brilliant innovations in the realm of genre, structure, and style reflect the features of his philosophy of life and of
life as it is portrayed by him.

The difference between Čexov and Tolstoj in the genres they selected is quite clear to any reader. Although there are quite a few masterpieces among Tolstoj's short stories and shorter novels, he expressed himself as an artist primarily in novels - on huge epic can-
vasses. Gravitation towards the genre of the novel and especially
towards the epic-novel could not be fortuitous for a writer who
cherished an epic breadth of world view and who united his psychological profundity with a thirst for traditional integrity as well. The
attraction of Čexov as an artist to the prose of 'small forms' - the
short story, the lyrical novella, the socio-philosophical tale - corresponded to his views on life which combined somber scepticism
with the poetry of a dream; if one looks at the broader perspective,
it reflected also the contemporary reality of his time.

In the 1880s and 90s one finds in general a crisis over large epic
forms of Russian literature. The best writers of that era - Korolenko, Čexov, Garšin, and, in the younger literary generation,
Gor'kij, Kuprin, Bunin, and L. Andreev - all write short stories
or short novels and, with the exception of Tolstoj, no great artist
attempts to write a full-fledged novel. In Tolstoj's epic philosophy of life we find a great force of opposition to 'prosaic reality',
that is, to stagnant forms of life. Depicting peasants, exiles, and
revolutionaries in Resurrection, Tolstoj discovers a new vocation
for epic characters. But Čexov finds no material either for epos
or for a novel in the life of the middle, Philistine circle which he
knew so well.

It is common knowledge that Čexov dreamed of writing a major
novel and was frustrated by the fact that he did not succeed. He attempted to realise his intention in 1888-1889, and wrote the following to Suvorin about the novel which he had begun: "I have already
outlined nine persons clearly. What intrigue! I have titled it Stories
from the Lives of My Friends and I am writing it in the form of separate, complete stories which are tightly interconnected by a common intrigue, idea, and dramatis personae. Each story has its own
title." Anticipating the bewilderment of his addressee over a novel
in the form of separate and complete short stories, Čexov reassured
him: "Don't think that the novel will consist of shreds. No, it will
be a real novel, a complete body where each person will be organi-
cally indispensable" (XIV, 330). (3)

Evidently Čexov himself was not completely certain that he was
writing a novel rather than a cycle of short stories - otherwise he
would not have attempted so insistently to convince Suvorin the opposite was true. It is significant that he did not even bring this plan
to completion; in all probability we read fragments of his uncom-
pleted novel in the form of various novellas, not suspecting that
they come from a 'novel'.

To shield Čexov from the criticism that large works were not easy
for him and to follow the logic of his own letter to Suvorin, it is
sometimes said that although he did not write a novel, all his short
stories taken as a whole make up one huge novel of Russian life at
the end of the last century. One can, however, look at the matter
differently: the greater part of Čexov's short stories - not to speak
of his longer tales - are mini-novels, histories of human lives,
condensed into a few pages.

Čexov's art consists simply in that while relating some small
fragment - either a single or a limited number of episodes from the
life of a man - he makes it possible to imagine the whole fate of that
person. Before our eyes the "Darling" changes from a young girl
with dimples on her cheeks to an elderly, timid, silent woman who
darts to and fro about the house; Ionyč from a youth who was not
without daydreams becomes a complacent and self-satisfied doctor
and homeowner. We see not only the beginning and end of the pitiful
transformation of these people, but it is as if we knew their whole
life from day to day.

How poor life must be in its internal content, how monochromatic
and impersonal must it be in its essence if one can write about it in
such a brief way! Yes, but at the same time the author's artistry
must be great if he is to be able, in an extremely laconic form, to
tell so much about man and man's soul, to show the path of personality development, the interconnection of diverse fates, the entire
unexpected complexity of life, and the sources and consequences of
human motives and actions.

Let us examine yet another 'mini-novel' - "On the Cart". It is
neither an episode nor a small scene, because there is nothing
interesting in itself in the teacher's trip to the city or in her meeting with Xanov or in any other incidental or episodical element found
in the external course of the story. No, here is the whole life of a
lonely woman as if she herself were narrating it, from the years
of tranquil childhood, from her happy memories of her family and
her mother's love through her wearisome existence in school and
up to the present joyless day. It is as if she told it to some attentive,
warm-hearted person who understood her as no one else could, sym-
pathized with her, and also cast a general glance at all such
teachers, hundreds and thousands of such lives, who bear from day
to day the burden of heavy work in some Godforsaken rural place.

Čexov broadened the possibilities of the smallest format infinitely -
he used it to encompass material from life which is significantly
richer and more complicated than that in the stories of his predecessors in Russian literature. The reason is that he was able to
create a picture with one stroke, a character with one hint, and a
fate with one episode.

Čexovian laconism stands opposed to Tolstoyan epic thoroughness
and to the plenitude and ramifications of artistic motivations and
interconnections which concerned an individual character as well as
the sujet of a work as a whole. Of course the laws of the genres -
the novel and the short story - are different. But, as has already

been mentioned, the very choice of the genre is predetermined to a great extent by the object to be depicted and by the author's outlook on life.

The stronghold of patriarchal ideals serves as the epic soil for Tolstoj's view of the world, which is all-encompassing and objective in its breadth and versatility. The complete range of vital connections and 'links' as a characteristic of the epos of a new era, in conjunction with a very subtle analysis of human psychology, make Tolstoj the powerful and versatile artist he is. Čexov is always more 'of the chamber', his artistic vision is very sharp, delicate, and intelligent, but not so broad or 'matter of fact'. Rather than an epic view of the world, Čexov has lyricism and irony, and a sober, delicate scepticism which flows through everything, not touching merely dreams and hopes.

Even in the most elementary scrap of artistic fabric we can discover this difference between the writers.

For example, in Tolstoj's style similes are usually distinctive by the sharp 'thingness' in which their power and novelty reside. When he describes the attack of the hussars in War and Peace, Tolstoj gives the impression of a volley of enemy fire. "Suddenly something swept through the squadron like a large broom." In depicting Nataša's mental state as she emerged from her grief, Tolstoj notes that her face smiles at Pierre with an effort "like a door opening on rusty hinges". So also a segment of a Tolstoyan landscape: "On the bare branches in the garden hung transparent droplets which fell upon the freshly fallen leaves. The earth in the vegetable garden turned a shiny, moist dark color, like poppy seed" (War and Peace, Vol. 2, Part 4, Chapter III).

Tolstoj's similes are usually drawn from the realm of nature or from simple ordinary life well known to all, but most of all they are drawn from rural life. A house, a beehive, cattle in the fields - this is the basic stock of similes in War and Peace. The connections between things and phenomena which Tolstoj establishes are simple and natural, 'objective'; it is as if they clarify that which is more complex with the aid of the elementary which is in the reach of all, and they have the unsullied clarity of common sense. As Tolstoj wrote in the second edition of Childhood, "I have never seen lips of a coral color, but I have seen brick-red lips; nor have I seen turquoise eyes, but I have seen some which were the color of diluted blueing and of writing paper. A simile is used in the following way: either to compare a bad thing with something better in order to show how good the thing being described is, or else to compare an uncommon thing with something quite ordinary in order to present a clear understanding of it" (Vol. 1, p. 179).

Čexov's similes serve neither of the purposes mentioned by Tolstoj. Čexov needs to stir up a swarm of vivid associations and to create an impression, sometimes using therein the most unexpected methods of influencing the reader's imagination. However, before demonstrating this essential difference between Tolstoj's and Čexov's similes, we must recall what they do have in common.

Like Tolstoj, Čexov usually tends towards similes of an 'unpoetic' type which are unelevated and common. Take, for example, the famous description of the storm in the beginning of "The Steppe": "On the left, as if someone struck a match on the sky, a pale phosphorescent streak flashed and then went out. One could hear that somewhere far away someone walked across an iron roof. They were probably walking across the roof barefoot because the iron rumbled hollowly" (VII, 91). In these similes one senses a protest against conventionally poetic descriptions with which vivid concreteness - the authenticity of sensation - does battle. Like Tolstoj, Čexov does not like to see eyes compared to pearls or clouds to an eagle's shadow. He repulses every touch of traditional bookishness, using in his similes the material of the life experiences of the average democratic reader, the gentried and plebeian intellectual, and the city dweller. It is not without reason that "matches" and "an iron roof" figure in his description of a storm on the steppe.

The simplicity and authenticity, the spontaneity of sensations, the 'naturalness' in the perception of nature startled one of the thoughtful readers of "The Steppe" - I. Dombrowsky, a Polish writer. "The French, the Germans, and even we, although we are Slavs", he wrote, having read Čexov's story, "simply flirt (I do not know how to translate that word into Russian) with nature; we dress it up in moon, stars, dew, in shades of light, and we always make of it only a more or less artistic decoration. Only a Russian describes nature for its own sake. In many such descriptions you simply smell the hay, manure, barns. If a Frenchman were to write about dew, he would place before you all the colors of the rainbow with which it glistens - if a Russian did, you would feel the dampness in your boots." (4) These words are equally true for Tolstoj and Čexov. Simplicity, life-like concreteness of images which are spontaneous, taken first-hand - both Tolstoj and Čexov have this in common. Whereas Tolstoj, with his similes and method of description in general, explains an object being guided by its objective connections, Čexov achieves a vivid impression through unexpected associations.

In "Anna Around the Neck", for example, when he wishes to give a picture of the character's appearance, Čexov says that Modest Alekseič's clean-shaven, round chin looked like a heel. Regarding his excellency's wife, "the lower part of her face was so disproportionately large that it seemed as if she had a large stone in her mouth".

The kiss which Lieutenant Rjabovič had received by mistake in the dark is described in the following way: "His neck, which the soft, fragrant arms had just embraced, seemed to him to be anointed with oil; a light, pleasant chill, as if from peppermint drops, trembled on his left cheek near his moustache . . ." (VI, 344).

Tolstoj would not write like that; there is in these similes a special effect of unexpectedness, a bold 'arbitrariness', and a 'subjectivity' of associations. A charge of internal irony is hidden in the sharp rapprochement of the seemingly distant characteristics of an object. This applies even to descriptions of nature. In The Seagull Trigorin

notices a cloud which "looks like a grand piano". We will find nothing
similar in Tolstoj. When describing the sun, sky, and clouds, Tolstoj very rarely turns to similes, perhaps because nature, whose
characteristics he is happy to transfer to man, stands itself 'beyond
comparison' in a literal sense. There comes to mind only the single
comparison of a cloud dissipating to a shell in the pages of <u>Anna</u>
<u>Karenina</u>. Instead, Čexov's fantasy in this sense is inexhaustible:
in "The Mail" a cloud is like "a cannon with a gun carriage", in "The
Beauties" "one little cloud looked like a monk, another was like
a fish, and a third like a Turk in a turban", in the story "Gusev",
"one cloud looked like a triumphal arch, another was like a lion,
and a third like scissors". Čexov's similes are new, paradoxical,
sometimes refined, but they are always exact and they stimulate
certain lyrical and ironic associations.

To the Tolstoyan epic 'completeness of objects', to his abundance
of immediate interconnections, relationships, and interactions,
Čexov contraposes his own art of seeing the world in unexpected
rapprochements, in details which outwardly seem to be accidental
but actually are deeply characteristic and expressive. Čexov aban-
dons all orderliness and strict sequence of artistic description.
Instead, as if by chance, a dropped detail - a detail in the description of a person or of nature, of events or circumstances, a fortuitous segment of a conversation and a hint to an unexpressed feeling
- gains new significance and value in Čexov.

For example, instead of describing thoroughly the breakdown of
a merchant's household, Čexov only mentions as if in passing that
"the rice in the <u>pirožki</u> [small pies, filled with meat, rice, cabbage,
etc.; sometimes they are made as a large pie (<u>pirog</u>)] was not completely cooked, the tablecloth smelled of soap, and the servants
made loud noises with their knives" ("Three Years", VIII, 467). Instead of going into details about the discord between the proprietors
of the estate and the common folk, the peasants, the author casually
notes that Aunt Daša, when talking with salesmen and peasants, "for
some reason always used to put on a pince-nez" ("At Home", IX,
236).

When the actors of the Art Theater asked Čexov to comment on
their roles, they received from the author answers which seemed
strange and even eccentric: Čexov spoke about Trigorin's checked
pants and fishing poles, and about the good tie which Uncle Vanja
wore . . . The author felt that this answered their questions completely and explained the typical trait of the personage, for behind
a given detail Čexov saw a person.

When applied to Čexov, the very word 'detail' (5) demands more
precision. Under detail we are accustomed to see something specific
and supplementary which explains to us the general character of a
personage or of an event. For Čexov, a detail does not complement
the meaning of an image or a picture - it encompasses it, concen-
trates it in itself, and radiates it from itself. In some superficial
little scene, in a fragment of a conversation, in a particular of
daily life, the character of a person, the mores and usages of a

milieu, and the ideals and beliefs of a hero suddenly come to life.

A fleeting sketch is quite characteristic of Čexov: "When this liberal, after having dined without a frock coat, went to his bedroom and I caught sight of the suspenders on his back, it was then quite clear that this liberal was a bourgeois Philistine and a hopeless one at that" (XII, 283). What might one think is the connection between the mention of the negligent afterdinner dress and the internal essence of the 'liberal'? But he is spread out before our eyes, well-fed, self-satisfied, complacent. And it is not necessary for him to say anything 'liberal' or for other persons to unmask him – he is there entirely in this stroke.

In "The Teacher of Literature" the hero, returning from his wedding in church to the house of his young wife, "stretched and sprawled out on the Turkish sofa in his new study and had a smoke . . ." It would seem to be an unimportant particular, but Čexov revives it again two pages later when describing the everyday life of Nikitin when he was immersed in the quiet joys of family life: "After supper he lay down on the divan in his study and had a smoke . . ." This Oblomovan [Oblomov, hero of a novel by Gončarov, characterized by apathy and inertia] trait all but becomes attached to the appearance of this personage who does not notice how gradually the slime of Philistinism overwhelms him and subordinates him to itself.

Many other details are interlaced with this one: the homemade lunch in a napkin which Manjusja sends to the high school for Nikitin and which he eats "with slow measured bites so as to prolong the pleasure", the conversations of Ippolit Ippolitovič, Manjusja's little pots of sour cream, the white cat rolling up into a little ball next to its mistress, and sleepy Muška yelping under the bed: "rrr...nga-nga-nga..." The dialogue, the rapprochement of diverse yet always characteristic details, gradually create the general impression desired by the author, and little by little, imperceptibly, but with complete artistic necessity they draw the reader towards a thought: "There is nothing more terrible, more insulting, or more tedious than banality." Tolstoj had grounds for saying of this story: "So much is said in it with great artistry in such small forms; there is not a single line here which does not pertain to the matter at hand, and that is a sign of high artistic worth." (6)

Observations, episodes, small scenes, and, in the broad sense of the word, 'details', all united into one artistic impression, create a picture of dynamic life, familiar to the point of actuality, and tinted in the most realistic colors. Tolstoj considered this method of Čexov to be an important artistic discovery, and compared it to impressionistic painting. "You see", said Tolstoj, "without any effort at all the man dabs on some bright paint that he happens to come across and there is no evident connection between all those bright splotches, but the general impression is remarkable. Before you there is a bright and extremely effective picture." (7) Tolstoj notes the absence of a direct connection between the "bright splotches" in Čexov, and this statement helps us to understand how the role of details differed between the two writers.

Tolstoj also knows well the power that an artistic particular has in making an impression. In a certain sense he is even more lavish with details than Čexov. With Tolstoj, however, particulars are connected by direct, spontaneous cohesions, but with Čexov they are connected by a juxtaposition occurring in the reader's mind. Following the dialectic of life, Tolstoj extracts something similar to a chain of details while retaining the causal connection and the sequence of transition from one detail to another. He wishes to create the impression of the completeness of a picture and of the continuation of the process of movement. Čexov does not connect details, but rather juxtaposes them, doing it, however, in such a way that we do not notice the gaps, breaks, and leaps, or the absence of a 'unifying fabric'.

In Čexov heterogeneous, various traits, "bright splotches", are brought together, and the author relies on the general impression which fuses them together. "The duty of smiling and speaking continuously", Čexov writes of the heroine of "The Nameday", "the sound of dishes, the servants' muddle-headedness, the long interlude between courses during the dinner and the corset which she was wearing to hide her pregnancy from the guests tired her to exhaustion" (VII, 140). The blending of a variety of signs of the physical and emotional state of the heroine permits the reader to empathize with her condition.

Tolstoj uses this device as an exception when he wishes to render those nuances of sensations and the atmosphere surrounding an action which are difficult to perceive. Such is the description taken from War and Peace, in which Tolstoj appears as a direct predecessor of Čexov. ". . . in the hot air, in the shouts of the peddlers, in the vivid, bright summer clothes of the crowd, in the dusty foliage of the trees on the boulevard, in the sounds of the music and of the white pantaloons of the batallion going on guard, in the rumble on the pavement and in the bright glare of the hot sun there was the same summer languor, satisfaction, and dissatisfaction with the present which one feels particularly sharply on a clear hot day in a city" (Vol. 3, Part 1, Chapter XVIII). This excerpt can serve as one of several examples of Tolstoj 'impressionism'. The summer clothes, the music, and the glare of the sun, are all mixed together like "bright splotches". Most often, however, Tolstoj strives to present the characteristics of the phenomena being depicted both in their proper sequence and in their fullness. For him artistic particulars are 'small bricks' of images, fitted very closely together.

We will recall, for example, the thoroughness with which Tolstoj describes the scene of Kitty and Levin's wedding in Anna Karenina. At first the author seems to glance over the decorations of the church and the crowd which had gathered. "The golden glow on the red background of the iconostasis, the gilded carving of the icons and the silver of the chandeliers and candlesticks, the tiles on the floor, the rugs, the gonfalons up by the choir, the steps of the ambo, the books darkened with age, the cassocks, the surplices – all were bathed in light" (Part 5, Chapter III). We find out how the guests, the priest, the protodeacon, the sexton, the singers, and the best man conduct themselves while awaiting impatiently the beginning of the wedding service. Finally the bride and groom appear. Tolstoj dwells at length on the details of the ritual - the litany, the exchange of the rings, stepping onto the rug, (8) etc. He depicts all the fluctuations of Levin's and Kitty's internal states, but in the process he does not forget to follow the figures in the crowd and the hum of conversations. In about two pages of Tolstoj's work the faces of Korsunskaja and Drubeckaja, of Count Sinjavin and Princess Carskaja, of Ščerbackij and of the lady in waiting Nikolaeva, of Koznyšev and Darja Dmitrievna, of Stepan Arkad'evič, of Countess Nordston, of Lvova, and also of the nameless 'common folk' - all these manage to flash by. Such a variety of particulars, faces, voices, and opinions creates the illusion of complete sequentiality, not a 'random' description, although of course each of Tolstoj's details is the result of a painstaking selection.

In "The Teacher of Literature" Čexov describes the wedding of his hero in a quite different way. He is not at all interested in the particulars of the setting, the decorations in the church, the rituals or the conversations in the crowd. In one or two sentences he mentions the "sputtering candles, the brilliance and the finery", the number of happy, content faces, and how the archpriest's choir sang magnificently. Instead, two almost insignificant details are moved to the foreground and presented as 'close-ups'.

It was very noisy in the church during the wedding ceremony, and the priest, looking over the crowd through his glasses, said gruffly, "Don't walk about the church and don't make noise; stand quietly and pray. You must have fear of the Lord." Because of its dissonance, this prosaic particular penetrates Nikitin's solemn mood and his thoughts of how his life had flowered and had taken shape so poetically since the time that he had fallen in love with Manjusja. It is as if the priest's words play a role in bringing the hero back to reality and serve as a threat to his dreams.

Even more significant is a second ironic detail. After the wedding ceremony the Brigadier-General came up to Manjusja and said to her in his aged, squeaking voice, "I hope, my dear, that you will remain a rose even after your wedding" (VIII, 364). In answer to this compliment on the part of the general, Nikitin produced a "pleasant, insincere smile". The recollection of this "pleasant" smile later came to Nikitin as a tormenting vision. Banality walks at the heels of the hero, even in the most solemn, bright minutes of his life, but when it becomes unbearable to him, when he understands the futility of his dream of quiet happiness, he will then recall with doubled hatred the word of the Brigadier-General - "rose" - and will feel a cold malice towards Manjusja. Thus the circle of artistic associations encompassing a few details is apparently closed.

It might sometimes seem that Čexov prefers secondary, accidental features in the characters and in the setting of the action to the major ones, and that he communicates not the essence of the matter, but rather something attending it. This, however, is not the case.

In this sort of detail, regardless of how secondary it might seem to be at first glance, there is always the hidden energy of a generalization. But the energy 'releases itself' and begins to act on the reader only in confrontation with many other details in the general course of the narration.

Čexov speaks rapidly about the most important items in the hero's visible fate, about the events which usually attract attention; he is simply imparting bare information to the reader. For example, in the story "The Darling" the writer tells us in a few words that Olen'ka fell in love with Pustovalov. "The match was quickly arranged and then came the wedding." Čexov's attention is concentrated on the uneventful daily life of the heroine. He is able to select the sort of moment, to seize the fleeting instant and to notice the small characteristic which, better than long descriptions, might shed light on the personality, customs, and attitude of a person.

> On Saturdays (Čexov writes) she and Pustovalov would go to the evening service and on holidays they went to early Mass, and returning from church, they walked side by side with gentle expressions on their faces. They both smelled nice and her silk dress rustled pleasantly. At home they drank tea with fancy breads and various kinds of jam, and then they ate pirog. Every noon the savory smell of borsch and roast lamb or duck drifted out through their yard and into the street, and on fast days there was the smell of fish, and nobody could go past the gate without feeling hungry. A samovar was always boiling in the office, and customers were treated to tea and bagels. Once a week they went to the baths and returned side by side, both red in the face (IX, 320).

Externally, this picture is completely objective - nowhere is there any direct judgment on the part of the author regarding the life of the Pustovalovs. But through his selection and rapprochement of these characteristic details Čexov tells us everything, and he speaks more convincingly than if it were expressed in direct judgments - for these scenes are quite true to life and they succeed in exposing the characters, ideals, and daily life of the protagonists. Čexov manages to show us the three spheres of family delights - church, food, and bath - and this is adequate for understanding all of the Darling's simple ideals, her concept of happiness, and the whole tenor of her narrow life. The reference to the tempting snacks and refreshments stimulates an interest in them and reveals their significance in the life of the loving couple. Gently, without any pressure, the author's ironic attitude is clarified by such words as "they ate pirog" and "side by side", which is repeated twice: "they walked side by side" from church and they returned "side by side" from the bath. A touching picture.

The principle of artistic juxtaposition and not of link-cohesion is what in Čexov's work determines not only the particulars of a characteristic, but also the entire structure of his stories. Each of Čexov's novellas or stories is usually a series of rapidly chang-

ing small scenes or 'takes', if one might use the cinematic term.
The writer is in perfect control of the techniques which permit him
at one point to speed up the movement of events, and at another
point to slow them down and select a single frame, or to present a
'long-shot' at one moment or a 'close-up' at another moment.

While telling of Olen'ka's life with Pustovalov, Čexov describes
only a single moment of their acquaintance as a solitary, unique,
concrete moment of life (". . . once Olen'ka was returning from
Mass, sad, in deep mourning. As it happened, one of her neighbors,
Vasilij Andreič Pustovalov, was walking with her from church...
. . ."). Everything which the author later relates appears as something ordinary and commonplace which took place many times. On
Saturdays Pustovalov and the Darling always went to church, and
every day at noon their yard smelled of borsch, etc.

Generalization of time in Čexov ("usually", "it often happened",
"every time") accompanies the complete concreteness and the artistic visibility of an episode.

> Usually (Čexov writes of Pustovalov) he stayed in the lumber yard
> until meal time, then he went out on business and Olen'ka took
> his place and she stayed in the office until evening writing up the
> bills and handing over goods.
> "The price of lumber is now increasing by twenty percent a year",
> she told her customers and acquaintances. "Goodness, we used
> to sell local lumber, but now Vasička has to go to the Mogilev
> region every year for lumber. And what shipping expenses!" she
> said in horror, covering both cheeks with her hands, "what ship-
> ping expenses!" (IX, 319).

There is all the concreteness of an unrepeated unique observation
in what Olen'ka says and in the way she pronounces these words,
but at the same time the author leads us to understand that this took
place many times either in the same way or in almost the same way.
A week ago, a month ago, yesterday, and today Olen'ka could be
sitting over the books in the office and bemoaning the rising shipping
expenses and covering both cheeks with her hands. This monotony
of life, when through a single episode one can imagine what happened
repeatedly, determines the tonality of a Čexovian narration.

Richness of interconnections as well as thoroughness help Tolstoj
portray the continuity of the process of life, eternal movement and
renewal. Tolstoj knows that any given scene is unique - an unrepeated moment of existence. In Čexov the scene - with its complete
reality - of this moment at the same time gives the impression of
a repeated, usual, recurrent action. In the structure and style is
reflected the mood, the tedium of a motionless life, a life which is
stagnant, undeveloping.

The specific objectivity of Tolstoj's epic tone consists in the fact
that each scene, each detail, each particular emerges as if at first,
as an integral part of this moment of life. Although he did not ignore
the artistic effect of a repeated particular, he used it in a very lim-

ited sphere – in the capacity of a portrait characteristic. It is
Karenin's prominent ears which everyone remembers, Princess
Mar'ja's radiant eyes, Anna Mixajlovna Drubeckaja's "tear swollen
face", etc. Here, with one detail, an image is created which is
strengthened in the reader's mind by recurrence. The external appearance which reflects the basic characteristics of a person has
such a stability and permanence (especially in comparison with the
fluidity of the psychological states and the continuous instability of
life situations) that Tolstoj finds it possible to find recourse to recurrences, which are usually foreign to him.

The Čexovian recurrent detail bears a more general significance.
It creates not only a portrait, but the daily tenor of life, the rhythm
and the surroundings of life which create a stable mood. When in
"The Betrothed" Andrej Andreič proudly shows Nadja the portrait
of "The Nude Lady with a Vase", it is a brilliant particular, a
characteristic little trait, and nothing more. But Čexov does not
forget this detail; he repeats it again. When Nadja sits down in the
train to leave the city, "she suddenly remembers everything: Andrej,
his father, the new apartment, and the nude lady with the vase . . ."
Upon returning home a year later, Nadja recalls her past, and once
more "Andrej Andreič and the naked lady with the vase sprung up
in her mind . . ." The repetition of a detail strengthens its meaning:
it is no longer a particular, but a generalized image of middle class
prosperity, the concept of which includes among other elements a
certain minimum of 'spiritual values' - pictures, books, and tunes
distinguished by their particularly bad taste.

Artistic repetitions and stable leitmotifs are also found in people's
speech. A word repeated two or three times, a remark or an expression which is connected with the hero are imprinted strongly
on the reader. We recall how Dymov in "The Flutterer" would come
smiling into the dining room with a warm invitation: "Please, gentlemen, have a bite to eat." In the story "Anna Around the Neck" we
see Petr Leont'evič's children stretching out their arms to their
drunken father and saying, "Don't, Papa dear . . . Please, enough,
Papa dear . . ." Sisoj, the old man in "The Bishop", is remembered
from his often repeated statement, "I don't like it! . . . don't like
it." The constant recurrence of words, remarks, and expressions
is not simply an arbitrarily chosen device on the part of the author.
This stylistic trait reflects the sensation of a monotonous and motionless life, where statements, words, and poses are repeated in
a cheerless cycle of dull existence.

In other stories by Čexov scenes and even entire episodes pass
unchanged before the reader two or three times. When he first became acquainted with the Turkin family, the hero of "Ionyč" found
the unique daily life of this little world to be 'interesting': the lady
of the house reading her novel, Kotik's energetic playing on the
grand piano, Ivan Petrovič's jokes, even Pava's pause with his
"Death to you, unhappy woman!" But, invited back to the Turkin's
four years later, the hero is surprised to see that nothing has
changed: Vera Iosifovna still reads her novels devotedly, Kotik plays

noisily on the grand piano, Ivan Petrovič is still trying to be witty
and still has his favorite expression, "Not badsome", and even Pava,
now a young man with a moustache, 'performs' his old tragic pose.
These repeated details project a feeling of the stagnation and inertness of daily life. If the hero does actually move, it is in a narrow,
previously determined circle. The fate of doctor Dmitrij Ionyč himself has already been pointed out by the signposts of repeated details:
we see the mark of time in that the doctor has put on weight, his
coachman Pantelejmon is turning red and fat, and his rides in the
horse-drawn carriage are becoming more and more majestic –
these particulars are modified three times.

In Tolstoj, the picture of daily life, the milieu and the atmosphere
of action, takes shape unnoticeably and objectively from multiple
features, specifics, and characteristics; in Čexov single vivid
strokes which are often strengthened by repetition replace the con-
sistency and the 'exactness' of the descriptions, and concentrate the
artistic content in themselves. Since Čexov omits a multitude of
features and specifics, when describing a person or event, in his
works a particular load – an emotional emphasis – falls on some
details. A detail begins to gravitate towards a poetic generalization,
a symbol.

"Čexov sharpened his realism to the point of its being a symbol"
(9) was the subtle observation of Vladimir Nemirovič-Dančenko [co-
founder (with Stanislavskij) of the Moscow Art Theatre], referring
to the realistic nature of Čexovian symbolics.

In general, one can speak only with reservations about Čexovian
'symbolism', 'impressionism', or 'naturalism'. Čexov did not narrow
his realism down to one of these artistic movements. Remaining in
the territory of realism, he opened up within it the possibility of
presenting more accurately the sensations of the subjects, the 'impressions', the 'bright splotches'. This had been considered to be
the privilege of impressionism. He also made efforts to be absolutely
simple and exact, to find the distinct 'flesh' of the world of objects,
but he did not as a result become a naturalist. Such is also the nature
of Čexovian 'symbolism', that there is not in it the slightest trace
of irrational mysticism.

In capitalistic decadent art onesided formal problems were the
main property of impressionist, naturalist, and symbolist movements, trends which broke with realism. Čexov remained true to
realistic, artistic content, to the truth of life, and therefore the
search for new forms of expressivity did not carry him to symbolism, naturalism, or impressionism properly speaking, but notice-
ably enlarged the stock of his artistic means.

In this sense Tolstoj was a predecessor of Čexov. The French
critic de Vogue wrote that Tolstoj is "a naturalist – if the word has
any meaning – because of his accurate imitation of nature and the
strictness of his scholarly study. Tolstoj is an impressionist because
by means of just a sentence he describes the physical sensation
of a sight, an object, and a sound." (10) Tolstoj, more than anyone
else, can be considered to support complete realism, but de Vogue's

statement has some truth in it. Among Tolstoj's diverse artistic
devices there are those which can be interpreted as impressionistic
or naturalistic. For example, doesn't Nataša's impression that
Pierre was something "squared" and "blue" have an impressionistic
character? But can one doubt that when Tolstoj depicted Nataša's
impression, he was describing her as a realist would, attempting
to catch only the uniqueness of her sharply individual feelings? Re-
fining the use of realistic resources does not suggest that Tolstoj
departed from the fullness and specificity of realistic depiction,
but is in essence subordinated to it and never turns into a practice
of neuroticism.

The most strict and consistent realists did not neglect the poetic
symbol, and there is a reason for this. In fact every artistic generalization is akin to a symbol. Gogol' stated that the city, as depicted
in Dead Souls, was a symbol of the "universal image of idleness".
Gončarov in his novel The Precipice and Ostrovskij in his play The
Forest, by the very titles of these works, underscored the symbolic
sense of certain particulars of the setting of the action. Finally,
isn't the sky over Austerlitz in War and Peace, appearing more than
once in Prince Andrej's consciousness, a poetic generalization which
is close to a symbol?

In Čexov we also have to deal with a realistic symbol, a symbol
"in the good sense of the word", as Lunačarskij [A. V. Lunačarskij
(1875-1933), Russian author and publicist, onetime Minister of Education, very often dissented philosophically from the leaders of the
Communist Party] said, "that is, we do not deal with reconciliation
to mysticism, or the fragmentarization of something of which we
are consciously aware into something too detailed or subconscious,
but rather with an effort to generalize actuality to the point of symbolic images . . ." (11) Symbols "in the good sense of the word"
are the image of a seagull, of a cherry orchard, of a "happy umbrella" in the tale "Three Years", or of Belikov's case [Belikov -
main character in Čexov's "The Man in a Case"].

Let us say that the most fleeting particulars and traits, when repeated and strengthened, can acquire symbolic meaning. In using
them, Čexov usually does not openly interpret anything, he does not
explain the sense of the symbol, but rather he makes it understood
from the very confrontation of details.

Love for Anna Sergeevna, the 'lady with the little dog', filled
Gurov's life and brought him under the windows of her home in S, a
dull district city.

> Just opposite the house stretched a long, grey fence studded with
> nails.
> "One would run away from a fence like that", thought Gurov,
> glancing back and forth from the windows to the fence (IX, 367).

It would seem that this is a mere detail from the city landscape, but
what a depth of poetic meaning there is in it! It unites the image of
the city itself - gray, provincial, dull - and the way of life of its

inhabitants and the boredom and the torpor of a dull life. The abominable gray fence deprives and conceals Anna Sergeevna from Gurov. It stands as a stronghold of banality, barring the path of the heroes' dreams and love. Gurov walked past the house "and loathed that gray fence more and more, and by now he thought with irritation that Anna Sergeevna had forgotten him and perhaps was already amusing herself with someone else – and that that would be quite natural for a young woman who had to look at that damned fence from morning to night". A thrice repeated detail becomes highly significant, a dreary image grows and rises, to use Gor'kij's expression, "to the point of a spiritual and well thought out symbol".

The role of repetitions and leitmotifs in Čexov deserves to be noted in yet another sense. When it is repeated, strengthened, and reflected like an echo in reverberations of thoughts, recollections, and associations, a detail often creates lyric intonation: it carries, as it were, the melody of the narration. The dialogue of motifs and of recurrent moods adds a special musicality to Čexov's lyric novellas and stories.

NOTES

(1) [From: V. Lakšin, Tolstoj i Čexov (Moskva, Sovetskij pisatel', 1963). Part III, Chapter VI, pp. 495-511; 511-516.]
(2) N.M. Ežov, "Anton Pavlovič Čexov (Opyt xarakteristiki)", Istoričeskij vestnik (August, 1909), book VIII, p. 515.
(3) [Numerals in parentheses in this selection refer to the volume and page number in Čexov's, Polnoe sobranie sočinenij i pisem (Moskva, Goslitizdat, 1944-1951).]
(4) From a letter from I. Dombrowski to L. Zlobina, November, 1895. Voprosy literatury (1960), 1, p. 106.
(5) [We continue to translate detal' as 'detail' and podrobnost' as 'particular' as we have done in the selection by Dobin. Lakšin, however, does seem to use them synonymously.]
(6) An entry in the diary of V.P. Lazurskij, July 11, 1895. Literaturnoe nasledstvo (Moskva, Izdatel'stvo AN SSSR), vol. 37-38, part II, p. 464.
(7) A note by P.A. Sergeenko, Literaturnoe nasledstvo, vol. 37-38, part II, p. 546.
(8) [The tradition being that the first to step onto the church carpet will have the upper hand in the marriage.]
(9) Vl. I. Nemirovič-Dančenko, Stat'i, reči, besedy, pis'ma (Moskva, Iskusstvo, 1952), vol. I, p. 107.
(10) Quoted from: F.I. Bulgakov, Graf L.N. Tolstoj i kritika ego proizvedenij, russkaja i inostrannaja (St. Petersburg, 1899), third ed., part II, p. 61.
(11) A.V. Lunačarskij, Stat'i o literature (Moskva, Goslitizdat, 1957), p. 654.

V

STRUCTURAL FEATURES IN ČEXOV'S POETICS (1)

A. DERMAN

1

Čexov occupies one of the highest places among those literary artists
who in their work not only use the resources allowed by scholarship
- they all use them, even those who deny that they resort to them
and state that they rely exclusively on their own intuition - but also
among those who repeatedly express the principle of creative cooperation between the artist and the scholar . . .

There is something scholarly in his approach to the structure of
a work; he divided it into distinct stages, and for each of them he
had carefully reasoned methods for the creative embodiment of his
ideas.

Regarding the first stage, one must say that if Čexov's poetics
is, as a whole, polemical, that is, if he presents new devices in
contrast to old ones, then it is especially polemical with even a paradoxical emphasis as far as it pertains to the first stage of structure,
which is the so-called 'beginning of the plot', (2) 'preface', 'introduction', 'prologue', etc.

His poetics of the 'story's beginning' amounted in effect to the demand that there be no overt 'complication' or, in an extreme case,
that it consist of no more than two or three lines. This, of course,
was quite a revolutionary step in relation to the poetics of the time,
which was dominated by Turgenev (who was its greatest representative). In Turgenev's main and longest works, that is, in his novels,
he went through dozens of pages with retrospective biographies of
his heroes before they appeared. Čexov wrote no novels; the short
story and short novel were the dominant genres in his works, and
that, perhaps, is partly the reason why the nature of his formal
requirements was adapted to the short story or the short novel.

There is no doubt, however, that the main reason for Čexov's
sharp hostility towards more or less extended 'introductions' was
based on something else: they seemed superfluous and in contradiction to his idea about the active reader. He believed that even without the help of specific introductions this sort of reader would reconstruct what was most important in the hero's past life; he would
do this through a skillfully depicted present, and if something in the
past remained unknown to such a reader, then to balance it, a more
substantial danger would be avoided: that of the diffusion of an impression which a superabundance of particulars creates. Čexov's
most merciless demands concerned the brevity of the 'beginning of

the plot', 'preface', 'introduction', etc.

This is stated with great expressiveness in the valuable memoirs of S. Ščukin, a priest, who appeared before Čexov as an author with a manuscript. Taking the notebook, Čexov remarked:

> "A novice writer should do the following: bend it in two and tear out the first half."
> "I looked at him with disbelief", Ščukin writes.
> "I say this in all seriousness", Čexov said. "Novice writers usually attempt, so to speak, to 'introduce a reader to the story' and half of what they write is superfluous. One should write in such a way that the reader understands what was going on not through any explanation on the part of the author, but rather through the movement of the story and through the conversations and actions of the characters. Try tearing out the first half of your story; you will only have to change the beginning of the second half a bit, and the story will be completely understandable. And in general, you shouldn't have anything that is superfluous. You have to discard mercilessly everything that is not directly related to the story. If, in the first chapter, you say that a rifle is hanging on the wall, then it absolutely must be fired in the second or third chapter. If it is not going to be fired, then it ought not to be hanging there." (3)

Instructions of this sort are rarely absent in letters to authors who had sent him their works. He was no less merciless in his own personal creative practice, and his severity steadily increased as time went by. If in Čexov's earlier works one could still find 'beginnings' in the spirit of traditional poetics, with some specific traces of an 'introduction' - they later disappear without a trace, and Čexov begins the story either with one (literally!) sentence introducing the very essence of the narration, or else he manages even without this. As an example of the first sort, we shall refer to "Ariadna".

> On the deck of a steamer travelling from Odessa to Sevastopol a rather handsome gentleman with a little round beard came up to me to ask for a light, and he said . . .

This is a bit more than the whole introduction: the note about the gentleman's appearance, strictly speaking, already belongs to the corpus of the narrative because this gentleman, being the narrator, is, at the same time, an important protagonist. Everything further is already the corpus of the work, the narrative itself. Too, it is impossible to remain silent about yet another fact. Evidently sensing some sort of unnaturalness in such a 'beginning' where a man goes up to someone he does not know to ask for a light and without any apparent reason relates to him a long, complicated and intimate story, Čexov took care to render this device harmless. Having allowed the narrator to speak a bit at first not on the main theme but on a closely related subject, the author observes: "It . . . was clear that he was somewhat upset and that he would rather talk about himself than about women, and that I would not escape without hearing some long story in the nature of a confession" (IX, 63).

Such a story, of course, follows later. There is, however, a second shock-absorber against artificiality: once he has begun the story, the narrator, that is, the gentleman with the little round beard, soon turns to the listener-author: "I'm sorry, but I must ask you again: is this boring you?"

"I told him that it was not at all boring, and he continued", this time, we might add, uninterrupted by the author to the very end of the story.

As has already been mentioned, Čexov did not remain at this level in his battle with 'introductions', but began to get along entirely without them. Take, for example, the beginning of his long story, "My Life".

The manager said to me: "I am keeping you on only out of respect for your esteemed father; otherwise you would have been fired long ago" (IX, 104).

Here there is absolutely nothing of the traditional 'beginning', 'introduction', etc. It is a characteristic segment of the life of the main hero, the first of a great many similar elements from which the life of the hero as a whole is formed and whose story is therefore called "My Life".

In all probability, the dominant characteristic of his early work - always short stories - was the cause of the author's persistent concentration for many years on the improvement of literary devices directed towards condensing the 'beginning of the plot' as much as possible, because there was simply no room for it in the outlets in which he was published - newspapers and humor magazines. Having mastered the art of a short introduction, Čexov valued this achievement, became its principal supporter, and remained faithful to it even after every limitation on his work had been lifted.

2

Apropos of the second structural element, that is, the development of the theme, it must be said that here Čexov's persistent demand for compactness stands out very sharply, as is quite understandable: at this stage the author must most often be on guard against the dangers of extending the description and making it too detailed, and of allowing repetitions and superfluous comments. It is quite natural that it was to this stage that Čexov's inventiveness in the art of condensing the narration was directed. It would not be out of place to illustrate the laconism of his compositional devices here. The peculiarities of these devices are most spectacular in those instances where the author confronted the problem of chronologically depicting a process extending over a period of years. For the sake of illustration let us take an example:

It is necessary that the life of Starcev, the hero of the story
"Ionyč", pass before the reader. At first he is presented as a young
country doctor - a fresh, naive, trusting person with a romantic
personality. Then he slowly begins to lose his color; he turns grey
and sinks into the mire of a dull Philistine life. The spirit of greedy
and senseless money-grubbing seizes him; he finally loses the image
and likeness of a human being and even is given a specifically
Philistine nickname: "Ionyč". This entire slow lifelong dying of a
man's humanity had to be shown on the background of a colorless,
dull, pitiful, Philistine environment which drags everyone imperi-
ously into its own morass.

This entire extended multiphased process which by its own nature
would seem to demand a great accumulation of large and small
characteristics is realized in a few short pages with a truly com-
manding persuasiveness!

One can say that the main literary device which Čexov uses here
is the arrangement of signposts along the path of Doctor Starcev's
life, between which the writer leaves a broad space which the reader
may fill in as part of his creative cooperation in the work.

These signposts follow various lines which often intersect: signposts along the path of the doctor's career; signposts along the path
of the evolution of his tastes; signposts along the development and
fate of his romance; signposts along the path of the lives of those
individuals who form his milieu, etc.

Here are the signposts which signify the success of Starcev's
career:

(1) Starcev went to town to enjoy himself a bit and to make some
    purchases. He walked at a leisurely pace (he did not yet own
    any horses) and all the while he sang:
    "When I had yet to drink
    Tears from the cup of life" (IX, 287). (4)

A little more than a year passes. How the hero spent this time is
not mentioned, but it is stated almost in passing that:

(2) He already owned a pair of horses and had a coachman named
    Pantelejmon in a velvet waistcoat (293).

Another four years pass, and there is a new, third signpost along
the path of Starcev's career.

(3) Starcev already had a large practice in the city. Every morning
    he hurriedly received his patients at Dyalizh, and then he left
    to make house calls in the city. Now he drove not with a pair
    of horses, but with a troika with bells . . . (297)

A few years later we see the final phase of Starcev's transformation
marked by the last signpost:

(4) Starcev has grown even stouter, he breathes heavily and now
walks with his head thrown back. When he rides in the troika
with bells, fat and red in the face, and Pantelejmon, also fat
and red in the face with his thick beefy neck, sits on the box,
extending his arms stiffly in front of himself as if they were
made of wood, and shouts to those he meets "Keep to the r-r-
right!" It is an impressive picture, and it seems that it is not
a mortal being driven, but a pagan god (IX, 302).

In this way the detailed depiction of the growth of Dr. Starcev's
material success and the simultaneous destruction of his moral and
spiritual being was replaced by Čexov with a step by step view of
his 'mode of transportation'. One could not, however, complain of
an insufficient expressivity in the sum total of the portrait of Dr.
Starcev as received by the reader.

But in other instances Čexov found it possible to manage even
without such signposts! Take for example the description in "Ariadna"
of Šamoxin's love for the heroine after he gained her affections and
when, as he put it, his love "entered into its final phase, its waning
phase".

I became her lover (says Šamoxin). At least for about a month I
was crazy, feeling only delight. To embrace her young, beautiful
body, to take one's pleasure of it, to feel each time upon waking
her warmth and to remember that she is here, she, my Ariadna -
oh, one cannot get used to this very easily! (IX, 79).

It would seem that all of this was intentionally thought up to prepare
the reader for a vivid story of the flowering of this passionate, in-
toxicated love, with the various shades of its further development.

No, the reader does not get a single line of this story! The words
"one cannot get used to this very easily!" are followed immediately
by "but nevertheless I did get used to it and gradually began to relate
sensibly to my new situation" (IX, 79).

3

Of the three classical elements of structure - the beginning of the
plot, the development of the plot, and the finale - it seems that
Čexov was most concerned with the finale. Evidently the popular
saying "The end crowns the matter" (5) was for him a living experience in the process of his work. It is not without good reason that
in his statements on matters of structure, considerations about the
finale occupy the foremost place. The sharp changes in Čexov's
poetics over the course of years are observable best of all in his
finales: both the theory and practice of the writer's early years not
only differ from those of his later period, but they are often in direct contrast.

Čexov's statements regarding his work on finales are character-

ized by their complete decisiveness. One of them which became quite
popular, thanks to its unique aphoretical expressiveness, is particularly valuable in that it refers to the structure of both his short
stories and his plays. When he finished working on Ivanov, Čexov
wrote the following in a letter to his brother Aleksandr:

> I was writing a play for the first time, ergo, mistakes are un-
> avoidable. The sujet is complicated and not at all foolish. I end
> every act as I do short stories: I carry each act calmly and
> quietly, but in the end I give the playgoer a slap in the face (XIII,
> 372).

Čexov did not attempt to explain further what he had in mind with
such an energetic formula, so it follows that he was certain that the
addressee would not err on that account. And so it was: in 1887,
when Čexov wrote that letter, the characteristic feature of the finales
of his short stories was tangibly clear: it was the surprise effect.
Here there is a situation deserving attention, but one which, however, is not immediately evident. We will recall that a surprise effect in a finale is strongly associated in our mind with the humorous
stories of Čexov's early period as, for example, "The Orator", who
makes the mistake of extolling in his panegyric not the deceased,
but rather a living person who happens to be present at the funeral;
"A Horse Name" which turns out to be only indirectly related to
horses; "Failure" where the groom, taken by surprise, is blessed
with a portrait of Lažečnikov [I.I. Lažečnikov (1792-1869) - a writer
known for his historical novels] instead of an icon; "The Drama"
where the writer uses a heavy paper weight to kill the lady driving
him insane with a reading of her drama, and so on ad infinitum.
What emerges from Čexov's letter is that he deliberately applies
this same literary device of an ending in his sombre drama! Moreover, in the letter, where he gives his brother only the most schematic idea of a literary genre which was new to him, he attempts
to emphasize that fact: it turns out that he uses the same device for
a dramatic work as for a humorous work.
It is certainly wrong to be surprised by this. In fact our erroneous
impression can be explained by the fact that in Čexov's early work
there is a predominance of humor which is strengthened further in
our mind in that we remember this sort of thing better. The effective
surprise endings of the non-humorous genres do not play a lesser
role in Čexov's early works than they do in his humorous works. We
recall such stories as "In Court" with its sudden assault on the
reader's nerves in the finale where it comes to light that the defendant accused of murdering his wife is escorted by his son. Or the
short story "The Beggar" in which he depicts the self-satisfied
Pharisee of a lawyer, who believes that his own cliche admonitions
have brought about the reeducation of Luškov, a drunkard and beggar,
but who discovers that it was not his own doing but that of Ol'ga, the
cook, who railed at him but in her heart wept over him and in his
stead did the work which Skvorcev had given him to do as a repay-

ment. We might also recall two other early short stories by Čexov:
"Without Title" and "The Bet" which stand apart in his literary leg-
acy by their philosophical character, which is reflected both in style
and theme. In the former story we hear of the abbot of a monastery
which was isolated from the sinful world. One day, having visited
the city, he related to the brethren how the life of the city dweller
passes in the depths of sin and temptation, and how great the power
of the devil is there. And then comes the ending: "When he left his
cell next morning, not a single monk remained in the monastery.
They had all rushed to the city" (VII, 11).

In the second story, a young lawyer bets a banker two million
rubles that he will voluntarily remain in prison fifteen years; but
then, having won the bet for all intents and purposes, he loses it
deliberately by escaping from prison, and leaves a note which ends
with the following remarks: "To show you my contempt for what you
live by, I am abandoning the two million which I once dreamt of as
paradise, but which I now scorn. To deprive myself of any claim
to this money, I am leaving this place five hours before the agreed-
upon time and thereby shall lose the bet . . ." (VII, 209).

It is clear that in both of these two philosophical stories the entire
structure is bound up in its 'surprise' ending. In particular, regarding "Without Title" (which in its first version was called "An Eastern
Tale"), Polonskij [Y.P. Polonskij (1819-1898), Russian poet and
editor] wrote to Čexov immediately after reading the story: "The
ending is not merely unexpected, but it is also significant". He was
correct in this. In the more dramatic and perfect stories of the
early Čexov, we do not notice, however, that the denouement contains an element of surprise. The reason for this is that we usually
associate surprise with amusing, funny, humorous stories; and when
there is no laughter, we get the impression that there is no surprise.
But, isn't the denouement of "Van'ka" - the naive address on his letter to his grandfather - a typical final surprise? And isn't the
denouement of "To Sleep, Sleep . . . !" also a surprise? And don't
we feel something of sudden tragic enlightenment when, in "Anguish",
the cabman Iona turns with his tale of deep sorrow to his horse, the
only, patient listener? And isn't the same thing true both in the
author's intention and in our understanding: "I give the reader a
slap in the face"?

It is necessary to take all of this into very careful consideration
in order to evaluate correctly the abruptness of the change which
later took place both in Čexov's opinions about finales and in his
creative practice. Only two years pass after he utters the aphorism
regarding the ending of Ivanov, and he writes the following to
Pleščeev in a letter about "A Dreary Story":

A narrative story, like the stage, has its own characteristics.
Thus, my feeling tells me that in the ending of a short novel of
a story I ought to deliberately concentrate in the reader the feeling of the entire story, and to do this I must mention briefly in
passing those people about whom I spoke earlier (XIV, 407).

Three years later, Čexov writes the following in a letter to Suvorin:

> I have an interesting sujet for a comedy, but still lack an ending.
> Whoever discovers new endings for plays will open up a new era.
> These damn endings do not come easy to me! Either the hero gets
> married or shoots himself - there is no other way out of it (XV,
> 388).

An exceptionally interesting situation! Čexov already recognizes the
necessity for a departure from the traditional 'denouement', from
the surprise effect ("he shoots himself"), that is, from the notorious
"in the face", but in practice he still uses that very sort of
denouement. However, he finally comes out the victor in this battle
with tradition: even for a work of drama, where "he gets married
or shoots himself" seemed somehow unavoidable to him, he creates
a finale without either one: we are thinking about The Cherry Orchard.
In his short novels as well as his stories, Čexov succeeds not only
in creating and elaborating, but also in strengthening the poetics of
an ending without a 'denouement'. Was it conceivable before Čexov
that a story in which the 'heroine' had gone through several love
affairs would end as in "The Darling"?

> She lies down and thinks about Saša, who is sleeping soundly in
> the next room. From time to time he mutters in his sleep: "I'll
> show you. Get out of here! Don't fight!" (IX, 327).

In the very nature of the finale there is a threatening danger for a
writer, a danger which in spite of its relative variety - elevated and
rhetorical, a bit sugary, spectacular, etc. - finally amounts to one
thing: the danger of unoriginal 'rounding'. Čexov used his own characteristic devices to do battle with this danger. One such device comes
forward with special clarity in "A Case from a Doctor's Practice".
A doctor comes to a sick woman who owns a factory, and is seized
by an oppressive mood replete with strong social feeling. He leaves
early in the morning.

> The singing of skylarks and the ringing of church bells was in the
> air. The windows in the factory buildings gleamed happily and on
> his way out of the yard and then down the road to the station,
> Korolev no longer thought about the workers, the pile dwellings,
> or the devil; rather he thought about the time, perhaps even in
> the near future, when life would be as bright and joyful as this
> quiet Sunday morning (IX, 314).

It would seem that as far as logic, psychology, and even rhythm are
concerned, one might put a period here: everything is said and a
typical 'ending' is made. But here the whole point is that the ending
is 'typical', is reminiscent of a curtain falling, is rounded in an
elevated style, and using a semicolon instead of a period, Čexov
adds, clearly adds two unpretentious 'lowering' lines: "and he thought

of how pleasant this was to ride on a spring morning in a fine troika
and how pleasant it was to warm oneself in the sunshine".

4

We have a classic example of a Čexovian finale characteristic of
the highest level of his creativity in "The Lady with the Little Dog" -
one of Čexov's masterpieces.

We have before our eyes a description of the story's two protagonists in one of the stolen moments of bitter 'happiness' which seldom fell to their lot.

> He went up to her and took her by the shoulders to caress her and
> say something cheerful, and at that moment he caught sight of
> himself in the mirror.
> His hair was already beginning to turn grey . . . The shoulders
> on which his hands lay were warm and trembling. He felt com-
> passion for this life which was still warm and beautiful, but prob-
> ably already near the time when it would begin to fade and wither,
> like his own life had . . . And only now, when his head became
> grey, did he come to love well, in a genuine way - for the first
> time in his life.
> Anna Sergeevna and he loved each other like people very close,
> and akin, like man and wife, like tender friends; it seemed to
> them that fate itself had destined them for each other, and they
> could not understand why each was married to someone else. They
> were like two birds of passage, male and female, snared and
> forced to live in separate cages. They had forgiven each other
> for everything that they were ashamed of in the past, they forgave
> everything in the present and felt that their love had changed them
> both.
> Formerly in moments of depression he comforted himself with
> any argument that came to his mind, but now he did not care any
> more for arguments, but rather felt profound compassion, he
> wanted to be sincere and tender . . .
> "Don't cry any more, my darling", he was saying. "You have
> cried enough, it is over now . . . Let's have a talk, we will come
> up with something."
> Then they talked for a long time consulting each other and spoke
> of how they might free themselves of the necessity for hiding, de-
> ceiving, and living in different cities while not seeing each other
> for long periods. How to free themselves from such unbearable
> fetters?
> "How? How?" he asked, clutching his head. "How?"
> And it seemed that in just a short while the solution would be found,
> and then a new, wonderful life would begin; and it was clear to both
> of them that the end was still far off and that the most complicated
> and difficult part was only just beginning (IX, 370-71).

This ending deserves very close attention. Here, with direct, exact words, the very thing which is the real essence of Čexov's finales in almost all the works of his mature stage of creativity, is distinctly pronounced 'aloud' the thing which he expressed elsewhere not so openly, sometimes only in an allusion.

Even if it is accidental, with no deliberate intention on the part of the author, that the quoted 'end' of "The Lady with the Little Dog" ends with the word 'beginning', it does not keep us from seeing that the same word could have been used in the finales of "The Duel" , "The House with the Mezzanine", "The Betrothed", "My Life", "An Unknown Man's Story", and many other stories, which are still read with deep interest in spite of the fact that 'the particular situations' from which they were created have almost completely disappeared into the past. These endings of Čexov's stories announce that in the life process depicted by the author a certain stage was completed - and only that. The process continues, a new phase begins which is more important than the one depicted, but it is the reader himself who must create it: Čexov places his courageous hopes on the creative cooperation of the reader, for whom he nonetheless has created all the necessary prerequisites for successful understanding.

In his excellent article "Čexovian Finales", the late A. G. Gornfel'd, (6) the well known scholar-critic whom Gor'kij held in high esteem, turned his attention to a peculiar feature of the finale in many Čexov stories: the author breaks with his hero at the moment when the hero falls to thinking, becomes absorbed in thought after experiencing the events described. This, of course, is not a chance repetition of a device. The thoughts and reflections of the hero are a projection of the presumed thoughts of the reader. They are the sort of thing which comprise the goal of the author's efforts. It is natural that the most intensive work in the reader's mind be directed towards the crowning of the work, toward the completion of the work when all the images and events before the reader's eyes which constitute the segment of life portrayed have passed. Hence the attention Čexov gave specifically to the finale. But if in his early years he concentrated in the latter all his resources to get an effect, in the most part for the emotional saturation of the reader's reaction, then in later years, while not ignoring this aspect of the matter, he nevertheless shifted the center of gravity towards arousing in the reader the deepest possible mental activity.

And so, turning attention to Čexov's prose beginning with 1894, that is, in the last decade of his life, we find the following in the finales:

In "Woman's World":

She (Anna Akimovna, the heroine) now was thinking that were it possible to draw a picture of the long day which she had just lived through, then everything that was bad and vulgar . . . would have been true, while her dreams . . . would have stood out from the whole . . . like something false or exaggerated (VIII, 333).

In "Rothschild's Violin" Bronza, the principal hero, reflects bitterly and resentfully just before his death:

Why is it that in this world there is such a strange order of things that life, which is given to man only once, passes without profit? (VIII, 343).

A student (in the story of the same name)

was thinking that truth and beauty . . . evidently always constituted the most important things in human life (VIII, 348).

In "A Case from a Doctor's Practice" Doctor Korolev, returning to the city early in the morning from a call to a patient

thought about the time, perhaps even in the near future, when life would be as bright and joyful as this quiet Sunday morning (IX, 314).

In "The New Dacha" the peasants think about their absurd relationship with the owners of the dacha:

What kind of fog is it which shrouded their eyes from what mattered most? (IX, 341).

This enumeration of Čexov's works where the principal hero falls to thinking in the finale, trying to comprehend all that he has undergone, could be continued up to the very end of Čexov's writings, including his swan song, "The Betrothed", at the end of which we read:

She went into Saša's room and stood there for a moment. "Farewell, dear Saša!" she thought, and her new life, broad and spacious, was pictured before her, and this life, still obscure, full of mystery, attracted her and beckoned to her (IX, 450).

Out of all of these leitmotifs of finales, we will distinguish only one which is particularly remarkable. In the short story "On Official Duty", Inspector Lyžin, under the influence of what he has undergone, surrenders to his customary thoughts about the connection of his personal life with the general order of things. Significant is the 'addition' to these customary thoughts, engendered by the picture of harsh social contradictions raised before the eyes of Lyžin, who started to feel his responsibility - keenly - to the victims of this general process.

He felt that this suicide and the peasant's misery lay on his conscience too; to tolerate the idea that these people, resigned to their lot, take upon themselves the heaviest and darkest burden in life - how terrible this was! To tolerate this, and to wish for oneself a bright, active life among happy, satisfied people and to dream constantly of such a life – would mean to dream of new suicides of people crushed by work and weariness . . . (IX, 355).

Regarding the sharpness and revelatory character of the given train of thought, the author interrupts at that moment:

Such were Lyžin's thoughts, and such thoughts had long existed hidden within him, and only now were they displayed so broadly and clearly in his consciousness (IX, 354).

It is in these words that we find the key to Čexov's finales as extremely important structural elements! He does not attempt to startle his reader or uncover before him some exotic, unusual area of life. Just the opposite: he attempts to take out of the shadows and put into light 'old' but 'hidden' thought, to direct it towards what is most familiar and constantly before the reader's eyes, to open his eyes even wider, to compel him to look more deeply into the depths of life, to help him to perceive this life which is taken for granted "broadly and clearly", to begin to think.

NOTES

(1) [From: A. Derman, O Masterstve Čexova (Moskva, Sovetskij pisatel', 1959). Chapter IV, pp. 74-88.]

(2) [Zavjazka – that point in the sujet where the plot actually begins to unfold; sometimes called the 'complication'.]

(3) S. Ščukin, "Iz vospominanij ob A.P. Čexove", Russkaja mysl' (1911), 10, p. 44.

(4) [Numerals in parentheses in this essay refer to the volume and page number in Čexov's Polnoe sobranie sočinenij i pisem (Moskva, Goslitizdat, 1944-1951).]

(5) [Equivalent to the Latin finis coronat opus, not 'the end justifies the means'.]

(6) Krasnaja nov' (1939), 8-9.

VI

THE STYLE OF ČEXOV'S TALES (1)

G. N. POSPELOV

The stories which he wrote at the end of the 1880s show that Čexov
was already surmounting the canons of <u>sujet</u> construction which had
become traditional in literature and that he was advancing new principles. This primarily affected the construction of <u>sujets</u> of novel-
like stories prevailing in Čexov - works wherein the basic goal consisted in disclosing the development of the principal hero's (or
heroes') character in relation to his disaffection with the social
milieu.

In the course of Russian literature, even from the time of the
first novels and novel-like stories which possessed a concentric
(and not adventurous) construction of the <u>sujet,</u> a certain principle
of <u>sujetal</u> correlation and development of the principal heroes'
characters received wide acceptance. This principle can be stated
as follows: in the course of the events constituting the <u>sujet</u> of a
work, the heroes and heroines with different characters and ideological positions which, for the author, had a positive or negative
meaning, were opposed to one another. Between these arose conflicts,
which were usually connected with love (romantic relationships or
rivalry). Such conflicts were resolved by having one of the heroes
prevail over the other, which thus expressed the author's 'verdict'
on the characters of the heroes and their ideological positions, and
at the same time expressed the underlying purpose of the work.

There was a sort of variant in the <u>sujet</u> construction which was
externally more simple but in essence more complex: in the love
conflict there was a basic conflict only between the hero and heroine
who had different characters and took differing ideological positions,
but the development and solution of the conflict was created so that
the <u>hero</u> in one way or another displayed the weak traits of his character and ideological stances and arrived at a moral self-negation.

Čexov does have novel-like stories embodying both of these variants of 'sujetal' structure, which had been worked out long before
his time: of this type are "The Wife", "The Flutterer", and "Ariadna".
To a certain extent the short novel "The Duel" also belongs here.

In the first of these, Asorin, the principal hero and narrator, with
his reactionary views and his narrow, egotistical self esteem, appears as an ideological antipode to his wife Natalja Gavrilovna, with
her inclinations towards charity and her sympathy towards the local
provincial intelligentsia. Asorin is a lonely, suffering man, and his
encounter with the representatives of this milieu (Doctor Sobol', the
landowner Bragin) brings him to a moral revolution and a rapproche-

ment with his wife and her 'party'. For the writer, this defeat of the reactionary Asorin has a fundamental and independent meaning. The writer does not show any inclination toward connecting Asorin's defeat with the general condition of Russian society. Rural liberals attempt to do battle with famine in the nearby villages and with the aid of the material assistance of Asorin, who had become reconciled with them, their campaign is rather successful.

Likewise, in the story "The Flutterer" the narrative is devoted entirely to contrasting the modest, honest, and talented Doctor Dymov with the pretentious, corrupt popular artist Rjabovskij, who seduces Dymov's empty, vain wife, Ol'ga Ivanovna, but soon casts her off. Dymov does not take vengeance on his wife and his rival, but he does suffer deeply, and overcomes his suffering by intense self-sacrificing work; it could be that this is why he undertakes the risky medical experiment which brings him to his tragic death. The affirmation of Dymov's moral superiority over Rjabovskij is the basic idea of the story. It is not complicated by any broader generalizations.

The other stories of this group are constructed in a similar manner. In this sort of sujetal construction the conflicts have, naturally, a basic decisive importance. They are therefore noteworthy to a certain extent for the drama of their content which is put sujetally in the foreground. Thus we have such conflicts as Asorin's quarrel with his wife and his attempt to leave home, Ol'ga Ivanovna's unfaithfulness and Dymov's sickness and death, Ariadna's secret relationship with Lubkov, and von Koren's hidden animosity towards Laevskij which comes to a head in their duel, which all but costs Laesvkij his life.

All of these belong to the relatively early stories of the period under review, which were written in the first half of the 1890s. In some of his later stories Čexov substantially complicated this traditional principle of sujet construction and filled it with new content. As before, the story was built on a conflict between the heroes who oppose each other in their personalities and beliefs, and, as before, this conflict is solved by a rather sudden and abrupt denouement. But at the same time the writer introduced into the narrative some very significant emotional reflections of the narrator about broad, general subjects which even exceed the boundaries of the reality depicted. These reflections took on the basic ideological load in the story, and the conflict being depicted lost its self-contained significance and tended to be subordinated to the general ideological-emotional tone developed by the narrator's reflections.

"The House with the Mezzanine" was written in that way. The ideological disagreements and arguments between the artist-narrator and Lida traverse the whole story and create its conflict. The conflict is resolved by Lida's victory in which she despotically separates the artist from her sister Zenja as soon as they have declared their love for each other, and in doing this Lida deprives him of his personal happiness. It would seem that the whole sense of the story is contained in this victory of the self-confident but narrow-minded

Lida over the disappointed, romantically inclined artist. However,
in his statements made in the presence of Lida and Ženja, the artist
not only denies the value of Lida's cultural-social work in the village, but he also draws a very gloomy picture of the state of
peasantry in general and expresses a romantic confidence in the
possibility of a free and happy life for all society. In the light of
these prospects his disagreements with Lida and his lack of success in love seem unimportant. On the other hand, his romantic
rapprochement with Ženja and the emotional ending of the story
which expresses his vague hopes ("Misjus', where are you?") receive, on the contrary, a sort of basic symbolic significance and
express the expectation of some unusual changes in the future.

The story "The Man in a Case" has a similar construction. In it
the collision between Belikov, aggressive in his political cowardice,
and the liberal Kovalenko leads to the disgrace of Belikov and to his
death. This collision, however, does not exhaust the ideological
tendency of the story, but actually contradicts it. It is the reflections of the narrator Burkin and Ivan Ivanovič which provide the
theme, revealing that 'caseness' completely dominates the whole
life of the Russian intelligentsia, that it makes this life unbearable,
and that not to protest against it is impossible, but to protest against
it is dangerous.

In all of Čexov there are comparatively few stories which are
based on a sharp sujetal antithesis of the characters of the main
heroes and the conflicts flowing therefrom. At the very beginning
of his mature work, he began to write stories whose sujets were
constructed in a different way. These are those stories in which
the internal, ideological-moral development of the hero's character is the basis for the development of events; external sujetal conflicts are relegated to the background and only motivate and sharpen
the content of this internal development. The evolution of the hero's
character represents his reevaluation of the foundations of his personal life, and - indirectly - it also represents to a certain extent
a reevaluation of the moral condition of all of Russian society and
in particular of that of its privileged classes. Step by step, although
with chronological zig-zags, Čexov recognized more clearly this
connection between the ideological evolution of his heroes and the
conditions of society, and expressed it with increasing clarity and
breadth. In this way he constructed the sujets of his most significant short novels, such as "The Black Monk", "An Unknown Man's
Story", "Three Years", "Ionyč", and "The Betrothed". Even in some
of his earlier stories this principle of sujet construction begins to
show itself rather distinctly.

In the story "The Name Day" there is no noticeable antithesis of
characters and there is no conflict which would result from it. But
a peculiar conflict does slowly unfold in the consciousness of the
main characters. Petr Dmitr'evič and his wife are at first completely subordinated to the ordinary moral standards of their milieu
(which consisted of nobility and civil servants), and, deceiving themselves and others, they play the role of happy hosts in the presence

of their guests. But later, when Ol'ga Mixajlovna reaches the point of extreme exhaustion and serious illness, they begin to recognize the falseness and vanity of their lives. The author himself clearly supports his heroes in their severe condemnation of their society, but this condemnation still does not acquire a broadened significance and refers only to the people depicted in the story.

The sujet of "The Black Monk" is likewise built on the evolution of the protagonist's character. Master (2) Kovrin strives to overcome his mediocrity with a sick conceit, with dreams about his lofty natural gifts, and with his deliberate estrangement from the world of conventionality and triviality, represented by Pesockij's managerial obsession. But step by step the true meaning of his groundless conceit is revealed, and Kovrin dies having contributed nothing to the sum of scholarly knowledge. His unsuccessful marriage to Tanja Pesockaja (3), her father's death, Kovrin's loneliness - all of these only intensify his personal catastrophe. Still, there is no broader negation of convention and social triviality in the story.

More encompassing and significant in content are those short novels of a similar sujetal quality, such as "An Unknown Man's Story" and "Three Years".

In the former there is a contrast of characters as the well as love intrigue arising from it. Here a terrorist-revolutionary, the story's narrator, is opposed in his internal nobility to Orlov, a high ranking metropolitan civil servant, an empty, depraved individual. Having deep contempt for Orlov and sympathizing with Zinaida Fedorovna, whom Orlov had seduced and abandoned, he takes her out of the country in futile hope of the personal happiness which he has never known. However, the point of the story is not to be found in this antithesis nor in the clash between the characters, but in the ideological evolution of the narrator. Living with the Orlovs as a lackey, he observes the useless lives of the ruling bureaucracy and realizes the futility of terrorist battle with this inert, slow-witted milieu. He resolves to search for other ideals which are not political, but moral, and attempts to embody them in his concern for the child of the woman he loves.

But in this story, as opposed to "The Name Day" and "The Black Monk", Čexov realizes the development of his principal hero's character in a considerably deeper and wider way. He not only contraposes it to the inert life of the ruling classes, but sees in it a reflection of the negative moral condition of Russian society. This is the meaning of the narrator's letter to Orlov. "Why are we tired out?" the narrator asks in the letter. "Why are we at first so passionate, courageous, and noble, but at 30 or 35 become completely bankrupt? Why is it that one man dies from tuberculosis, another puts a bullet into his head, a third seeks oblivion in wine or cards, and a fourth, to deaden his fear and grief, tramples beneath his feet the picture of his pure, wonderful youth?" And later the narrator says that he dreams about a life which is "holy, lofty, and solemn like the vault of heaven". In the light of such thoughts and moods, the relationships and events which constitute the sujet of the story acquire a significantly deeper and broader meaning, about which the readers of that period were bound to think and reflect.

The short novel "Three Years" was constructed along the same lines. In it too the basic meaning consists not in the opposition of Laptev, the educated merchant, spoiled by the 'warehouse', to the representatives of a working and enlightened intelligentsia, Jarcev and Kočevoj, nor is it the family love conflict of Laptev and Julija, whose unhappy marriage exposes the mutilating power of the 'warehouse' riches even more strongly. The ideological meaning of the story is in Laptev's moral development; bit by bit he begins to become aware that he has been ruined not only by his father's 'warehouse' but by the 'warehouse' of the whole of Russian life. "Look at me", Laptev says to his brother, ". . . I am afraid every time I take a step, it is as if they flog me; I lose courage in the presence of the nonentities, idiots, and creatures who are worth immeasurably less than myself; I am afraid of yard-keepers, door-keepers, policemen, gendarmes, I am afraid of everybody, because I was born of an oppressed mother and from childhood I was oppressed and intimidated." This summation of Laptev's moral development sheds a new light on the characters and events in the story, giving them a much deeper and wider meaning than they would have otherwise. The readers understood that people could be oppressed from childhood not only in 'warehouses', and that not only those who are intimidated from birth are afraid of yard-keepers and policemen.

The stories "Ionyč", "The Teacher of Literature", and "The Betrothed" have similar construction. Throughout this entire group of stories the sujetal role of the conflicts differs from the stories of the first group. The conflicts present in them either lack great dramatic intensity or, if such intensity does exist, it is realized weakly in the course of events which lie at the base of the sujet. Thus in "The Black Monk" there is a detailed narration about Kovrin's happy wedding, but only a mention of how his scholarly career collapsed and how Pesockij died, and furthermore absolutely nothing is said about how Kovrin abandoned Tanja for another woman. So also in "The Teacher of Literature" Nikitin's whole life takes shape externally as one which is completely happy, lacking any external conflicts, and only slowly does the growing internal dissatisfaction, the awareness of the banality of his life, overshadow the hero's spirit towards the end. So also in "An Unknown Man's Story" all the dramatic events take place in the heroine's life, and the narrator enters only as a witness. In the story "Three Years" Laptev and Julija's unhappy family life changes slowly and gradually without tense or dramatic events. In "Ionyč" the relationship between Ionyč and Katerina Ivanovna does not lead to actual clash between them, but changes into one of estrangement in the four years during which they did not meet. In "The Betrothed" the basic conflict - Nadja's break with Andrej Andreič - proceeds gently, with no dramatic complication. It is not drama of external conflicts which interests the writer in these stories, but the tension in the situation of the main characters and in their lives in general.

But in Čexov's work there is still another group of novel-like
stories in which he applies his new principles of <u>sujet</u> construction
with even greater boldness. These are the stories in which the inner development of the protagonist's character is slow, impercep-
tible, and has no significance in itself; instead, the basic significance is acquired by the deep antagonism into which he enters as a
result of his changed beliefs, an antagonism with the entire social
milieu, the moral tenor of its life, and, through it, the conditions
of society. In these stories the gloomy atmosphere of Russian life
unfolds not only in the general statements of the main hero or narrator, but also directly or indirectly in all of the daily relationships of the heroes, in the minutiae of day to day life, and in the
hero's impressions of them. The stories "A Dreary Story", "Ward
No. 6", "My Life", "At Home", and "The Gooseberries" are written
in this manner. Here Čexov's <u>sujetal</u> innovation is revealed with
particular clarity. Insofar as their <u>sujetal</u> quality is concerned,
these stories are very close to the writer's later, mature plays,
in particular to <u>Uncle Vanja</u> and <u>The Three Sisters</u>.

Thus in "A Dreary Story" unexpected and unpleasant changes take
place in old Professor Nikolaj Semenovič's (4) family life. His ward
Katja undergoes serious failures both on the stage and in her personal life, and his daughter Liza is enamoured of an unworthy man
and marries him secretly. But all this affects the professor very
slightly. He lives immersed in his personal internal drama which
is the bitter end of his long career as a scholar-teacher. He is "en-
venomed by new thoughts, the sort which he had never known earlier";
finally he understands that in his thoughts, feelings, and aspirations
"there lacked something general to unify them", and that there had
never been a 'general plan' to his activity. And now it seems to him
that his "popular name . . . has betrayed him". In conjunction with
this, his attitude towards his environment changes. Everything seems
ugly, banal, and dull to him. Now he is startled by the stupidity of
his colleagues, the mediocrity of his students, the lack of intelligence and dignity in scholarly literature, the lack of decency and
staunchness on the part of the intelligentsia, the routine in the
theaters, the pettiness and egotism of the members of his family,
etc. He even begins to hate "people who use violence".

The <u>sujet</u> of this story is thus constructed as a series of episodes
unconnected by a 'unity of action' but bound together by the unity of
the hero-narrator's thoughts and moods as well as by his impressions, characteristics, and recollections. This unity of the
hero's experiences, sustained by the author, dominating the particulars of day to day life and permeating these particulars, is often
called the 'undercurrent' of Čexov's works. Such a 'current' appears
especially strongly in the group of stories under discussion.

In this regard, the short novel "Ward No. 6" is written with particular brightness and significance. It can seem that the <u>sujet</u> of the
story is constructed on Gromov and Ragin's common interests and
on the antithesis of Ragin and Xobotov's characters, which gives
rise to the conflict between them. But in fact here too, in the center

of the narration is the constant active antagonism of the hero with surrounding life.

Very soon Ragin becomes the victim of the atmosphere of the deceit and cowardice which at that time reigned in Russian intellectual circles. After brief attempts to improve the city hospital, he becomes reconciled to the impossibility of radical change, and to justify his weakness he adopts those arguments often used by the Russian Philistines of the time. It was a peculiar 'philosophy', with an attitude of compromise and irresponsibility, moral weakness, and laziness. "Why", thinks Ragin, "should one keep people from dying if death is the normal and regular end of a human being?" Why should one alleviate suffering? It obviously does "lead a person to perfection", etc. But Ragin's irresponsibility and laziness are concealed not only by this sort of 'philosophy', but also by his aspiration to improve himself with his lofty ideas about progress. Not a single person in the local society could, in that sense, match him as an interlocutor, and he began to visit Gromov, who was suffering from a persecution complex and who also eased his soul with similar conversations. On these grounds there arose a constant conflict between the irresponsible dreamers and the irresponsible careerists. Externally, it ended with Ragin's defeat and Xobotov's victory.

But in essence it remains unresolved. Therefore the entire life of this little city, with its banality and emptiness, and Ward No. 6 itself, with its stench and dirt, its stupid and cruel guard Nikita, its iron bars on the windows from which one could see the prison – these emerge as symbolic: they signify the condition of the entire Russian intellectual-Philistine society, the political oppression it experiences, its cowardice and empty its dreaminess.

The short novel "My Life" is constructed in a similar way. The deep moral discord which the protagonist-narrator Misail Poloznev experiences with his family and with the whole local bourgeois-noble society – Misail's aspirations to take to plain living and to place himself in conflict with the daily norms of society, the contempt his relatives and friends feel towards him – is the basic 'stimulus' of the narration and penetrates all of the episodes in the sujet and the details of the depiction. However, the love conflicts – Misail's brief marriage with Maša and Cleopatra's affair with Doctor Blagovo – only set off and deepen this basic conflict, which remains unchanged from the beginning to the end of the narrative.

Such also is the sujetal construction of the story "The Gooseberries", in which the external groundwork of the sujet consists of the story of Cimša-Gimalajskij the younger, but the basic ideological load is carried on through the reflections of his elder brother, the narrator, who is in deep conflict not only with the main hero but with the whole tenor of the life embodied in his brother's personal fate.

The final group of Čexov's novel-like stories is particularly close to stories of a different genre – the 'ethological' (5) type.

Čexov's originality here also consists in bringing into his narration generalizing emotional statements from the narrator or from

the heroes themselves, which carry a considerable ideological load
and subordinate the depiction of characters and events to their meaning.

The short novel "The Peasants" is quite characteristic of this.
Separate episodes from the life of the Čikildeev family and that of
the story surround the lyric culminations found at the beginning and
end of the story: the episode where Marja and Ol'ga go to church and
the concluding episode where Ol'ga and Saša leave Zhukovo to go
back to Moscow. Proceeding from the impressions of the dramatis
personae themselves, the writer speaks here of the beautiful and
happy life which could exist but does not. In the light of these romantic reflections village life appears particularly oppressive and
dreary.

Even more characteristic of this is "A Case from a Doctor's Practice". In it Čexov describes the boring, repressed Philistine life in
the home of Ljalikov, a factory owner. This life, which embodies the
inertness and vulgarity of the Russian bourgeoisie in general, is presented from the point of view of the narrator, Doctor Korolev, in
the light of his reflections about the vicious, senseless existence of
Ljalikov's workers and about the bright, happy life which, perhaps,
would come in the not too distant future.

The structure of "On Official Duty" is also interesting. The oppression and submissiveness of the peasants, their heavy exhaust-
ing labor, and the darkness and hopelessness of the life of the lower
social strata as opposed to the happy, carefree life of the landowners
are exposed in the depiction of two or three secondary characters -
the policeman Lošadin, the landowner von-Tauniz, and the suicide
Lesnickij, an agent from the Zemstvo. Onto the foreground of the
story come the representatives of the civil service and especially
Inspector Lyžin, who recognizes these scandalous contrasts of Russian life and responds to them with his disturbed thoughts.

Thus even in this group of stories all the narrations are subordinated to the pathos of generalizing emotional reflections which belong either to the author or to the heroes and impart peculiar and
significant expressiveness to the particulars of the life being depicted.

Such are the general principles from which Čexov built the sujets
of his stories.

In stories sujets always are realized, as they say, in the narration
about them. In the dynamics of depiction always inherent to stories
and in some way to dramatic works, a twofold distinction must be
made. It is necessary to distinguish between (a) what takes place
in the heroes and their lives created by the author's mind, and (b)
to what extent and by what means everything which takes place in
the lives of the heroes is encompassed in the author's or narrator's
narrative.

Such a differentiation is particularly important in studying the
style of Čexov's stories. The new general principles of sujet construction which Čexov used could produce their artistic effect only

under the condition that they be accompanied by the specific devices of narration which suit them.

Having understood this, Čexov began to use special devices to overcome old traditions. He repudiated the thoroughness, leisurely pace, and verbosity which distinguished the works of the most eminent Russian writers of the mid-nineteenth century. He attempted to overcome the bulkiness of the structure of the narrative. Having mastered the technique of short stories even in his early period of activity - stories which were short not only in the size of their sujets but also in their lack of verbosity - he applied quite similar principles of narration to the stories of his mature period. This was not a mechanical transfer of the system of devices of a humorous short story into the confines of a 'serious' story. In Čexov's mature stories the old system was given a new content and thereby acquired an entirely new function.

As has already been shown, the emotional reflections of the heroes, narrators, or the author-narrator upon the oppressive conditions of Russian social life and their dreams of a different, free, and happy existence acquired in Čexov's stories a basic ideological load, a fundamental importance. They had to subordinate to their pathos the whole narrative of the events in the life of the heroes and their relationships to the conflicts which constitute the sujets.

Due to this, the narrative itself about the sujet had also to disclose and to realize that kind of meaningful subordination both in a qualitative and in a 'quantitative' sense. It had to correspond internally to the emotionally reflective culminations of the story and be coordinated with them in its own meaning. It had to bear an echo and imprint of their emotional reflectiveness. It had also to be concentrated around these culminations. For this reason it could not be long, bulky, verbose, and could not possess a self-contained complex structural organization.

It follows that the events themselves, the sujet of the work, had to be distinctive in their internal focus, conciseness, and brevity. It was necessary to emphasize not the episodes which had in themselves a decisive significance for the relationships and personal fates of individual heroes, but rather those episodes which revealed the general condition of their life, its permanent conflicts, which by that very fact were coordinated in their meaning with the emotional-meditative culminations of the story.

For this reason Čexov's stories usually begin directly from basic sujetal episodes. The prehistory of the heroes, their preliminary characteristics, and the motivations of sujetal conflicts are all kept to a minimum and presented in the course of the narrative. The narration of events is rather brief and develops rapidly. It does not linger over intermediate phenomena nor secondary explicatory episodes and it almost never contains digressions from the basic sequence of events. It does contain gaps of entire periods in the heroes' lives, gaps which extend for days, weeks, and even months or entire years. Much which is essential to the personal lives of the heroes remains behind the scenes of the narrative. Reflecting on this kind

of narrative, the reader gradually realizes all the more that drama
in the lives of Čexov's heroes is formed not by their personal fates
but by the general conditions of their milieu and the general atmosphere of civic life in Russia which these reflect. The heroes of the
novels and the author-narrator brood over this. The thoughts of
the heroes gently and unnoticeably merge into the thoughts of the
author himself and with this they strengthen the emotional mood of
the story.

The story "At Home" was constructed exactly in this way. It belongs, basically, to that group of Čexov's stories in which the sujets
are built on the constantly manifested antagonisms of the main heroes
with their social milieu. However, in this story, the conflict, which
does not contain any specific ideological purpose, ends with a compromise.

Vera Kardina arrives at her relatives' estate on the steppe with
a thirst for "space and freedom". On the very first evening she asks
her Aunt Daša whether they beat people there, and expresses her
fear that she will find it boring to live there. Her fears soon turn
out to be well grounded. No one is beaten at the estate, but Vera's
grandfather has retained the most blatant attitudes of the age of serf-
dom, Aunt Daša treats her servants cruelly and is constantly changing them, and Vera herself, in a fit of dissatisfaction with life, gives
in to these ways and shouts at the defenseless, oppressed Alena.
Vera's family lives in constant contact with other families of the
nobility and with the educated employees from a nearby factory. This
happy and active local 'society' shows a lack of serious interests and
the emptiness of its spiritual life. Although Vera is constantly visiting
people, she is very bored, thirsts for something, does not know what
to do with herself, and the following summer she marries Doctor
Neščapov who is externally quite impressive but in essense empty
and boring. She marries him simply to bring some change into her
life.

The sujet of this story encompasses the whole year of Vera's life
'at home'. Under the pen of many other writers of Čexov's time, a
similar sujet might have been given a broad and detailed treatment.
The protagonist could enter into moral as well as material conflicts
with his relatives, the owners of the estate. The intellectual-land-
owner milieu could be shown through a whole series of carefully described persons, and the tenor of its life could be shown in the relations of these people to one another and to the main hero. The basic
day-to-day family intrigue could be unfolded in a complex web of
loves, rivalries, etc.

None of this happens in this particular story. Although Vera becomes more and more dissatisfied with life in her family's home,
her relations with her grandfather and aunt never become aggravated. Likewise, she does not experience any rapprochement with
her new friends and none of them, Neščapov excluded, receives any
individual characterization. The relationship between Vera and
Neščapov remains completely passive and uncomplicated by any
rivalry.

In other words, this story has no external conflicts. Its sujet is
formed out of a handful of short episodes interconnected like a chronicle. Out of the whole of Vera's life with her family in the course of
a year we find depicted in the total narrative only the two summer
days of her arrival at the estate (the road, the welcoming, the evening conversation with her aunt, the morning walk, and Neščapov's
visit) and two days of the following summer, when she came to the
decision to marry (the jam making, the evening conversation with
a worker, the morning scene with Alena, and Neščapov's new visit).
The whole long winter life is depicted descriptively - in the general
characteristics of the milieu and Vera's condition. Only one narrative episode - the conversation with her aunt about boredom and the
possibility of marriage - concludes the middle, descriptive part of
the story.

But with all their conciseness, the sujetal episodes quite clearly
reveal the conditions of the milieu in which Vera lives. This is
greatly aided in that the episodes of the sujet alternate with episodes
of a lyric character. These are Vera's reflections, which are either
preceded by those of the author or else easily enter into them. Such
is the lyric beginning of the story which presents the dreamy mood
of a person upon arriving at the steppe from a city and the impressions from 'charming' pictures, "the likes of which are not to
be found near Moscow". It is the description of the steppe, in which
the motifs of 'space' and 'freedom' stand out in contrast to the sujetal
depiction of a thoughtless and despotic life. The lyric image of the
steppe passes through the entire story, repeated four times in the
impressions and thoughts of Vera, and symmetrically completes
the whole work.

In addition, this description of the monotonous and boring life at
the estate in the middle of the sujet passes over into Vera's noctur-
nal thoughts about "what to do?" and "where to go?" and these constitute the lyrical culmination of the story. These thoughts express
the girl's feelings about the sacredness of work for the people and
her bitter recognition that she is spoiled and unsuited to the heavy
working conditions of a rural teacher or doctor, as well as her condemnation of the hypocritical conversations of the intelligentsia
about the necessity of educating the people. These thoughts are so
significant, so concrete in their particulars, that they cannot belong
to Vera herself - one clearly hears the voice of the author in them.

The lyrical culmination of the story, vaguely reminiscent of the
description of the steppe, fixes the whole tone of the narrative and
of the description in the sujetal episodes. It predetermines the hidden emotional mood of the narrative and the brevity which stems
from it.

Such are the devices of narration stemming from the construction
of sujets in Čexov's stories. With the help of these devices Čexov
prompted in his readers a specific emotional understanding of Russian social life. He thus sought to show that the state of dissatisfaction and dreaminess which his heroes underwent arises not so
much from the situations in their personal lives as from more hid-

den reasons stipulated by the oppressive political atmosphere dominant in the nation. Čexov created new principles of narration which corresponded to his new content. He created relatively brief narrative works which possess <u>lyricism</u> barely seen through the prose narration.

Čexov did not discover these principles at the beginning. They developed slowly in his stories and only in the very latest ones did they achieve tangibility and perfection. The stories of the late 1890s and 1900s represent the most perfect expression of his style.

NOTES

(1) [From: G. N. Pospelov, <u>Problemy literaturnogo stilja</u> (Moskva, 1970), pp. 308-323.]
(2) [As in M. A. or M. S. At that time in Russia it meant more than a current Ph. D.]
(3) [In Russian, if a husband's name is Pesockij, his wife will be Pesockaja.]
(4) [Actually, Nikolaj Stepanovič. Pospelov errs.]
(5) [Descriptive of morals and customs.]

VII

IMAGERY IN ČEXOV (1)

VADIM NAZARENKO

. . . The key to the understanding of verbal imagery is not found in
a narrow linguistic sphere. A word becomes image-bearing only
when it proves itself able to evoke the images of the real world which
are alive in us. The most sophisticated means of linguistic imagery
of A. Efimov's sort can turn out to be fruitless. (2) But even the
most simple word can be a powerful image. The power of a word to
create an image does not <u>per se</u> reside in the word, but rather in
the way the word acts upon us. That is why a narrowly linguistic approach to the problem cannot reveal the basis of the artistry of the
language of literature.

Thinking in images is not the property and privilege of the writer
alone. All of us think in images - more or less. The worth of the writer
consists then not simply in that he thinks in images, but in the
strength and scope with which the ideas are born through his image-
bearing thought processes.

It is clear that the mere ability to narrate something coherently
and vividly does not yet constitute authentic art. Art begins with typi-
fication. I shall explain this through one of many possible examples.

It had been a long time since I had read Čexov's "The Man in a
Case". As could be expected, I remembered quite well the essence
of the story - the figure of the 'anthropos' Belikov, which contained
such-and-such a common and satirical meaning. I did not recall how
the story was constructed or along which specific lines the movement
of the narration progressed. I did not recall specifically that the
story of Belikov is told by the teacher Burkin.

And then, when I reread the story a short time ago, I noticed what
an extremely important role its beginning has (which precedes the
actual story about Belikov) and so does its ending - which takes place
after the story about Belikov has been concluded. For the sake of the
present discussion it would be rather instructive to turn our attention
at least to these two specifics of the structure of the story.

It begins as follows:

The belated hunters settled down for a night's rest in the barn of
Prokofij, the village elder. There were only the two of them. (And
then we read) They did not sleep. Ivan Ivanyč, a tall, lean, old man
with a long moustache, was sitting outside the door, smoking his
pipe; the light of the moon made him visible. Burkin was lying on
the hay inside, hidden in the darkness.

What role does this description of the locale of the interlocutors play in the narration? It is most likely that A. Efimov would find no "linguistic means of imagery" here. After all, there aren't any tropes. It is quite possible that not only A. Efimov but many others would consider this description to be a particular necessary for 'verisimilitude'.

Actually, verisimilitude is present. It is quite natural that Ivan Ivanyč before going to sleep does not smoke in the hay-filled barn, but rather outside. It is also normal that Burkin, a non-smoker, would go into the barn and carry on the conversation from there. However, we would understand nothing of Čexov's artistry were we to limit it here solely to verisimilitude.

Now we draw near the end of the story. Everything about Belikov has already been said. Then:

> The high school teacher went out of the barn . . .
> "What a moon, what a moon!" he said, glancing up . . .

Burkin's exit is essential for artistic unity. First, he gives emotional emphasis to the heaviness of the story about Belikov when, having told it, he wants to breathe some fresh air. However, the meaning of Burkin's exit is much broader. He stares at the moon, and this is immediately followed by the author's words about what Burkin is feeling:

> On a moonlit night, when you see a broad country road with its huts, haystacks, and sleeping willows, your soul becomes quiet; in its rest, concealed in the shadows of the night from work, anxiety, and sadness - the street is gentle, sad, beautiful, and it seems that stars also look down with kind, tender emotion, and that evil no longer exists in the world and that all is well . . .

A bitter remark by Ivan Ivanyč immediately shatters this moon-inspired illusion. In him, as we understand it here, the generalizing work of thought and feeling, provoked by the story about Belikov, continues. "And indeed the life we lead in the city, in stuffiness, in the crush, the useless papers we write, the vint we play - isn't this a case? . . ." Ivan Ivanyč asks suddenly. And the story about Belikov suddenly begins to broaden in its internal meaning. "The man in a case" begins to signify not simply a specific breed of callous bureaucrat. In the capacity of a "case", the conditions of life of those times begin to come forth on a broad front. Ivan Ivanyč suddenly feels that both he and Burkin are "people in a case".

The development of the story and the broadening of the idea depend upon the simplest of circumstances - that Burkin went out of the barn; this alone makes the consequent structure of the artistic thought possible. Here you understand that the narrator Burkin was not put in the barn just for the sake of verisimilitude. That which unfolds at the very end of the story was foreseen and prepared earlier by the placement of the interlocutors.

Here in all its glory appears the theatrical mastery of the author who had the talent to find the most expressive 'stagings' in the development of a depicted reality. It turns out that the simple, business-like reference to where the people sat before the beginning of the conversation becomes a link of imagery which is all the more important for the deep meaning of the story.

Yet another example. Before the story about Belikov begins there is the following paragraph:

> They told various stories. Among other things they talked about how Mavra, the wife of the village elder, a healthy and not a stupid woman, had never left the village in which she was born, had never seen a city or a railroad, and had spent the past ten years behind the oven, venturing onto the street only at night.
> "There is nothing remarkable in that!" said Burkin . . .

And then, as if by association, the story about Belikov begins.

What is the artistic purpose of this paragraph, this mention of Mavra, who walks by night?

The logic of verisimilitude is certainly present here once more. One is informed that the conversation about Belikov arose, say, by accident (as happens in life). The story about Mavra, who also lives in her own sort of "case", serves as a natural transition to the story about Belikov. But we would err if we were to reduce the matter simply to this.

The story comes to its end. Burkin has already gone out of the barn and admired the moon; Ivan Ivanyč has already made his comment; Burkin has already answered him with the terse: "No, it's time to sleep now. See you tomorrow." But the narration stretches on. It would seem that everything is already clear; what purpose do these following particulars serve?

> Both of them went into the barn and lay down on the hay. And when both covered themselves and began to doze off, they suddenly heard light footsteps: tup, tup . . . Someone was walking not too far from the barn; whoever it is walked a bit, stopped, and a minute later began to walk again: tup, tup . . .
> "That's Mavra walking", Burkin said.
> The steps died away.

What is the purpose of this? Is it simply to confirm pictorially what was mentioned at the beginning - the fact that Mavra walks at night? Of course not.

Mavra's footsteps have a special meaning for the story: Burkin and Ivanyč listen closely to them for a reason. This attentiveness is depicted, very subtly by the writer. With just four words, (3) "The steps died away", we feel how Burkin and Ivan Ivanyč held their breath listening to these footsteps. But when they became quiet . . . Ivan Ivanyč 'exploded' and began to talk:

"To see and hear them lie and then call you a fool because you
endure those lies; to suffer wrongs, insults, not to dare to say
openly that we are on the side of honorable, free people, and to
lie, to smile - and all of this for a crust of bread, for a warm
corner, for a petty civil rank which isn't worth a damn - no, a
man cannot live like this any longer!"

Here the theme of the man in a case acquires its clearest and
broadest disclosure; a revolutionary protest against a grasping, de-
humanized life rings forth. The thought of a life in a case has so in-
flamed Ivan Ivanyč that he cannot now sleep at all, "He stood up,
went outside again, sat down at the door, and smoked his pipe", -
at which point the story is broken off.

It is Mavra's footsteps, suddenly audible, which served as the
stimulus for this seething thought. Before that moment they both
had already "covered themselves and were beginning to doze off".

As is evident, the point is that it is Mavra's footsteps which definitely turn the theme of the story away from an exposure of the
teacher-bureaucrat Belikov towards exposing the conditions of life
which have deadly effects on man. End the tale with the story about
Belikov - and the "case" would only come to the personal characteristics of the 'anthropos' and to the peculiarities and abnormalities
of his bureaucratic existence. But Mavra . . . She is "a healthy and
not a stupid woman". But she too is in a case, although in a different
kind of case than Belikov. That is why Mavra's footsteps in the night
evoke such an oppressive feeling; they sound a warning alarm about
the cruelty of life, about the necessity of changing it.

Therefore the brief mention in the beginning of the story of the
village elder's wife who walks by night is not simply a realistic detail, but the most important link of the figurative thought of the narration.

The reference to Mavra in the beginning of the story and the sound
of her footsteps at the end are artistically juxtaposed very exactly.
This juxtaposition tells us a great deal, it tells that which was not
said by the writer in words. We should notice that these two particulars of the opposed ends of the story can in no way be syntactically
and linguistically interconnected. They are connected only structurally. But what a strong connection it is! In this instance - as always
in real art - you see that it is the structure which speaks.

NOTES

(1) [From: Vadim Nazarenko, Jazyk iskusstva (Leningrad, Sovetskij
pisatel', 1961). Chapter 1, pp. 71-76.]
(2) [A. Efimov, a well known specialist in stylistics. In an article
"Image-bearing speech of an Artistic Work", Voprosy literatury, 8
(1959), he maintains that only tropes and similes can be considered
as the lexical media of imagery.]
(3) [In the original Russian - two words.]

VIII

ČEXOV'S LYRICO-DRAMATIC STORIES (1)

V. V. Golubkov

> Remember that those writers whom we call immortal or simply
> good and who intoxicate us have one highly important feature in
> common: they go somewhere and beckon you, and you sense, not
> with your intellect, but with all your being, that they have some
> goal, like the ghost of Hamlet's father which had a reason for
> coming and disturbing his imagination . . . The best of these
> writers are true to life and they present life as it is, but since
> their every line is saturated with the awareness of a goal, you
> feel life not only as it is, but also as it ought to be, and that is
> what captivates you. And we? We! We describe life as it is,
> period. Beat us further with whips, if you wish. We have neither
> immediate nor remote goals, and there is complete emptiness in
> our souls . . .

These hot, sad words of Čexov, written to Suvorin on November
25, 1891, mark a turning point in Čexov's activity. At that time he
recognized quite clearly what he called the sickness of contemporary literature - the absence of moving towards a goal, of guiding
ideas which give justification and social purpose to a writer's activity.

The indication in Čexov's letter that the sickness which afflicted
the literature of the 1880s was neither hopeless nor fatal is significant.

"I do not know", wrote Čexov, "what will have happened to us in
ten or twelve years; then, perhaps, the situation will have changed
. . . I am not to blame for my sickness, nor is it for me to cure
myself, for my sickness, I daresay, has hidden but good purposes,
and it has been sent to me for a good reason . . ."

From the beginning of the 1890s until the end of his life, Čexov's
troubled search gradually increases, the problems of social life
disturb him more and more deeply, and in his creative activity he
is no longer satisfied with the role about which he had written to
Suvorin earlier, on May 30, 1888: "An artist ought not to be the
judge of his characters nor of what these characters say, but rather
he should be an impartial observer." Now Čexov wants to be a judge
of his heroes and to influence the reader as much as possible.

To be sure, Čexov did not live long enough to be able to work out
a clear social-political philosophy. But his search, his dissatisfaction with limited, uninspired banality, his belief in man, in the
Russian people and its future, gave irresistible ideological force to

his works.

The best of Čexov's stories which can be called lyrico-dramatic belong to that period.

Čexov wrote this sort of story still in the 1880s; for example, "The Hunter" (1885) which, as is well known, was noted by Grigorovič, "Anguish" (1886), "Happiness" (1887), "The Fit" (1888), and others, but in the 80s stories like these were exclusively episodical and were submerged in the mass of his humorous and satirical stories.

In the 90s, such stories determined the basic line of his writings, and if they alternated with other works, the latter were for the most part tales and dramatic works which resembled them in content.

Among the most brilliant of Čexov's lyrico-dramatic stories are "The Flutterer" (1892), "The Student" (1894), "The Teacher of Literature" (1894), "Anna Around the Neck" (1895), "The House with the Mezzanine" (1896), "The Peasants" (1897), "On the Cart" (1897), "A Case from a Doctor's Practice" (1898), "The Lady with the Little Dog" (1899), "The New Dacha" (1899), "The Betrothed" (1903), and others.

What were the ideological and artistic peculiarities of these stories, and what gives us the right to call them lyrico-dramatic stories?

First of all, they are marked by Čexov's strong preoccupation with man in his yearning for happiness, freedom, truth, and man's inevitable collision with his social environment and its traditional beliefs and prejudices. Dramatic conflict always lies at the base of these stories; sometimes it is a conflict of the social order (for example, in "The New Dacha"), at other times it is a conflict of a family sort (as in the story "The Lady with the Little Dog"), but more often it is both of them.

There is yet another peculiarity connected with the dramatic nature of these stories: that is the penetrating lyricism coloring the characters of the main heroes. This lyricism gives the story a mood of light melancholy and a dream of what is beautiful, of what ought to be.

Sometimes a character in the story communicates this lyrical mood, as for example, Ivan Velikopolskij in "The Student" or Ol'ga in "The Peasants"; sometimes (and this is quite natural) it is the hero-narrator, as in "The House with the Mezzanine" or "About Love"; and sometimes the author speaks directly from himself, cleverly weaving his own personal feelings and philosophical reflections into the story's fabric.

The description of the sea in "The Lady with the Little Dog" has the nature of a lyrical digression.

Not a leaf stirred on the trees, cicadas shrieked and the monotonous hollow rumble of the sea carried up from below spoke of the rest, of the eternal sleep which awaits us. It rumbled below even when there was no Yalta, no Oreanda, it rumbles now and shall rumble just as dispassionately and hollowly when we are no more. And in this constancy, in this complete indifference to the life and death of each of us is hidden, perhaps, the pledge of our eternal salvation, of the continuous movement of life on earth, of perpetual progress towards fulfilment.

This lyrical digression is an organic part of the story; it does not contradict the traits of Gurov or of Anna Sergeevna; it is in a certain degree consonant with their mood, but in a still greater degree it communicates the melancholy reflective mood of Čexov himself, who was living out the final years of his life in Yalta.

The third peculiarity of lyrico-dramatic stories is the complexity of their structure and of their intonation.

Whereas the humorous and satirical stories are constructed on a single basic tone which always penetrates the whole story, the lyrico-dramatic stories, besides two basic intonations (dreams of a better life and dramatic intensity), usually include elements of humor and satire. Moreover, to the extent that Čexov, uncovering the conflict of hero and environment, shows his ironic or even inimical attitude towards this environment, humor and satire necessarily occupy a significant place in the lyrico-dramatic stories. This is quite understandable: the more full and more vivid the satiric illumination of the environment which subordinates the hero to itself or provokes him to battle - the more deeply it is possible to reveal the conflict at the base of the story.

The new content of lyrico-dramatic stories also demanded new supplementary artistic devices of the author.

Earlier, in his humorous and satiric stories, Čexov selected very simple, often primitive characters with clearly expressed dominant traits (despotism, cowardice, servility, ambition, etc.); now complex characters, combining different psychological properties, become the main object of his depiction.

To disclose comic characters it was sufficient to have a single episode or scene, a vivid portrait and a skillfully constructed dialogue. But for lyrico-dramatic stories an additional element was indispensable: a complex sujet was required, one which would permit varied interconnections of the dramatis personae.

Earlier, Čexov advised writers to refrain from author's characterizations in their stories and suggested that they write in such a way that the heroes show themselves through their actions, through their relations to other persons, and through their particular mode of speech. "It is best to avoid describing the emotional state of heroes", he wrote to Al. P. Čexov [his brother, Aleksandr] on May 10, 1886. "One must try to make that known through the action of the heroes." Now Čexov uses direct reference, the hero's internal monologue, extensive psychological landscape, and lyrical digressions - in a word, the most varied means which further the revelation of human psychology.

One of the devices most characteristic of Čexov's lyrico-dramatic stories is duality of structure.

Exposing life's contradictions and the conflicts brought about by them, Čexov naturally had to turn to an analysis of intimate emotional experiences which were usually unnoticed at a fleeting glance.

Like Gurov (the hero of "The Lady with the Little Dog") he understood that people often have two lives: "One open, seen and known by everyone who needs to, full of conventional truth and conventional fraud . . . and another one passing in secret", so that "everything which was important, interesting, indispensable, of value to him (i.e., Gurov), everything in which he was honest and did not deceive himself, everything which was the core of his life went on in secret from others; but everything which was a lie, in him his cover . . . all this was in the open".

Čexov made a conscious artistic device out of this juxtaposition of two lives – one, which everyone sees, external, the other, internal, unnoticed, and often of little interest to others.

Take, for example, the story "Anguish". First and foremost is that which is in plain sight of everyone: Iona's occasional fares, one replacing the other, the yard-keeper, and the cabmen in the inn. They see the external side of Iona and his horse: some see it as humorous, amusing, others see it as commonplace and familiar – but they all pass over his sorrow, for each has his own troubles, and none of them cares about the other. But in Iona Čexov shows what takes place behind the scenes and creates the undercurrent of the story: by means of psychological analysis and internal monologue he shows Iona's inescapable woe and his terrible solitude . . .

How is the device of psychological analysis used in the story? It is as if Čexov is reincarnated in his hero:

> Iona's anxious, tormented eyes search the crowds scurrying on either side of the street: out of all these thousands of people is there not one person who would hear him out? But the crowds hurry by without noticing him or his grief . . . His grief is immense, boundless . . . It has managed to conceal itself in such an insignificant shell that no one could see it, even in the daylight with a lantern.

The story ends with Iona going to the stable where his horse is, and "he tells her everything".

Iona's conversation with the horse is a conversation with an imaginary interlocutor and in essence is an internal monologue. But this original form of internal monologue is completely justified and prepared by the whole previous course of the story. Iona must have an interlocutor, a living person with whom he can share his woe and who, in turn, will pity him.

The first interlocutor is a military officer, a person from a completely different world, and naturally Iona finds no compassion in him. The next fares are somewhat more simple, and from them one might expect greater attention, but they too treat Iona with the same complete indifference. The yard-keeper with whom Iona then speaks is closer to him socially, and the cabmen in the inn are certainly his own sort of people, and it would seem that Iona's grief would be particularly understandable to them. In spite of that, Iona does not find what he needs, either in the yard-keeper or in the cabmen.

When all means accessible to Iona for talking to people are exhaust-
ed, there remains one thing: to find a release from his insufferable
emotional state in a conversation with an imaginary being. But to
whom can Iona speak, if not to his horse?

Such is the logic of the story, giving a psychological basis for the
unexpected and - at first glance - strange ending.

The device of structure on a dual level is applied by Čexov in an
especially vivid way in the story "Polen'ka". The external level is
an ordinary conversation between a salesman in a haberdashery
and a lady customer:

"For goodness sake, a ruble for it isn't too high at all!" - the
salesman assures her . . . "It is a French trimming, octahedral
. . ."
"I still need a beaded corselet with gimp buttons", says Polen'ka,
sighing for some reason or another. "And do you have bugles in
the same color?"

This is spoken in a loud voice, and everyone can hear it.

Simultaneously another conversation is taking place, quietly, in
a whisper, and it exposes the deep drama in the relations between
Polen'ka and the salesman.

Polen'ka bends still lower toward the counter and asks softly:
"And just why did you leave us so early Thursday, Nikolaj
Timofeevič?"
"Hm. Strange that you noticed it", the salesman says with a smirk.
"You were so carried away by that college student that . . .
strange, that you noticed it."
Polen'ka blushes and remains silent . . .
"I also need bead lace", says Polen'ka, raising her guilty eyes
to the salesman.
"What kind do you need? Bead lace on tulle is black or colored
. . . And I will never come to see you again", Nikolaj Timofeevič
adds in a low voice . . .

To communicate subtle, intimate experiences, Čexov, in his stories
of the 1890s, uses a device about which he once wrote to I. L. Leont'ev
[Penname: I. Ščeglov - a minor writer of the end of the 19th century,
author of Memoirs in which he wrote about Čexov]: "In very short
stories it is better to understate than to say too much." It is a device
of reticence, allusion, and details which create in the reader a strong
impression and stimulate his creative fantasy.

In "The Peasants", Čexov had to present and evaluate the interrelation of the grandmother ("a toothless, raw-boned, hunch-backed
old woman") and her granddaughters, Saša and Motka. Čexov uses
this detail: the grandmother began to whip the girls with a switch,
because although they had been told to look after the geese, they
had let them go into the vegetable garden:

Saša cried with pain and fear and meanwhile a gander, stretching out his neck, waddled up to the old woman and hissed something or other, and when he returned to his flock all the other geese greeted him approvingly: honk-honk-honk!

The lyrical mood of Čexovian stories is usually concentrated in its final segment.

The moods and feelings communicated by this device can be of various sorts.

At the finale of "The Student" it is a feeling of youth and the dreams of happiness proper to youth:

The feeling of youth, health, strength – he was only 22 years old – and the inexpressibly sweet expectation of happiness, a mysterious, unknown happiness, gradually overpowered him and life seemed to him to be delightful, miraculous, and full of high significance.

In "The Teacher of Literature" we find disappointment in vulgar prosperity and dreams of some sort of "new, exciting, conscious life which is not in harmony with peace and personal happiness". The story ends with the words: "There is nothing more terrible, more insulting, more dreary, than banality. Flee from here, flee this very day, or else I shall go out of my mind!"

A feeling of tender, pure love is found in "The House with the Mezzanine".

When Ženja's first timid love was unexpectedly crushed by the crass interference of her sister, there remained in the artist's soul a beautiful memory and a hope that happiness would return. The story ends with the words,

And even more rarely, in those moments when solitude torments me and I feel sad, I recollect vaguely, and for reasons of which I am not certain I begin to feel that I, too, am remembered and awaited, and that we shall meet again.
"Misjus', where are you?"

In what does the ideological-artistic meaning of such lyrical endings lie?

Will the student's dreams of unknown happiness come true, shall the teacher of literature be able to flee, and what shall he find in his new life? Will the artist and his Misjus' meet? – all of this is unknown and is left to the reader to decide.

But a clear answer in this case is not essential. The significance of the lyrical endings of Čexov's stories is that they arouse in the reader dissatisfaction with the present and a thirst for a bright future.

This feeling on the part of the reader was expressed very well by Gor'kij in a letter written to Čexov in the beginning of the year 1900 apropos of the story "The Lady with the Little Dog":

You do a great deal with your little short stories, arousing in
people an aversion to this sleepy, half dead life - the devil take
it! . . . Your stories are gracefully faceted little bottles contain-
ing all the scents of life, and - believe me - a sensitive nose shall
always discover among them that subtle, pungent, and healthy
smell of 'that which is real', truly valuable and necessary, which
is always there in each of your little bottles.

The complexity of the content of lyrico-dramatic stories is also reflected in the individuality of their language.

In stories such as "Anguish" and "Polen'ka" sharp changes of intonation are met not infrequently: comic speech passes into lyrical,
dramatic speech is followed by lyrical. Various devices of lyrical
speech - such as emotional expressivity, musicality, etc. - demand
special attention when studying Čexov's literary craft.

For a more detailed study of lyrico-dramatic stories one should
turn to such examples as "The Flutterer", "Anna Around the Neck",
and "On the Cart".

"THE FLUTTERER" (1892)

A new story called "The Flutterer" was published in 1892. Čexov
did not immediately decide on that title. He first called the story
"The Philistines", and then "A Great Man". Although he rejected
these initial titles, they are still of indisputable interest for us,
for they aid in understanding the author's intention, as one must especially say about "A Great Man". Having rejected the phrase as a
title, Čexov repeats it several times in the text, and finally applies
it to the hero, Doctor Dymov.

The whole content of the story leads to the conclusion that the
basic question raised in it is the problem of what constitutes a 'great
man', of false and of authentic greatness, or, in other words, of
the social value of man.

Taken in the broad sense of the word, the whole structure of the
story shows that the above is true. To this bear witness the interrelation of characters, the structural devices employed in the creation of characters, the sujet of the story, and the language as taken
in its ideological-artistic significance.

In the basis of the system of characters in the story lies a simple
scheme: he-she-he, that is, the artist Rjabovskij - Ol'ga Ivanovna
(the 'flutterer') - Doctor Dymov. Close to each of them are secondary characters: Rjabovskij's fellow artists, the friends and acquaintances of Ol'ga Ivanovna, and Doctor Korostelev - Dymov's friend.

Such a scheme may at first glance seem ordinary, a pattern common in novels and stories, but with Čexov it acquires its own peculiar
flavor and is filled with the greatly significant content typical of
lyrico-psychological stories.

We have before us not only various people but, as it were, two
worlds: Rjabovskij, Ol'ga Ivanovna and their friends, on the one hand,

and Dymov and Korostelev, on the other. The former consider themselves select people, exclusive, unlike the crowd; these are artists,
musicians, poets, actors - all singled out by the mark of talent.
Čexov does not deny their giftedness. "Each already had a reputation and was considered a celebrity, or if this were not yet true,
he had brilliant hopes for it."

Their fault was that each suffered from conceit. They viewed
themselves as some sort of aristocrats of the spirit, and looked
down their noses at others - including Doctor Dymov, the husband
of Ol'ga Ivanovna - as dull.

> In the midst of this aristocratic and free company spoiled by fate
> . . . Dymov seemed foreign, superfluous, and even small -
> although he was tall and broad shouldered. He looked as if he were
> wearing someone else's coat and his little beard was like a sales-
> man's. However, had he been a writer or an artist, they would
> have said that with his beard he reminded one of Zola.

But Dymov belonged to a different world, a world of socially useful
toilers, of talented scientists through whose unceasing energy science
moves forward; humble people, yet strong in mind and moral purity.

This juxtaposition speaks for itself. Only people like Dymov are
really valuable, 'great people', and even Ol'ga Ivanovna saw this.
When Dymov died, she "suddenly realized that he indeed was an unusual, rare, and - in comparison with those whom she knew - a
great man . . ."

Even a general outline of the story leads to an understanding of
the writer's intention.

However, its ideological sense will be revealed more fully and
deeply if one turns to its sujet and to those artistic means which or-
ganically are part of the sujet - that is, to portrait, landscape, and
the mode of speech peculiar to each of the characters.

The sujetal construction of "The Flutterer" is one of the best of
Čexov's artistic achievements. This sujet transmits a very compli-
cated content, but it is nonetheless simple, clear, and harmonious.
It unfolds according to a dramatic plan; it has an 'exposition' (Ol'ga
Ivanovna's wedding and happy life with Dymov), a 'complication'
(Ol'ga Ivanovna and Rjabovskij's trip on the steamer), a 'develop-
ment of action' (the interrelations of Ol'ga Ivanovna, Rjabovskij, and
Dymov), a 'culmination' (Ol'ga Ivanovna's break with Rjabovskij and
Dymov's sickness), and a 'denouement' (Dymov's death).

The sujet is enclosed in a chronological frame: the action begins
in winter, continues through spring, summer, and autumn, and ends
with winter again; the landscapes (e.g., the summer and autumn
landscapes on the Volga) and even reference to the time of the year
are, in some degree or other, connected with the experiences of the
main heroes, with the basic stages in the development of the action.

The sujet, in all its unity and integrity, clearly breaks down into
three sujetal lines: the story of Rjabovskij, of Ol'ga Ivanovna, and
of Dymov. In these three lines, which develop parallelly and stand

in contrast to each other, a psychological analysis of the dramatis personae is present and the dramatic meaning of the work is revealed.

Rjabovskij's story is presented in a satiric light. The hero's external appearance and manners, his speech, and, most important, his attitude toward people - everything in him which was artificial, theatrical, and designed for effect - is described satirically.

Rjabovskij was handsome, but he flaunted his handsome features and loved to posture before his female admirers. In the scene on the Volga steamer, after his declaration of love, he "looked at Ol'ga Ivanovna with adoring, grateful eyes, then, closing his eyes, he said, smiling languidly, 'I am tired'". He continued to show off to Ol'ga Ivanovna and then, when love was already gone: "He came up to her in some sort of gray short frock-coat with flecks and a new tie and asked languidly, 'Am I handsome?'"

Rjabovskij's posturing and clowning appear clearly in his speech. The scene in which he appears before Ol'ga Ivanovna as a profound judge of her sketches creates a comic impression; here he speaks with an unnatural language:

"So . . . that cloud of yours shrieks; it is not lighted as in the evening. The foreground is somehow chewed up and something, you understand, is not quite right . . . And your hut is choked with something and squeaks pitifully . . . This corner ought to be made darker. But in general - not badsome. (2) I praise it."

Rjabovskij also displays this sort of verbiage in moments of emotional enthusiasm when, on that quiet moonlit July night he stands with Ol'ga Ivanovna on the deck of the Volga steamer and speaks about how

in the sight of the fathomless skies and of sad, dreamy banks which speak of the vanity of our life and of the existence of something higher, eternal, and blessed - it would be good to sink into oblivion, to die, to become a memory. The past is banal and uninteresting, the future is insignificant, but this wonderful night, unique in our lives, shall soon end, it shall flow into the eternal - why, then, live?

These romantic reflections about life and death, reminiscent of Čexov's reflections in "The Lady with the Little Dog" which have psychological justification therein, are obviously used here as a parody.

For Rjabovskij it is only a beautiful approach to the declaration of love which is to follow.

But when, after two months, love has gone, and Rjabovskij becomes openly coarse while talking with Ol'ga Ivanovna, here too he is playing a role - that of a martyr:

"Ol'ga, I ask only one thing", the artist said imploringly with his

hand on his heart, "just one thing: don't torture me! I want nothing
more from you! . . . "
She began to sob again and went behind the partition . . . Rjabovskij
clasped his head and paced once from corner to corner, and then
with a determined face, as if wishing to prove something to someone, he put on his cap, threw his rifle over his shoulder, and
walked out of the hut.

The story of Ol'ga Ivanovna takes place parallel to that of Rjabovskij.
It shows how much in common Ol'ga Ivanovna had with the psychology of 'great' people like Rjabovskij. She has petty ambitions.
The quiet, moonlit night on the Volga and the presence of Rjabovskij
caused her to dream that she would become

a great artist and that somewhere there far away beyond the moonlit night, in eternal space - success, glory, and the people's love
awaited her. When she gazed into the distance a long time without
blinking, she imagined crowds of people, lights, solemn strains
of music, shouts of rapture and herself in a white dress and
flowers raining down on her from all sides. She also thought that,
next to her . . . stands a really great man, a genius, one chosen
by God.

None in her circle of friends and acquaintances ever told her that
she was and always would be a dabbler and that she would never be
a celebrity. Just the opposite:

Those whom she called famous and great received her as one of
their own, as an equal, and prophesied to her in one voice that
with her talents, taste, and intelligence, if she would not squan-
der her energies, she could become something great. And Ol'ga
Ivanovna believed that glory and a brilliant future awaited her.

Like other quasi-great people, she looked down on common people
with pity:

She looked at Korostelev and thought: "Wouldn't it be boring to be
so simple, undistinguished, known to nobody, and with such a
crumpled face and poor manners?"

Like Rjabovskij she enjoyed playing a beautiful role, and she was
carried away by a beautiful phrase. When she wanted to explain to
her friends why she had agreed to be Dymov's wife, she spoke of
him: "Isn't it true that there is something strong, powerful, bear-
like in him?" Ol'ga Ivanovna liked this expression so much that when
they started to talk about her latest whim - her participation in the
wedding of a certain telegraphist, she said of him to her husband:
"A handsome young man . . . and he has in his face, you know,
something strong, bear-like."
She once spoke of her husband to Rjabovskij: "This man oppresses

me with his magnanimity."

"This sentence", says Čexov, "pleased her so much that, upon meeting artists who knew of her affair with Rjabovskij, she always spoke of her husband, making an energetic gesture with her hand, 'This man oppresses me with his magnanimity.' "

One of Ol'ga Ivanovna's peculiarities was that she was very emotional, and was easily carried away, but these emotions were shallow and short-lived. Her love for Rjabovskij was also a transitory passion and not a deep feeling. If she did not let Rjabovskij out of her grasp, if she was jealous and followed him, it was not love but offended pride and a feeling of resentment that he preferred others to her. However, in all her feelings - among which were fear for herself and egoism - Ol'ga Ivanovna was sincere, spontaneous, and she was liked by many because of that. This childlike spontaneity probably attracted Dymov too, causing him to forgive his wife for that which, most likely, he would not forgive in another woman who was cunning and false.

D. Makovickij [Lev Tolstoj's family doctor] stated that when Tolstoj read "The Flutterer", he said of Ol'ga Ivanovna: "One gets the impression that after his death she will remain exactly the same person."

In fact, Čexov showed very clearly that innocent selfishness was Ol'ga Ivanovna's basic quality, and to speak of sudden change in her life after undergoing the tragedy is impossible: she was and would remain a 'flutterer', shifting easily from one fancy to another, loved by others for her buoyancy and spontaneity but loving only herself.

Dymov's story is told in a parallel way to that of Rjabovskij and Ol'ga Ivanovna and in contrast to it. However, Čexov tells it in a special way - through the medium of small details and of the testimonials of other people.

In the development of the sujet, Ol'ga Ivanovna and Rjabovskij are in the foreground, on the brightly illuminated proscenium, but Dymov is in the shadows. Little is said of him, and he himself says little.

How did Dymov relate to Ol'ga Ivanovna's friends in the first month of his married life? What did he think, what did he feel when Ol'ga Ivanovna left for the Volga with the artists? What did he suffer when he learned of his wife's betrayal? What was the basic cause of his death? What was he as a man of science, as a scholar?

Čexov answered all these questions, but in a completely different way than he did in regard to his other heroes.

Speaking of Rjabovskij and Ol'ga Ivanovna, Čexov, to elucidate their experiences, shows them in action and uses the device of the author's analytic remarks and the hero's internal dialogue.

In relation to Dymov, these devices are employed to a significantly lesser degree: Čexov allows the reader to conjecture independently about everything, using very scant remarks and allusions in the story.

Dymov loved Ol'ga Ivanovna with a boundless, selfless love; he deeply believed in that which was best and truest in her, and he forgave her everything: her idleness, her flippancy, her empty life, her indifference to his work and interests, and the conceit of the 'great' people surrounding her. But how is all this shown in the story?

Dymov goes to the dacha to see his wife. "He had not seen her for two weeks and he missed her terribly. Sitting in the train . . . he felt hungry and tired all the while, and dreamed that he would dine at ease with his wife and then tumble into bed. And it was pleasing for him to look at his bundle in which was wrapped caviar, cheese, and white salmon." But in the dacha he found two unfamiliar dark haired men with short beards and a fat, beardless actor; Ol'ga Ivanovna, although she was sincerely happy to see him, sent him back immediately to Moscow for her rose colored dress, flowers, and gloves which she needed for the telegraphist's wedding. "Dymov quickly drank up the cup of tea, took a roll, and, smiling meekly, went to the station. The two dark haired men and the fat actor ate the caviar, cheese, and white salmon."

This cup of tea and roll instead of caviar and white salmon and Dymov's meek smile express much: the childish selfishness of Ol'ga Ivanovna, and in particular Dymov's submissive love.

Or how does Čexov describe the scene of the meeting of Dymov and Ol'ga Ivanovna when she had just returned from the Volga? Here too the reader guesses about Dymov's experiences not on the basis of his words (which are so common, so insignificant in content) but through the description of his manner, in juxtaposition to that of Ol'ga Ivanovna.

When Ol'ga Ivanovna caught sight of his "broad, meek, happy smile and gleaming joyful eyes, she felt that to deceive this person was so base, abominable, and so impossible and as beneath her as it would be for her to slander, steal, or murder . . ."

"What is it? What is it, darling? Missed me?" he asked tenderly . . . "Missed me? . . . Let's sit down! . . . Like that . . . Eat some grouse. You have starved yourself, poor thing! . . ." He glanced at her tenderly and laughed happily . . .

And how is Dymov's mental state conveyed in that part of the story where he is convinced of his wife's unfaithfulness? The reader expects scenes of jealousy, of a decisive talk between husband and wife, and, perhaps, a separation.

There is nothing of the sort. Externally, life does not change. There are the same evening gatherings on Wednesdays. "The actor read, the artists sketched, the cellist played, the singer sang, and always, at half past eleven, the door to the dining room opened and Dymov, smiling, said: 'Please, gentlemen, have a bite to eat!' "

Dymov suffers more than many others would in his situation, but he suffers silently, and Čexov does not speak about him directly, but rather indirectly, most of all through the new expression on his face: "As if he had a guilty conscience; he could not look his wife in the eyes, and he did not smile happily upon meeting her."

The exceptional culture and delicacy on the part of Dymov appear
now in those rare moments when he is with Ol'ga Ivanovna; it was at
mealtime, and he would invite his friend Korostelev and carry on
conversations about medicine "only to give Ol'ga Ivanovna the opportunity to be silent, that is, not to lie".

When, because of her jealousy towards Rjabovskij, Ol'ga Ivanovna
could not control herself and began to sob loudly, "Dymov . . . went
to the bedroom and, embarrassed and confused, said softly: 'Don't
cry loudly, Mama! What for? Better be quiet about it . . . Better
not let people see, hear? . . . What is done is done . . .' "

To weaken and soften his grief somehow, Dymov gives himself
entirely to medicine and research and achieves very great success.

In this regard, the following brief scene is very telling:

One evening, when she (Ol'ga Ivanovna) was standing in front of
her pier-glass dressing for the theater, Dymov entered the bedroom dressed in tails and a white tie. He smiled meekly and, as
in the past, joyfully looked his wife in the eyes. His face glowed.
"I was defending my dissertation just now", he said . . .
"Successfully?" Ol'ga Ivanovna asked.
"Yes!" - He lauged, and craned his neck to see his wife's face in
the mirror; she continued to stand with her back to him and arranged her coiffure. "Yes!" he repeated. "You know, it is quite
possible they will offer me the position of assistant professor in
general pathology. It's in the air."
It was evident from his blissful, radiant face, that had Ol'ga
Ivanovna shared his joy and triumph with him, he would forgive
her everything, both present and future, and would forget everything, but she did not understand the meaning of 'assistant professor' or 'general pathology', and besides, she was afraid of
being late for the theater, so she said nothing.
He sat for two minutes, smiled guiltily and left.

Here Dymov stands before the reader in full stature both as an
emerging great scientist and, more important, as a great person
with a pure, loving heart, not understood and alone.

Dymov remains so up to the final hours of his life when, fearing
for his wife and protecting her, he suffers inwardly and dies alone.

At the end of his story, Čexov gives a general evaluation of his
hero through the words of Korostelev:

"He is dying because he sacrificed himself . . . What a loss for
science! . . . This man, compared with all of us, was a great,
extraordinary person. What gifts! What hopes we all had for him!
. . . My God, he was the kind of scholar that can no longer be
found. Os'ka Dymov [diminutive of Osip, Dymov's first name] ,
what have you done? Ah, my God!
"And what moral strength! . . . A pure, good, loving soul - not
a man, but a crystal . . . And he worked like an ox, day and
night, and no one spared him . . ."

In spite of the fact that little was said about Dymov, the reader accepts this testimonial and completely agrees with Čexov's views on the value and beauty of the human soul.

"ANNA AROUND THE NECK" (1895)

In contrast to the story "The Flutterer" which is a family drama in content, "Anna Around the Neck" can be called a social-dramatic story.

The concept of social contradiction, which was so characteristic of Čexov's era and for all of prerevolutionary Russia, is at the base of the story. It is the contradiction between the higher and lower strata of society, between the strong and the weak in their historically established interrelationships: for the strong it was despotism and certainty in their right to coerce and oppress; for the weak it was consciousness of their lack of civil rights, fear, and the submissiveness instilled in them from childhood.

In "Anna Around the Neck" there are allegorical images which illustrate that feeling of panicked fear before the strong who have power; this feeling abides in Anna, the main character, and to a significant degree it determines all her behavior.

At one time in her childhood the high school principal always appeared to her to be a most impressive and fearsome power, approaching like a stormcloud or a locomotive about to run over her; another such power about which they always talked in the family and which they feared for some reason was His Excellency; and there were a dozen other lesser powers . . . And in Anna's imagination all of these powers fused into one, and in the shape of one huge, frightening white bear they moved on those who were weak and guilty, like her father . . .

For Čexov the terrible power which morally mutilated and crushed Anna and her father was the system of social relationships which existed in his time.

Such is the meaning of "Anna Around the Neck".

Judging from Čexov's "Notebooks" this story was conceived to show how a difference in social position influences the characters and relations of people and to show the unnatural forms of life and dramatic conflicts which are created by the poverty and lack of rights of some and by the richness and power of others.

The first outline of the sujet of "Anna Around the Neck" which we read in the "Notebooks" says that the story's dramatic conflict was to encompass three characters of opposing social position: a poor girl and two predators who took advantage of her poverty:

The poor girl, a high school student, has five younger brothers; she marries a rich civil servant who begrudges her every piece of bread, demands obedience, gratitude (he made her happy), mocks her relatives: "Each person must have his obligations." She suffers everything, is afraid to contradict lest she fall into her previous poverty. An invitation to a ball from a superior. She creates a sensation at the ball. An important person falls in love with her, makes her his mistress (she is secure now). When she notices that the superiors are fawning on her, that her husband needs her, then at home she tells him with scorn: "Go away, blockhead."

In later notes Čexov again returns to the story's sujet and, in part, to the last episode ("Go away, blockhead!"). The psychology of Anna's husband - a rich civil servant - interests him and he outlines his first portrait as emphatically satiric, level:

And he too stood before her now, with the same fawning, sugary expression with which she was accustomed to seeing him in the presence of the powerful and the noble; and with delight, with indignation, and with contempt, knowing that nothing would happen to her for it, she said, pronouncing each word distinctly: "Go away, blockhead!"

In preparing the story for publication, Čexov brought in other characters: a third 'predator' (the rich Artynov) and poor people - Anna's father and brothers.

Thus the first variant of the story came into being, and it was printed in the newspaper Russkie Vedomosti in 1895.

The social conflict placed in the foundation of the story was expressed both in the relationships of the characters and in the development of dramatic action.

The characters are sharply divided into opposing sides: the predators and their victims. The dramatic sujet develops along two closely connected lines: one descending (the fate of her father), and the other ascending (Anna's fate).

It is completely clear to the reader that the sujet line of Anna's father proceeds downward. The man is poor, materially insecure, only a teacher of penmanship. Even among high school teachers he stands on the lowest rung of the official ladder; he is weak by nature, crushed by the death of his wife and now again by the loss of his daughter, whom he himself has handed over to the predators. It scarcely can be doubted that his position is hopeless and that poverty, solitude, and life catastrophe await him.

The problem of the sujet line of Anna is more complicated. Subjectively, in her own consciousness, her life follows an ascending line: she is not a victim, she believes in the power of her beauty and youth and goes voluntarily to meet her shameful fate. But objectively, in the reader's moral assessment, Anna is nonetheless a victim of social conditions: having succumbed to the temptation of a brilliant and probably precarious, temporary success, she loses herself, her moral personality, and all that which was good in her before her marriage.

The complexity of Anna's character and situation and that of her father prompted Čexov to pay close attention to the psychological motivation of their actions. Insofar as their life was interwoven with the life of Anna's husband and her possessors, Čexov also had to reveal the psychology of the latter in some detail. Psychological portrait, description of the surroundings, and also interior monologue served Čexov as the basic means of elucidating the experiences of Anna and the other protagonists of the story.

Reworking the story, Čexov deepens Anna's character and elaborates more precisely the motives of her relationship to her husband. To do this, he brings in some supplements to the portrait of this man – Modest Alekseič.

In the first variant which was printed in Russkie Vedomosti, the following was said of Modest Alekseič: "He was a civil servant of medium height, rather portly, with long sideburns but no moustache . . ."

In the final text, printed in Čexov's collected works, (3) we read: "He was a civil servant of medium height, rather portly, flabby, very well-fed, with long sideburns but lacking a moustache."

And further – in the first variant: "The chief characteristic in his face was the absence of moustache, the cleanly shaven, naked spot which gradually merged into his cheeks."

In the reworking he added something to the word cheeks: "into his fat cheeks which quivered like jelly."

These additions help one better understand Anna's feeling of aversion towards her husband: "The soft movement of his flabby body frightened her; she felt terrified and disgusted."

Anna's aversion was aggravated by Modest Alekseič's character – by his callousness and stinginess. Čexov emphasized these features too in the reworking of the story.

Instead of helping Anna's father and brothers, Modest Alekseič read them admonitions.

"But he gave them no money. To make up for it he gave Anna rings, bracelets, and brooches, saying it is good to have these things for a rainy day."

So it reads in the first version.

In the rewriting there was an addition: "And often he opened her chest of drawers and inspected to see if all these things were still there."

Modest Alekseič's stinginess and distrust, his suspiciousness about his wife, are communicated not with dialogue and not with a new sermon, but by one single description of his movements: the reader sees Modest Alekseič unlocking the chest of drawers and inspecting the objects therein – and the reader then makes conclusions about him as a person.

One other reason for Anna's aversion and hatred for her husband was his open groveling before all who had power over him.

After His Excellency honored Anna with his attention, Modest Alekseič began to fawn upon his wife too. In the first version of the story literally the same thing is said of him as had been written in a notebook previously: "And he also stood before her now, with the same fawning, sugary expression with which she was used to seeing him in the presence of the powerful and the noble."

On reworking, Čexov strengthened the elements of servility in the portrait of Modest Alekseič: "He stood with the same fawning, sugary slavishly deferential expression, which . . ." etc.

It was bad enough that Modest Alekseič himself was a groveller, but he demanded the same sort of slavish deference from his wife too.

"Bow to this old lady!"
"But I don't know her."
"That doesn't matter. It is the wife of the Director of the Treasury Office! Bow, I tell you", he grumbled urgently. "Your head won't fall off."

Čexov reproduced this dialogue in its entirety in the new edition. But he made an addition: "Anja [Anja, Anjuta - diminutive of Anna] bowed and, to be sure, her head did not fall of, but it was painful."

It is clear how much all these supplements - for the most part, of a descriptive portrait nature - gave to the reader: they deepened one's understanding of Anna and especially of the hatred towards her husband which slowly accumulated in her soul.

To explain Anna's situation even further, Čexov makes insertions when rewriting the story (this time along the path of direct characterization).

Instead of the words "Anna had as little money as before her marriage" (as it was in the first edition), Čexov speaks extensively:

She did everything her husband desired and was angry at herself because he had cheated her as he would a complete little fool. She had married him only for his money, but now she had less money than before her marriage. Before at least, her father would give her a twenty kopeck piece, but now she didn't get a penny.

All of this leads the reader to understand the scene showing Anna and her husband together for the last time (later we see her either in 'society' or with Artynov); this is the scene where she calls her husband a blockhead.

One must read the story very carefully, especially all the additions to it which we have pointed out, in order to understand how much bitterness, indignation, contempt, and thirst for revenge accumulated in Anna; so much accumulated that at her very first opportunity she could immediately free herself from her usual fear of her husband and say:

"Go away, blockhead!"

This was the rebellion of a slave who could rise up against her master only because she was now under the protection of another, more powerful master.

Such was one order of Anna's thoughts and feelings which was connected with her relationship with her husband.

Čexov presents another series of her experiences which is also germane to understanding her character and fate. He also makes these experiences more accurate and deep in his creative reworking of the story: to a significant degree, he does this by using interior monologue and psychological portrait.

This series is about Anna's thirst for life and her confidence in a happy future.

Anna's views on happiness were, it is true, very limited, impoverished, Philistine - riches, finery, amusements, success with men - but these were firm views, most likely learned in childhood when Anna's mother, a former governess, was alive. "Her late mother . . . always dressed in the latest fashion and always fussed over Anja. She dressed her elegantly, like a doll, and taught her to speak French and to dance the mazurka perfectly."

Faith in her happiness does not desert Anja in the most difficult moments of her life. Thus after her wedding she rides in a train with her husband, depressed by the realization of her terrible mistake, but when the train stops at a small station surrounded by summer houses she steps onto the platform, shakes hands with some acquaintances, and smiled happily.

She noticed (Čexov wrote in the first variant of the story) that Artynov was watching her, and she spoke with a lady friend in French, and because music was heard and the moon was reflected in the pond and because Artynov, that well known Don Juan and rogue, was looking at her greedily and with curiosity - she was already humming a waltz . . . and she returned to the compartment with the feeling that at the station they had assured her that she would certainly be happy, come what may.

In the reworked text some words are changed and some insertions made: "When she noticed that Artynov was watching her, she narrowed her eyes coquettishly and began to speak loudly in French, and because her own voice sounded so beautiful and music was heard . . . . (further as in the first version) And when the train began to move . . . she was already humming a polka . . ." (further as in the first version).

The changes which we have noted in the text were obviously calculated to emphasize more strongly Anna's certitude that her power was in her beauty and that it would certainly bring happiness to her.

It is interesting that in the new version Anja hummed a polka, not a waltz. Čexov probably found that the brisk and happy rhythm of the polka better expressed the mood of light-hearted Anja than did the rhythm of the waltz.

Čexov worked particularly on the ball scene - the scene which depicts the moment of the break in Anna's life.

"They went to the ball . . ." Further on in the first variant Čexov tells briefly of how Anna went up the stairs of the Nobility Club, entered the hall, recognized her friends in the crowd, etc.

Looking over the text, Čexov considered that it was essential to give a more detailed, step by step description of Anna's impressions of the Nobility Club which was so unlike the depression she experienced from the maddeningly boring government apartment of her husband.

After the words "They went to the ball" comes an insertion:

Here is the Nobility Club and the doorway with the porter. The anteroom with hangers; fur coats, scurrying servants and ladies in decollete shielding themselves with fans from the piercing draught; it smells of illuminating gas and of soldiers.

And Čexov adds further "An orchestra was already thundering in the great hall . . . Anja glanced over the hall and thought 'Ah, how lovely!' "

"A huge officer came up and 'invited her to waltz,' " Čexov wrote in the first variant. He later changed the words "came up" to "sprang up as if from the ground" - which were more picturesque and more expressively corresponded to Anna's elated mood.

Speaking of Anna's success during the dances, Čexov, in the reworked text, again emphasizes her confidence in herself and in her awaited happiness. Instead of the words of the first version: "She was a success with the men and realized it", Čexov writes: "She was a success with the men, that was clear - it could not have been otherwise . . ."

In this way the central decisive episode - the mazurka - was approached.

The description of the mazurka in its vividness and plasticity of presentation is one of Čexov's greatest artistic achievements; this scene deserves to be considered equal to similar masterpieces of Tolstoj such as his description of Nataša Rostova's first ball.

We will allow ourselves to reproduce Čexov's description in its entirety as it appeared in the first edition:

She danced the mazurka with the same huge officer. He walked with an air of importance and moved his shoulders and chest and stamped his feet with an expression as if he were quite unwilling to dance, but she flew about, exciting him with her beauty and her uncovered neck; her eyes burned with fervor, her movements were passionate, but he became all the more indifferent and he held his hands to her condescendingly, like a king.
"Bravo, bravo!" was heard from the crowd.
But little by little even the huge officer broke through; he grew animated, excited, and now, yielding to her charm, was carried away and his movements became light and youthful, but she only twisted her shoulders and glanced coquettishly, and at that moment it seemed to her that the whole ballroom was watching them, and that all these people were thrilled and envied her . . .

Yet as good as this picture was, Čexov felt it necessary in the reworking to add still a few touches which made the picture even more expressive.

With a few brief insertions and word changes he sharpened his contrast between Anna and the tall officer.

Instead of "He walked with an air of importance" Čexov wrote: "He walked with an air of importance, heavily, like a hulk in a uniform." Instead of "stamped his feet with an expression as if he were quite unwilling to dance", Čexov wrote in the new version: "He barely stamped his feet – he was loath to dance."

These changes made the external appearance of the officer even more vivid and besides, they explained his mood in a different way: he did not pretend that he did not want to dance, but he actually started to dance without any enthusiasm; being an experienced dancer, he reluctantly made familiar movements, hence: he "barely stamped his feet". Such a change in presenting the officer was necessary since otherwise the following paragraph beginning with the words "But little by little even the huge officer broke through" would not have been understood.

Čexov also made additions to the description of Anna. Instead of the words "but she only twisted her shoulders and glanced coquettishly", Čexov wrote: " But she only twisted her shoulders and glanced coquettishly, as if she were already a queen, and he a slave". The insertion was made with the same high level of contrast; it depicts Anna more clearly and at the same time it is a sort of transition to the following scene: the crowd parted and His Excellency comes to Anna. So begins a new period of her life.

Anna enters a world which is new to her – a world of the provincial aristocracy, of Artynovs and of 'ladies of high society'. She "knew that she was created solely for this noisy, brilliant, happy life of music, dances, admirers . . ."

Her attitude towards her family and father changes immediately. When Anna, as requested by the governor's wife, was in charge of a booth at a charity bazaar, her father, among other people, came up to her. In the first, newspaper text this scene was presented as follows:

> Petr Leont'ič, already pale but still steady on his feet, came up to the booth and asked for a glass of cognac. Anja blushed, expecting him to say something out of place, but he drank it up, threw down a ten ruble note from his roll, and walked away with an air of dignity, not saying a word.

From this scene the reader could draw the conclusion that only her father's condition shocked Anna – that she feared that, being somewhat unsober, he would do or say something out of place at the ball and thereby place her in an awkward, ridiculous position.

But reworking the text, Čexov makes a substantial addition showing that this was not quite the point. After the words "Anja blushed, expecting him to say something out of place" Čexov adds parenthetically "She was already ashamed that she had such a poor, common

father." This new feeling of Anna's explains why, after the ball, she
gradually becomes distant from her family, "she visits them less
and less often", does not help them, and casts them to the whims of
fate.

Čexov, passing over to the new period in Anna's life, makes the
governor (His Excellency) and Artynov basic characters. In the reworking of the story Čexov does not leave these characters unattended
– he makes them more specific through the devices of portraiture.

In the first edition the scene where His Excellency makes his acquaintance with Anna begins:

> It was His Excellency with two decorations who was walking towards
> her, looking directly at her and smiling. "Delighted, delighted",
> he began.

In the reworked story there is a large interpolation which depicts the
main features of this predator:

> It was His Excellency wearing a dresscoat with two decorations
> who was walking towards her, . . . Yes, His Excellency was walk-
> ing towards her, because he was looking directly at her and giving
> her a sugary smile and working his lips as he always did when he
> saw pretty women.

A similar addition was made to the portrait of His Excellency in the
scene of his visit to Anna on the day following the ball: "Looking at
her with a sugary smile and working his lips, he kissed her hand and
asked permission to visit again . . ."

This portrait of the old libertine makes it clear that Anna endured
his attentions only in the face of extreme necessity, and also that
shortly afterwards Artynov assumed the first role among her admirers.

To an extent greater than that of the others, the image of this third
predator is shown through his appearance, dress, and manners.

Artynov is the only hero in the story who does not say a single
word, yet the reader pictures him clearly and does not confuse him
with anyone else.

We first see him in the beginning – in the scene on the platform of
the small station near the summer houses.

Even in the first (newspaper) version Čexov presents an extensive
portrait of Artynov in this scene:

> Here too was Artynov, the owner of the whole town of dachas, rich,
> tall, stout, dark-haired, very well-fed, with bulging eyes and in
> a strange costume. He wore a peasant shirt open on the chest,
> riding boots with spurs, and a black cloak fell from his shoulders
> and dragged on the ground like a train. Behind him walked two
> Russian borzois with their sharp muzzles to the ground.

In this portrait everything which ought to have made an impression

on Anja was noted! Artynov's interesting appearance, his preten-
tiously original clothes, and, most important, his wealth.

In rewriting the text, Čexov strengthened even further the features
of Artynov's 'irresistibility'. To show what sort of impression Anja
made on him, Čexov introduced a new detail into the portrait: "Artynov, that notorious Don Juan and playboy, was looking at her greedily and with curiosity."

This detail is very significant: it shows Artynov's most characteristic trait in his attitude towards women and it prepares the reader
for the role which he will later play in Anja's life, and in addition,
this detail specifies one more feature of Anja: Artynov's 'greedy'
attention did not offend Anja at all - on the contrary, it flattered her
ego quite a bit that a man with the reputation of a local Don Juan was
interested in her.

We see Artynov a second time at the ball - to be exact, at the charity bazaar, near Anna:

Wheezing asthmatically, Artynov, the rich man with the bulging
eyes, came up, but he no longer had on that strange outfit in which
Anja had seen him in the summer; he wore tails like everyone else.
Without taking his eyes off of Anja, he drank a glass of champagne
and paid a hundred rubles for it, then he drank some tea and paid
another hundred - in complete silence, suffering from asthma.

Once more in the portrait of Artynov his eyes call attention to themselves: he stood silently, not taking his eyes off of Anja.

This silent, persistent gaze of Artynov - the conqueror of women's
hearts - somehow brings to mind a boa constrictor gazing at a rabbit
which it has chosen to devour.

The last time that we see Artynov is during a drive with Anja along
Old Kiev Street; he is sitting on the box of the coach in place of the
coachman.

In general, it is truly a 'romance without words', told exclusively
through verbal portraiture.

In conclusion, it is fitting to pause on the second, descending sujet
line of the story, which reveals the fate of Petr Leont'ič, Anna's
father.

As in certain other of Čexov's dramatic stories such as "The Flutterer", "Anna Around the Neck" is built on the principle of a dual
level of sujet - a characteristic feature of Čexov's works.

In the foreground are Anna, her husband, and her admirers. The
story is mainly about them, and the reader gets the impression that
these are the main heroes, through whom the ideological scheme of
the author is revealed.

Anna's father and brothers stand in the background; they might be
taken for secondary figures, introduced into the story only so that
the character and fate of the main hero can be revealed more clearly.

One might interpret "Anna Around the Neck" in that way at the
first reading.

But, if one penetrates more attentively to the content of the story, and if one contrasts Anna's story with that of her father, then it becomes clear that the second sujet line has an independent role and that, as far as the understanding of the deep social thought of the story is concerned, the image of her father contributes no less than that of Anna.

Likewise, just as in "The Flutterer" the dramatic thought of the story is revealed not through the image of the frivolous, empty Ol'ga Ivanovna, but through the image of her husband, Doctor Dymov, whose spiritual story takes place almost exclusively behind the scenes, so in "Anna Around the Neck" the truly tragic hero in the final account turns out to be not Anna, but her father – in spite of the fact that Čexov does not seem to devote sufficient attention to him.

Petr Leont'ič is presented in the story in six rather short scenes and primarily through a psychological portrait.

The most significant of these portrait sketches are the first and the last scenes, since the whole fate of the hero is shown in them. When they saw the newlyweds off at the train station,

> Petr Leont'ič, in a top hat and a schoolmaster's coat, already drunk and very pale, kept reaching toward the train window with his glass and said beggingly:
> "Anjuta! Anja! Anja – just one word!"
> Anja leaned towards him from the window and he whispered something to her; enveloping her in the sour smell of wine, he breathed in her ear – she could not understand a word – and made the sign of the cross on her face, bosom, and hands, and his breathing became unsteady and his eyes glistened with tears. Anja's brothers, Petja and Andrjuša, school boys, pulled him back by his coat and whispered with embarrassment:
> "Papa dear, enough – Papa dear, don't . . ."
> When the train moved, Anja saw her father running a bit behind it, staggering and spilling his wine, and how pitiful, kind, and guilty a face he had.
> "Hurra-a-ah!" he shouted.

This first scene tells how much Petr Leont'ič loved his daughter, how he was sorry for her and felt guilty towards her, but nonetheless hoped that the marriage, perhaps, would be successful, how his children loved him, and how weak and pitiful a person he was.

And now the final scene. An inveterate drunkard, Petr Leont'ič met Anja several times on the road when she was driving with Artynov – he "took off his top hat and was about to shout something, when Petja and Andrjuša held his arms and pleaded: 'Don't Papa dear, . . . Please, enough Papa dear, ...' "

There is a great external connection between these two scenes: the same drunken Petr Leont'ič in the same top hat, and Anja again drives away from him, and he again tries to say something to her, and his children still hold him back, but what a difference there is in the meaning of these scenes!

Earlier there was the closeness between father and daughter and a certain hope for her happiness, but now there is alienation and despair.

Čexov's mastery is evident here not only in that by contrapositioning two analogous short scenes he could show the essence of Petr Leont'ič's life, but that by these scenes he still provided unity and completeness to the whole story.

The perfection of its structure is one of the reasons why "Anna Around the Neck" is rightly counted among Čexov's best stories.

"ON THE CART" (1897)

Among Čexov's lyrico-dramatic stories it is necessary to single out a group of stories in which one of the aspects of this genre - lyricism - appears with exceptional clarity.

One must pay particular attention to these stories since they are significant in the study of the artistic mastery of Čexov the lyricist.

Of the stories in this group, Čexov by the second half of the 1880s had written "Dreams" (1886), a story valued very highly by D. Grigorovič for its plasticity of artistic depiction, "On Easter Eve" (1886), and "Happiness" (1887); the last of these Čexov himself called a quasi-symphony and considered "the best of all my stories". (4) However, most of these stories were written in the 1890s. These were "In Exile" (1892), "The Student" (1894), "The Head Gardener's Story" (1894), "The House with the Mezzanine" (1896), "On the Cart" (1897), "A Case from a Doctor's Practice" (1897), and "The Lady with the Little Dog" (1899).

One must also include in this group Čexov's final story, written shortly before his death - "The Betrothed".

What is the basic feature of these stories which may tentatively be called 'lyrical'?

It consists in that Čexov, truthfully depicting reality in 'lyrical' stories, directs his main attention toward revealing his attitude towards this reality, or, as Gor'kij said of him in 1900, toward showing "his concept of the world and his role in it". While depicting life, Čexov - in Gor'kij's words - "illuminates its boredom, its absurdity, its yearnings, and all its chaos from a higher point of view. And although this point of view is elusive, not lending itself to definition . . . it was always felt in his stories, and becomes all the stronger." (5)

This "higher point of view" did not, in Čexov, take the form of a specific system of philosophical and socio-political opinions, as for example, in the case of Tolstoj and Dostoevskij, and it was for him a source of a lyrical elucidation of human life.

It was a faith in man, a deep dissatisfaction with the present and dream of a bright future, not the dream of an Oblomov or of a Manilov, (6) but an active one which incites to action, to battle.

Čexov's dream is always directed towards a goal: it takes its shape by the situation of a given hero, but in addition it always has a broader, general meaning and becomes a symbol of man's yearning for a fulfilling life.

Old Semën ("In Exile") has worked out his own original system for reconciliation with his hard life: he believes that all yearnings for freedom, for a life which is truly alive, are stupid and a temptation from the devil. "It is the devil tempting you", he says to his co-worker, a young exiled Tatar, who dreams of his homeland and his young wife.

"Do not listen to the accursed one. Do not give way to him. When he tempts you with a woman, defy him and say, 'I do not want this.' When he tempts you with freedom, rebuke him, saying, 'I do not want that either.' One needs nothing. No father, no mother, no wife, no freedom, no yard, no stick! Nothing, damn it!"

Semën scoffs at the exiled 'gentleman' who dreams of living in Siberia by his own work, and who wants with all his heart to bring his wife and daughter there. "Catch the winds in the field! Take the devil by his tail - damn it! What strange people, Lord, have mercy on me a sinner."

Through the lips of the young Tatar, Čexov flatly condemns such a mode of reconciliation.

"He good . . . good, and you - bad! You - bad! Gentleman is good soul, but you - beast, you - bad! Gentleman - alive, but you - dead . . . God made man to be alive so there would be joy, and grief and woe, but you don't want nothing. So you are not alive, but stone, clay! . . ."

The Swedish legend forming the basic content of "The Head Gardener's Story" has an even more symbolic meaning.

A doctor, a most remarkable person, in whose breast "beat a wonderful, angelic heart", had settled in a small town. He loved and helped everyone, and everyone loved him. "Adults and children, good and bad, honest men and swindlers - all respected him and knew his worth."

And this man . . . was found murdered. The murderer was arrested. At his trial he stubbornly denied his guilt, but all the evidence pointed to him and did not give rise to any doubt.

"Defendant!" the Chief judge addressed the murderer. "The Court finds you guilty of the murder of the doctor and sentences you to . . ."

The Chief judge had wanted to say 'to death' but he dropped from his hands the paper on which the sentence was written, wiped away the cold sweat and shouted:

"No. If I am rendering an incorrect judgment, then let God punish me, but I swear that this man is not guilty! I regard it inconceivable that a man can exist who would dare to kill our dear doctor. Man is incapable of falling so low . . ."

They set the murderer free and no one reproached the judges for making an unjust decision . . .
"Let the verdict of not guilty bring harm to the townspeople (so the head gardener (and with him, Čexov) ends the story) but in turn consider what a beneficial effect this faith in man had on them, a faith which does not remain inactive; it breeds feelings of generosity in us and always induces us to love and respect each person. Each one! And that is important."

The lyrical content of his stories demanded new devices of artistic mastery from Čexov.

The chain of events in these stories occupies a secondary place. Sometimes there are either no events or else they are kept to a minimum. In the story "Happiness" there are three characters: two shepherds, one old, one young, watching over a flock of sheep in the steppe, and a horse patrol. All three speak about buried treasure and happiness, but during the whole conversation they do not 'act', but remain almost motionlessly in place; the shepherds lie down, and the horseman stands near his horse, leaning on the saddle. There are no events - the entire interest of the story is in the dialogue, which is very vivid and expressive, in the discourses and daydreams of the old man, and in the lyrical tone of the narrator and author.

Sometimes an extensive sujet is presented, as for example in "The House with the Mezzanine" and particularly in "The Lady with the Little Dog", but such a sujet is permeated with lyricism: almost every event is accompanied by lyrical statements on the part of the hero, on the part of the author directly, and Čexov's point of view appears quite clearly in each.

The basic conflict of these essentially lyrical stories is not the collision of persons, as takes place in stories with a predominance of dramatic conflict, but a collision of feelings, of the hero's yearnings; the conflict in these stories is not so much external as internal.

The artistic devices primarily used in these stories are aimed towards emotional expressivity - toward the strengthening of the intonational aspect of the work. Structurally, it is the contrast of images and the repetition of impressions, and linguistically it is the use of emotional words, expressions, turns of syntax, musicality, and closeness to metric speech.

One of the stories most characteristic in this respect is "On the Cart", written by Čexov in 1897.

Judging by the original scheme of this story - as Čexov entered in a notebook - the story was to have had a plot based on a chain of events. Here is the plan:

A woman teacher in a village. From a good family. Brother is an officer somewhere. Orphaned, became a teacher by necessity. Day after day, endless evenings, without sympathy, without endearment; personal life dies, no satisfaction since there is no

time to think of high goals, and you don't see the results . . . In
the coach of a train slowly passing by she caught sight of a lady
who looked like her dead mother, suddenly she imagined that she
was a girl, felt as she did fifteen years ago, and kneeling on the
grass, she said tenderly, kindly, imploringly: O Mama! And
coming to herself, she quietly wandered home. Earlier she had
written to her brother but did not get an answer, he probably forgot. She became coarsened, hardened . . . Now she would stand
when the inspector or trustee entered and said of them: "they"
(7) . . .

In this scheme the general idea and basic tone of the story were
specified, and the central episode (the recollection of her mother)
was outlined, but when the story was actually written, significant
changes were brought into the original plan and into the content.

"On the Cart" is the description of the trip of Marja Vasil'evna,
a teacher, from the city where she had gone for her pay to the village Vyazovie, where her school is located. This trip took several
hours, from morning till evening.

The story is contained in the frame: "At half past eight in the
morning they left the town. . . . And this is Vyazovie. Here we
are."

The trip itself was of no interest to Marja Vasil'evna. "She had
been a teacher for thirteen years. One could not count how many
times in all these years she had gone to the city for her pay."

This was an ordinary trip in a wagon, 'on a cart', and the things
which happened on the road were ordinary. Xanov, a landowner,
passed them on the road, driving in a coach and four; in the afternoon they stopped by a tavern in Lower Gorodishche to rest and
drink some tea; while passing through a stream swollen by spring
floods, Marja Vasil'evna got soaked and ruined the sugar and flour
which she had purchased in the city.

The episode of her imaginary meeting with her mother was the
only exceptional thing, but this still was not a real but an illusionary
'event' characteristic of the teacher's inner condition.

The basic content of the story is not in this chain of events, but
in the heroine's experiences, her impressions of the world about
her, and her feelings, recollections, and dreams.

The lyrical content also determined the story's devices, its structure, and language.

The basic structural devices are contraposition, which gives nuances and emphasis to lyrical experiences, and recurrence of these
experiences.

At the very beginning of the story a sharp contrast is given between the spring landscape and the way it is perceived by the teacher.

"The road was dry and a wonderful April sun shone warmly." One
must recall that Čexov loved spring and understood quite well the
spiritual uplift, the feeling of joy which overwhelms people in spring.
"The snow has not yet left the ground", he wrote in the story "In the
Spring" (1881), "but spring already seeks to enter the soul. If you

have ever recuperated from a serious illness, then you know that
blissful condition when your breath weakens from vague presenti-
ments and you smile for no reason at all. Evidently, nature, too,
now experiences such a feeling."

It would seem that Marja Vasil'evna ought to have experienced a
spiritual uplift of this sort in April, but for her "neither warmth,
nor the languid, limpid forests warmed with the breath of spring,
nor the black flocks flying in the field above the huge puddles that
looked like lakes, nor that sky, wonderful and bottomless, where,
it seemed, one would very happily go - none of this presented anything new or interesting."

Marja Vasil'evna's experiences are in sharp contrast. On one
hand there is the monotonous, boring, oppressive present, but then
there are the wonderful, moving recollections of the distant past
when she lived with her family and was "young, beautiful, and
smartly dressed", and her even more beautiful dreams of the future
- that she would marry Xanov and devote the remainder of her life
to saving him from his colorless life and downfall.

The contrast between the reality in which the teacher has been
living and her dreams - whether directed towards the past or to
the future - is the basis of the story and permeates it from beginning to end.

This contrast is found in conjunction with repetition. Marja's experiences, her thoughts about what is, was, and shall be, are repeated constantly, replacing each other systematically. This change
of moods and their orderly transition give the story a certain
emotional rhythm.

Marja Vasil'evna rides on and thinks about her school, and "about
the impending examination for which she will present four boys and
one girl".

At that moment she is overtaken by Xanov, who, in spite of his
forty years, "is still handsome and liked by women". Marja
Vasil'evna thinks about Xanov, about how he was with her at an examination and she liked him, and how she felt shy sitting next to him.

Thoughts about school arise anew: how difficult it was to work because no one helped her - neither the president of the Zemstvo, (8)
nor the inspector, nor the trustee of the school who was a semi-
literate peasant and the owner of a tannery.

"He is really handsome", she thought, glancing at Xanov. Marja's
thoughts now take a new direction: she thinks of Xanov and is surprised that with his wealth, interesting looks, and good education,
he cannot lead a normal life or help others, even to the extent of
repairing the road on which they are now travelling. He is kind,
gentle, and naive - he knows that rough life no better than he knows
the prayers at the examination . . .

But reality rudely disturbs these dreams.

"Hold on, Vasil'evna!" said Semën. The cart lurched severely and
almost overturned . . ."

And again thoughts about Xanov - how good it would be for both of them if she were his wife.

"She thought again about her students, about the examination, about the janitor, and about the school board . . ."

But "she wanted to think of his beautiful eyes, of love, of the happiness which would never be".

And so, dreams and reality alternate with each other until the end of the story.

A certain digression from this structural device is found in the scene in the tavern, an extensively detailed scene of ordinary life, presenting Marja Vasil'evna in the environment of peasants, among whom she lives and to whom she has been called to teach and educate.

Here Čexov depicts the peasants of his time with the same mastery of a writer-realist as he does in his "The Peasants" and other stories about the old countryside.

The peasants consider the teacher one of their own, and her appearance at the tavern is not of special notice, but she is an educated person, a 'lady', and one must treat her with respect. Some drunken peasant swears, and Semën stops him:

"Why are you swearing, you there! . . . Don't you see there's a lady present?"

He is first met with a reply which is not favorable to Marja Vasil'evna:

"A lady . . . " somebody in the corner mimicked.
"Lousy pig . . ."

But in general the peasants' attitude was positive.

"Wait, brother! . . It's the teacher from Vyazovie . . . We know her. A fine lady."
"A respectable lady."

When the peasants were leaving the tavern, "the same drunk who had first offended her went up to Marja Vasil'evna and shook her hand; others, following his example, also offered their hands in parting . . ."

This brief but very lively scene shows the crudeness of the environment in which the teacher lived. It also shows that the possibility of her having some cultural influence on the peasants is far from hopeless.

But there was still much coarseness as is shown in the following scene where Semën fords the stream, not wanting to go to the bridge as Xanov did, and thereby causing Marja Vasil'evna great annoyance. However, she "only threw up her hands in despair and said: 'Ah, Semën, Semën! What are you, really!' "

If the interchange of reality and dream, the contrasting repetition of feelings, is the basic principle in the structure of the story, then one must add to this that in Marja Vasil'evna's repeated impressions there is movement and intensification. In the beginning, she is indifferent: "It was all the same to her", and she thinks only about the present. But with every new impression, all her recollections of her past life and all her dreams of happiness are strengthened, and all her thoughts of the present become more obsessive and sharpened. In the conclusion of the story - after the episode of fording the stream, where the teacher's helplessness and her bitter lot are displayed in all their force - we find in sharp contrast an illusory picture of a happy life, and this picture unites the dreams of the past and those of the future.

When, shivering from the cold, Marja Vasil'evna catches sight of a lady in the passing train who resembles her long departed mother,

> vividly, with striking clarity . . . she imagined her mother, father, brother, their apartment in Moscow, the aquarium with the little fish, everything, up to the smallest detail; suddenly she heard a piano playing and her father's voice . . .; a feeling of joy and happiness suddenly seized her and with delight she pressed her temples with her palms and called out tenderly, imploringly,
> "Mama!"

And she began to cry, not knowing why. At the very same moment Xanov drove up in his carriage, and seeing him she imagined happiness such as never existed and she smiled, nodding to him as an equal and close friend, and it seemed to her that her happiness and exultation shone everywhere, in the sky, in the windows, and in the trees . . .

The climax of Marja Vasil'evna's experience is in this lyrical finale. (9) This is a generalizing, synthetic picture, in which the best recollections of the past and the brightest dreams of the future are fused.

The lyrical content of this story demanded of Čexov not only a particular sort of structure, but also the use of appropriate language.

The most essential element in the story's lexicon and syntax is the reflection of the contradiction between dream and reality. Where the road, Semën, the school, and daily life are described, the language is clear, and, if it is the language of the characters, it is characteristic of the individual who is speaking. On the other hand where Marja Vasil'evna's recollections and dreams are presented, or where the author himself gives an evaluation of the life portrayed, the language becomes emotional, musical, and rhythmic.

Here are examples of both types of language:

<u>They turned off of the highway onto a country road: Xanov in front, Semën following</u>.

(A short sentence, but the words are selected so successfully and exactly that the reader visualizes this picture.)

The team of four horses went along the road at a slow pace, strain-
ing to pull the heavy carriage through the mud. Semën ma-
noeuvered about, sometimes leaving the road to go by way of a
hillock or a meadow, often jumping down from the cart and helping the horse.

(Again a very clear picture, built on a selection of simple words,
often encountered in conversation, but of the perfectly exact sort
which were indispensable in the given situation.)

Such was also the language used to describe the tavern.

Here Čexov considers it necessary to describe first with complete
exactness what Marja Vasil'evna saw when she entered the tavern.
He says that "carts stood" near the tavern, that they "carried large
containers of oil of vitriol" and that these carts stood "on dung-
strewn ground where snow still lingered" - everything is so clear
that one could draw a picture from this description.

The atmosphere of a country tavern of that time is sketched just
as clearly and distinctly:

There were many people in the tavern, all of them drivers, and
it smelled of vodka, tobacco, and sheepskin. A loud conversation
was in progress and the door, connected to a pulley weight, kept
slamming. In the store behind the wall, someone was playing an
accordion without stopping.

Here we find the same thing as before: short sentences, careful word
selection, everything very realistic, objective, with no evaluation
on the part of the author, graphic and typical to the highest degree.

This simple language is interspersed every now and then with
another language full of emotional epithets, and, sometimes, similes.
Marja Vasil'evna sees Xanov:

Next to old Semën he seemed well proportioned and vigorous but
there was something hardly noticeable in his gait, which betrayed
him as one who was already poisoned, weak, and doomed . . .
"And it is inexplicable", she thought, "why God gives good looks,
affability, and sad sweet eyes to weak, unhappy, helpless people,
why are they so attractive."

And when, after this, Marja Vasil'evna returns to her sad thoughts
about the conditions of her life in school, Čexov finds other, equally
emotional epithets to express these thoughts:

She had to collect money from her students for firewood and for
the janitor's pay, turn it over to the trustee, and then implore
him, this well-fed, insolent peasant, as an act of charity, to send
them firewood . . . And because of such a life she aged, became
coarsened, homely, angular, clumsy, as if she were filled with

<u>lead</u> . . .

The language is particularly emotional in the concluding scene of the story, which has been quoted above: this scene culminates not only the presentation of Marja Vasil'evna's mood, but, in harmony with this, the emotionality of the story's language.

Lyricism finds its expression, apart from the lexicon, in the peculiarities of syntactic construction.

If, in the description of objects, everyday life, etc., Čexov uses simple sentences, he prefers more complex structures of speech when he depicts the more or less complex and contradictory experiences of the heroine.

These structures consist of compound sentences with repeated conjunctions: and-and-and, or-or-or.

> Here was her past, her present, and she could not imagine a different future - only the school, the road to the city and back, and again school, and again the road . . . . And whether it was spring, as now, or a rainy autumn evening, or winter - it was all the same to her.

Yet another example:

> And because of such a life she aged . . . and is afraid of everything, and she rises at the arrival of a member of the <u>Zemstvo</u> or of the trustee of the school, not daring to sit down, and when she speaks about any of them, she uses a respectful 'they'. And nobody likes her, and her life goes on in boredom.

Marja Vasil'evna's thoughts and dreams are sometimes presented by interrogative or exclamatory sentences:

> "He only donates globes to the school", she thinks of Xanov, "but who needs his globes here?"
> "To be a wife! . . . To be a wife! . . ."
> On the platform of one of the coaches of the train stood a woman, and Marja Vasil'evna glanced at her briefly: Mother! What a resemblance! . . .

Finally, the musicality and rhythm of speech also constitute one of the peculiarities of Čexov's lyrical stories. The emphatic use of rhythm to whatever degree possible without destroying the naturalness and vivacity of speech is given in the very beginning of the story.

"<u>Šossé býlo súxo</u>" ('the highway was dry') - thus from the very first words a rhythmic perception of the text is presented; "<u>prekrásnoe aprél'skoe sólnce síl'no grélo, no v kanávax i v lesú ležál ešče sneg</u>" ('a wonderful April sun shone warmly, but snow still lay in the ditches and in the forest') also rings out like a musical phrase.

"I vsegdá, neizménno, xotélos' odnogó: poskorée by doéxat" ('and she invariably wanted only to get there as quickly as possible') - there is no doubt that the rhythm here is felt very clearly.

This musical element in the presentation of the story's lyricism is so overpowering that the reader carries it into those parts of the story where there is no regular pattern of accented syllables and where rhythm cannot be shown graphically.

This is especially true in the final part. If the reader were to read the final scene aloud, he would unwittingly make pauses and modify the tempo of the speech as in reading verse, permitting variety in the construction of rhythmic units, and would unconsciously strive to reproduce the musical sounds of that scene in which the story's lyricism appears with the greatest strength.

Čexov called his story "Happiness" a symphony. The story "On the Cart" has equal right to such a name.

NOTES

(1) [From: V. V. Golubkov, Masterstvo A. P. Čexova (Moskva, Gosudarstvennoe Učebno-Pedagogičeskoe Izdatel'stvo, 1958), pp. 119-125; 126-159.]
(2) [This incorrect expression shows Rjabovskij's clowning.]
(3) [Edited by Čexov himself and published in 1901.]
(4) Letter to Ja. P. Polonskij dated March 25, 1888. A. P. Čexov, Sobranie sočinenij v 12ti tomax (Moskva, Goslitizdat, 1956).
(5) M. Gor'kij and A. Čexov, Perepiska (Moskva, Goslitizdat, 1951), p. 124.
(6) [Oblomov, a character of Gončarov's novel of the same name and Manilov, a character of Gogol''s Dead Souls are futile, purposeless dreamers.]
(7) [When speaking of a single person, 'they' in Russian is a sign of exaggerated servility or respect.]
(8) [Zemstvo - a colloquial name for institutions of local government which had authority in education, public health, etc.]
(9) [The actual ending of the story - which follows the excerpt - is more sober.]

IX

ON ČEXOV'S STYLE (1)

V. V. VINOGRADOV

In Čexov, the devices of socio-professional speech characterization
reached great depth and stylistic subtlety. (2) Commenting on the
style of A.M. Fedorov's play <u>An Ordinary Woman,</u> he wrote the
following in a letter to the author: "Volodja is good . . . but, he
should be a mechanic or have been one. Then such expressions as
'The steam is released', and 'The wheels will start to move now',
will not be empty, but will flow, as it were, from a depth." (3)

It is obvious that even in a work of artistic realism there is no
complete and direct correlation between the literary reproduction
of a social style of speech and its socio-dialectal basis. However,
the principles and tendencies which determine the degree of verisimilitude in daily speech and in the character depicted are very important. For example, take Čexov's story, "A Happy Ending": the
characteristics of social-speech style of 'a person of experience',
a bourgeois with pretensions to education ("I am of the educated
class. I can say that I am with Prince Kanitelin the same as I am
with you right now. . .") combine with the typical attitudes of banal
rhetorics to form the style of head conductor Styčkin's speech. The
basic principle here is the structural deformation of ordinary expressions and of literary bookish locution: "Semën Ivanovič recommended you from the point of view, that . . ." (226); (4) "I am
a man of the educated class, with money, but were one to look at
me from a point of view, then what am I? An old bachelor, like a
Catholic priest" (227); "Whence shall I go and to whom shall I turn,
if all people are unknown for me?" (227); "To think various ideals"
(227); "You are to my liking, and suit me in your qualities" (230);
"I understand everything gentlemanly" (230); etc.

Another characteristic of his speech is his nonsensical use of
expressively colored cliches in a lofty style: "but I am in a position
to <u>feed at my side a beloved being</u> and children too" (226); "But I
lack just one thing - my own home and hearth and life's companion,
and I lead a life like a wandering Hungarian who moves from place to
place without any satisfaction" (226); "And therefore I most ear-
nestly implore you, Ljubov Grigor'evna, to settle my fate with your
assistance" (227); "I believe that the main thing in a woman is not
that which is on the outside, but what is <u>found within,</u> that is, that
she have a soul and all the properties" (227). (5)

Semantic deviations from the norms of literary usage are also
significant, as are distortions based on folk etymological, quibbling
distortions. For example: "I lead a well-grounded and appropriate
life" (226); "And therefore I wish very much to be united in the bonds

of Hymen, (6) that is, to enter into lawful marriage" (227); "and in
the arrangement of people's happiness has her profession" (227);
"For me beauty and appearance in general play a secondary role"
(227); "Strictly speaking, intelligence is not needed in a woman because then she will get a high opinion of herself and will think various
ideals" (227); "Well, but now as far as what is substantive is concerned" (228); etc.

The syntactic structure of the head conductor's speech also contributes to such peculiar phrase constructions as: "Just between ourselves, let me tell you that besides my salary, I also have money
in the bank . . ." (226); "I have no one to confide in, and, when I
am sick, there is no one to give me a drink of water and so forth"
(226–227).

These and other qualities of head conductor Styčkin's speech style
still do not completely define either his character, his 'artistic image', or his function in the structure of the story. Moreover, the
artistic and esthetic functions of these as well as characteristics
of the social speech style of a pretentious Philistine of the 'educated
class' become clear only in the dynamic structural development of
Čexov's novella, which he gave an ironic title, "A Happy Ending".

The first characterisation of Styčkin comes from the author himself: "Styčkin, a bit embarrassed, but, as always, serious, practical,
and strict, was walking about the room, smoking a cigar and saying
. . ." (226). Styčkin's self evaluation, full of utter complacency and
great self esteem, is repeated more than once in his speech. It is
natural that the expressive quality of those emotionally elevated
attributes which Styčkin applies to himself, especially since they
come from himself, acquire for the reader a deeply ironic and
sharply lowered evaluation. "My position is quite solid . . . I am
a practical and sober man, and I lead a well-grounded and appropriate life, so that I can be an example to many others" (226); "I
am a man of the educated class, with money . . ." (227); "I am a
practical person and a man of character" (227); "I am of the educated
class. I can say that I am with Prince Kanitelin the same as I am
with you right now, but I am a simple man" (228); "If you get a husband who is practical, sedate and thrifty, then, considering his salary and your earnings, he could come to like you very much and you
both will live in harmony" (229); "I am a practical and sober man
and, if you like me, then . . . what could be better?" (230); "I am
a strict, solid, practical man, I understand everything gentlemanly,
and wish that my wife would also be strict and would understand
that I am her benefactor and the most outstanding person" (230).

Thus in Styčkin's self-evaluation almost the same attributes and
evaluations of his character which appeared first in the author's
narrative style vary, develop, and extend. However, the expressive
semantic functions of these phrases as well as their characteristic
or characterological value in the structure of the entire narrative
change completely. The image of automatic, standard, rigid speech
builds up the self-characterization of this smug dullard.

The revelation of Styčkin's image in his speech occurs along several lines: (1) in his statements about his "life companion", and about how to "settle my fate" and be united with some worthy person in the "bonds of Hymen"; (2) in his exposition of his philosophy of life, of his relationship to women and his future wife, etc.; (3) in his practical calculations, in the combination of his bourgeois verbal romanticism with a sober and petty miserliness; and (4) in the constant revelation of the peculiarities of Styčkin's eroticism.

The basic disclosure of Styčkin's image is in his dialogue with Ljubov Grigor'evna, a sedate, "buxom lady of about forty who was engaged in matchmaking and quite a few other things of which one ordinarily speaks only in a whisper".

This euphemistic characterization is expanded and revealed further in the second part of Styčkin's dialogue with the matchmaker. (7) "They remained silent for about five minutes. The matchmaker sighed, looked askance at the head conductor and asked, 'Well, my good fellow, do you want anything in the bachelor line? I have some nice goods. One is a French woman, and the other is of Greek decent. They are very worthy' " (228).

Here Čexov reveals the basis or summit of Ljubov Grigor'evna's activity. Her style changes (cf. addressing him in the familiar thou, my good fellow). The phraseology is significant: "in the bachelor line", "I have some nice goods", "very worthy" (cf. "and so, my good fellow, we do not make money out of weddings"). In general, this entire scene, which is acted out after a five minute pause in the conversation, signals a sharp break in the development of the sujet of the story and is connected with the intensification in the development of the dialogue. It is interesting that the third act or third scene also begins with a reference to a pause: "A silence follows."

Thus, Čexov's novella "A Happy Ending" falls into three dramatic segments. The first is the philosophizing, self evaluating monologues of head conductor Styčkin which are interrupted by the laconic replies of the matchmaker.

"A fine thing", the matchmaker sighed.
"This is feasible . . ."
"This is feasible", she repeated. "What sort of bride would you like, Nikolaj Nikolaevič? . ."
"Of course, fate itself decides such matters, but you know, each has his own tastes. One person likes brunettes, another likes blondes . . ."
"To be sure . . ."
"I might also find someone with a dowry."

In Styčkin's monologues, aside from his repeated self evaluations and expressions of desire "to accommodate himself" to his bride, statements regarding the qualities of women and wives are emphasized. These statements are dialectical in their own peculiar way. In them appear the conflict between the demands of Philistine esthetics, the principles of 'pleasantness', and practical expediency.

They are presented in the form of adversative judgments and complex sentences which correspond to them:

> "For me beauty and appearance in general play a secondary role
> because, as you yourself know, you can't eat beauty for supper
> and a beautiful wife is always a lot of trouble . . . Of course it
> is very nice if a wife were a bit plump, but that is not important
> as far as mutual happiness is concerned; the main thing is intel-
> ligence."

The critical statement about woman's intelligence also leads to a
negative conclusion in the solution of the problem concerning the
necessity and importance of the female mind. "Strictly speaking,
intelligence is not needed in a woman because then she will get a
high opinion of herself and will think various ideals." Styčkin's
ideas about education enter in here:

> "One cannot get along without education nowadays, but there are
> various kinds of education. It would be nice if my wife spoke
> French and German with different intonations, very nice; but
> what good would that do me, say, if she did not know how to sew
> on a button?" (227-228).

The question of dowry and of rich and poor brides is solved with
the same sort of contradiction and dialectic and with an obvious
humorous bent. A particularly biting and significant place is given
to the relationship of love and "personal benefit", of passion and
money, in the selection of a bride.

> "I don't need a rich woman. I would not allow myself to sink so
> low as to marry for money. I would not want to eat my wife's
> bread, but she should eat mine, and appreciate it. But I don't
> want a poor woman either. Although I am a man of means and
> although I am not marrying for personal profit, but for love, still
> I cannot take a poor woman because, as you know, prices have
> gone up and there will be children."

The most interesting thing here is his peculiar understanding of the
word love. Styčkin's concept of love combines elements of cold
blooded calculation with the idea of a husband as benefactor.

Phraseological repetitions are characteristic: "The most important thing is that she respect me and feel that I have made her happy"
(228); "I . . . wish my wife would also be strict and would understand that I am her benefactor and the most outstanding person"
(230).

In the second act of this dramatic novella - in conjunction with
the fact that the price of Ljubov Grigor'evna's services "regarding
a bride" seems expensive to Styčkin - a change of ideas and plans
takes place in the head conductor. He begins to urge her more fre-
quently: "Have a glass, I beg you." An idea begins to develop - to

take the matchmaker as a bride.

Styčkin silently <u>looked her over from head to toe</u> and said:
"Fifty rubles . . . that makes six hundred rubles a year . . .
Have a glass, I beg you . . . You know, Ljubov Grigor'evna,
with such dividends you would have no trouble making a match for
yourself . . ."
"For myself?" laughed the matchmaker. "I am an old woman. . ."
"Not at all . . . You have a nice figure, your face is full and white,
and all the rest."
The matchmaker was embarrassed. Styčkin was also embarrassed
and sat down next to her.
"You are still very attractive", he said. "If you get a husband who
is practical, sedate and thrifty, then, considering his salary and
your earnings, he could come to like you very much and you will
both live in harmony" (229).

The third part of the dramatic dialogue also begins with a pause:

A silence followed. Styčkin began to blow his nose loudly . . .
Another minute passed in silence. Styčkin stood up and began to
walk about the room in excitement.
"I don't need a young wife", he said. "I am an older man, and I
need the type of person . . . somewhat like you . . . staid and
solid . . . with your sort of figure . . ." (8)

The ending repeats the beginning: Styčkin "sighed deeply and began
to expound to his fiancee his views on domestic life and on the duties
of a wife . . ."
This brief examination of the structural development of Čexov's
"A Happy Ending" does not merely illustrate the complex devices of
artistic literary reworking and <u>sujetal</u> organization involving a
character's unique style of social speech; it also illustrates a particular set of categories and principles of stylistically artistic literature and poetics, through which both the structure and the essence
of the content of socially tinted common speech undergo a change.
Into this area enter the complex problems of the relationship between
an author's speech and that of his characters, as do problems of
internal expressive and <u>sujetal</u>-semantic changes both in their forms
and in their structural properties.
***
. . . The matter of the expressive qualities of words, phrases, and
constructions - still so little investigated in the stylistics of language
and speech so far as various structural types and systems of social
speech are concerned - consists of a large, complex sphere of problems concerned with the combination, shift of contrasts, and strengthening of expressive colorations of speech and their influence on other
means of stylistic expression and the interaction with it.
Cexov's story "An Evil Affair" was first published in <u>Peterburgs-</u>
<u>kaja Gazeta</u> (1887, No. 54, p. 3, in the section "Flying Notes") and

174

then later - with changes in punctuation and in one word, <u>hoarsely</u> in place of <u>boldly</u> in the phrase: ". . . says the pilgrim, chuckling boldly" - in the collection of Čexov's stories <u>In the Twilight</u> (St. Peterburg, 1887) and likewise in all subsequent editions of this collection (2nd to 13th, St. Peterburg, 1888-1899) and, finally, with changes in punctuation only, in editions of Čexov's collected works. In this story the forms of the narrative style and the dialogue of the protagonists are arranged broadly and freely upon the dramatic co-ordination of the general expressive tone.

This unity of expressive tone in the general style of "An Evil Affair" was noted and mentioned by D.V. Grigorovič. In a letter to Čexov dated December 30, 1888, he gave the following evaluation of the story:

> In its preservation of harmony and in the endurance of its general gloomy tone, your story "An Evil Affair" is simply a model; from the very first pages, although one does not yet know what will happen, one begins unwittingly to get a feeling of horror, and a premonition of something sinister seizes control of one's mind. (9)

The story begins with an anxious question: "Who goes there?" There is no answer. A gloomy situation is described with suitable words, constructions, and expressive colorations.

> The watchman sees nothing, but above the sound of the wind and the trees he can clearly hear someone walking ahead of him in the alley. The March night, <u>cloudy</u> and <u>foggy, has blanketed the land</u>, and <u>it seems to the watchman that the earth, the sky, and he himself with all his thoughts have merged together into something huge and impenetrably black</u>. He can only grope his way about.

Then comes the tragicomic scene between the burglar, who is playing the role of a lost old pilgrim, and the watchman, who, though thoroughly frightened, pretends not to be afraid.

> "Who goes there?" the watchman repeats, and it <u>begins to seem</u> to him that he hears whispering and smothered <u>laughter</u>. "<u>Who is there</u>?"

The author emphasizes the aged voice and senile pilgrimish manner of the burglar's speech. A dialogue follows:

> "It's me, master . . ." answers an <u>aged voice</u>.
> "And who are you?"
> "I . . . am just a passer-by."
> "<u>What do you mean, just a passer-by</u>?" the watchman shouted angrily, hoping <u>to disguise his fear</u> with the shout. "The devil brings you here! <u>Wandering about</u> in a cemetery at night, <u>you forest spirit</u>!"

"Is this really a cemetery here?"
"Why? What else? Of course it's a cemetery. Can't you see?"
"O-ho-ho . . Queen of Heaven!" There is a sound of the old man sighing.

Then we hear the old man's manner of speech, with its salutations and interjections and with its emotional repetitions of words and expressions.

"I don't see a thing, master, not a thing . . . How dark it is, dark.
It's pitch black, dark, master! O-ho-ho . . ."
"And just who are you?"
"I am a pilgrim, master, a wanderer."

The nightwatchman's replies become more garrulous, extensive.

"What devils, night people . . . Pilgrims to boot! Drunkards."
The watchman mutters, calmed by the tone and sighs of the passer-by. "One will sin with you!" They drink all day and the devil drives them at night.

Then there is a recollection of the watchman's first impressions and feelings:

"Say, it seemed to me I heard not just you, but two or three of you."
"Only one, master, just me. There was just one . . . Oh-ho-ho, our sins . . ."

This whole dialogue takes place in complete darkness. But then the watchman and the pilgrim make physical contact, and a new associative series of questions and corresponding answers arises. The watchman now treats the pilgrim as a lost drunk. This corresponds to the watchman's becalmed imagination.

The watchman stumbles onto the man and stops still.
"How did you get here", he asks.
"I lost my way, good man. I was going to the Mitrievskaya mill and I lost my way."

Thus the clear delineation of the passer-by's personality emerges. Nearby locales are mentioned by name. All of this somehow confirms the watchman's surmise that the passer-by was wandering about drunk and wound up in the cemetery.

"Whew! Is the road to the Mitrievskaia mill through here? You dunderhead! To get to the Mitryevskaya mill you have to go quite a bit over to the left - straight from the city on the state highway. You've walked an extra two miles, you sot. I suppose you guzzled a few too many when you were in the city?"

"It was a sin to be sure, master, it surely was . . . Verily, it
was, and I shall not hide my sin. But how should I go now?"

Now, as the alleged passer-by attempts to lure the watchman further
away from the church, his speech is brighter, sharper and more
varied ways assumes the idiom and properties of a devout old man's
style.

"God grant you health, father. Save you, Queen of Heaven, and
be merciful. But if you only could guide me, good man! Be merciful, guide me to the gate!"

Along with this, in the watchman's replies - he has become completely calm and devoid of fear - a growing familiar, condescend-
ingly-protective brusqueness and even some contempt are seen.

"The gate will be there. Open it and go with God. Watch yourself,
don't fall into the ditch. And when you are out of the graveyard
go all the way along the field until you get to the state highway."

In answer to the wanderer's request to lead him there:

"Well, as if I have time. Go there by yourself."

And the wanderer exaggerates even more the way an old man would
make a request:

"Be merciful - make me pray to God for you. I don't see a thing,
it's pitch black, so dark, master . . . Dark, so dark! Guide me,
gracious master!"

The expression gracious master is the highest in the prayerfully
friendly relationship of the wanderer towards the watchman, who
answers independently and sternly:

"Oh sure, as if I have plenty of time to lead people. If I played
nursemaid to everyone I'd never finish leading people about."
"For the sake of Christ, take me there. I can't see and I'm afraid
to walk alone in a cemetery. It's sinister, master, sinister, I
am afraid, it is sinister, good man . . ."

The watchman agrees to take the wanderer as far as the gate.
    The landscape which the author has drawn is full of darkness and
anguish.

The watchman and the wanderer begin to move away. They walk
together, shoulder to shoulder, silently. The damp penetrating
wind hits them directly in the face and the unseen trees moaning
and creaking sprinkle large drops on them. The avenue is almost
completely covered with puddles.

The watchman continues to get better acquainted with the wanderer, who "visits holy places and prays for good people".

Then the descent into the denouement begins. Images of dead men and pilgrims are evoked. Now the pilgrim plays the main role and his responses become more extensive and colorful.

"The little dead are sleeping, our dear ones are asleep!" the wanderer mumbles, sighing deeply. "The rich are sleeping, and so are the poor and the wise and the foolish and the good and the evil. They are all worth the same. And they will continue to sleep until the sound of the trumpet. The kingdom of heaven be theirs, rest in peace."
"Now we are walking here, but the time will come when we too shall lie here", says the watchman.

The watchman barely sustains the dialogue. His replies are brief and monotonous.

"Yes, yes. We shall all lie here. There is no man who will not die. O-ho-ho. Our deeds are evil, our thoughts are devilish. Sins, sins! My soul is cursed, unsatiable, my belly is greedy! I have angered the Lord, and there shall be no salvation for me either in this world or in the next. Bound up in sin like a worm in the earth."
"Yes, everyone must die."
"That's certainly the way it is."
"It is easier for pilgrims to die than for people like me . . ." says the watchman.

At this point, in his description of various kinds of pilgrims, the wanderer begins to drop the mask of a pilgrim and the expressiveness of his speech begins to change radically.

"There are all sorts of pilgrims. There are the real ones who fear the Lord and watch over their souls, and then there are those who wind up in graveyards at night and please the devil . . . yes! Why if he wanted to, that sort of pilgrim could crack your head open with an axe handle and free your soul from your body."

The dumfounded watchman says:

"Why do you use such words?"

The pilgrim answers:

"No reason . . ."

The pilgrim sees the gate.

"Well, here's the gate, it seems. It certainly is. Be so kind as to open it, buddy."

The salutation "buddy" is used in place of the former "master" and "gracious master".

However, the former style of the pilgrim's language is preserved in one more fragment of conversation:

"O-ho-ho . . .", the pilgrim sighs quietly. "Now that I think of it, I have no reason to go to the Mitrievskaya mill . . . Why the devil should I go there? I would much rather stay here with you for a while, gracious master . . ."

An element of mockery enters into the wanderer's manner of speaking and churchly expressions disappear. He assumes another role which at first merely discourages the watchman but then creates in him a "heavy, cold dread".

"Why do you want to stay with me?"
"Well . . . it's more cheerful with you . . ."
"It looks like you've found a joker. I see you like to make jokes, pilgrim."
"Sure I do!" says the pilgrim, chuckling hoarsely.

This expression (formerly "chuckling boldly") is evidence that the wanderer has completely torn off the mask of a pilgrim.

"Am I really a pilgrim? I'm no pilgrim at all."
"Then who are you?"
"A dead man . . . I have just risen from the grave . . . Remember Gubarev the locksmith who hanged himself at carnival time? That's me, Gubarev . . ."
"Tell me another!"

Terror again seizes the watchman and then the wanderer exposes himself as a burglar and a potential murderer. The style of his speech changes once more. His expressions become coarse, brusque, imperative.

"Sto-op! I say stop and you'd better stop . . . Don't struggle, you filthy dog! If you want to stay alive, then hold still and shut up until I tell you . . . It's only that I don't want to spill any blood or else you would have been dead long ago, you mangy . . . Stop!"

The watchman's stance, his external appearance of terror, his thoughts and emotions are all given in detail.

The watchman becomes weak in the knees. He closes his eyes from fear and trembling all over he presses close to the fence. He would like to yell, but he knows that his shouts would not reach any dwelling . . . The wanderer stands next to him and holds him by the arm . . .

The length of this terrible dramatic scene which passes in silence
is fixed exactly.

> About three minutes pass in silence.
> "One is in fever, the second is asleep, and the third is seeing
> pilgrims about", mumbles the wanderer. "Great watchmen – they
> earn their money! Yes, brother, robbers have always been
> smarter than watchmen! Stand still, quit shaking . . ."

Again the time is specified: "Five, ten minutes pass in silence. Suddenly the wind carries a whistle."
The pilgrim's specialty is thus revealed once and for all –
theft.
In the ending the premonition of "something very evil" which seized
the watchman as he ran to the church is shown subtly and dynamically.

> Having a foreboding of something very evil and still shaking with
> fear, the watchman hesitantly opens the gate, and closing his eyes,
> rushes back . . .
> When he has run down the big avenue, he notices a small dim light
> in the dark. The closer he gets to the light, the more horrified
> he feels, and his foreboding of something evil becomes all the
> stronger.

The story ends with these dismal words:

> A short time passes and the howling wind carries through the grave-
> yard the frantic, uneven sounds of the tocsin . . .

Thus the problem of expressive speech in artistic literature becomes
a problem of expressive tone (and sometimes expressive background)
as well as expressive dynamic variations in the form of the entire,
unified literary structure.

***

The problem of an individual writer's style is bound up with isolating
the stylistic core, the system of expressive means which is always
present in the works of that writer, at least in the limits of a given
period of his creativity. Observations regarding a later change in
his stylistic system may provide a basis for conclusions regarding
the further evolution of his style. Thus the reproduction of the general system of a writer's style is based on a careful preliminary
thorough analysis of his works. Such an analysis should have a historical dynamic character. It is impossible to isolate the totality
of basic stylistic elements in an author's work without reconstruct-
ing the rules or uniformities of the movement of style in his individual works as they appear in their structural enfolding.
In illustration, we turn to several stylistic features of Čexov's
story "The Coroner". (10)

The district doctor and the coroner were riding to an autopsy on
a fine spring afternoon.

The coroner relates a strange story "while gazing at the horses
thoughtfully". He is talking about what is puzzling and obscure in nature
- about how one often runs across events even in daily life which
definitely do not lend themselves to explanation.

> "I know of several strange deaths which only spiritualists and
> mystics would attempt to explain, but would cause a clear-headed
> person to raise his arms in bewilderment. For example, I know
> of a certain educated lady who foretold her own death and died
> for no apparent reason on the very day she had predicted. She
> said she would die on such-and-such a day, and she did" (142).

This is a peculiar sort of story-discourse. On the whole, the subjective expression is connected with motifs of mysteriousness and
strangeness. At first it appears that the story concerns a casual
acquaintance - "an educated lady". The doctor's comment emphasizes the sharp difference between the coroner's attitude to the
mysterious and his own: he is a sober materialist. " 'There is no
effect without a cause', said the doctor. 'There is a death and therefore there is a cause of it.' " The doctor does not use such words
as 'mysterious' or 'strange'. He speaks ironically about 'wonders':
"As far as the prediction is concerned, I see very little out of the
ordinary there. All of our females, educated or not, have the gift
of prophecy and presentiment." In this way two different styles -
individual as well as social-typological - come into conflict. (11)

The coroner continues his story. The objective tone is, in general, preserved. True, in the description of the lady the expressiveness is deepened. Compassion, perhaps admiration, but at least
a delight towards her is shown.

> "Maybe so, but this lady of mine, doctor, is quite unusual. There
> was nothing womanish in her prediction and her death . . . She
> had, if you like, only one female trait - beauty."

A portrait is drawn - delicate, attractive, with an abundance of
details; it is positive, clear, and emotional. Words are repeated
and given special emphasis: intelligent woman, intelligent (eyes),
full of . . . intelligent, pleasant frivolity, and synonyms: thoughtful (an open and thoughtful face) and thinking, as well as cheerful,
full of very infectious gaiety (cf. "with a mocking, typically Russian smile in her eyes and on her lips", etc.). The coroner's monologue ends with the following words:

> "Could there possibly be any mysticism, spiritism, gift of presen-
> timent or the like here? She used to laugh at all that."

In the second part of the novella the coroner's narrative becomes
concrete and descriptive of day-to-day life. A strange tale unfolds -

the death of the woman who was described at the beginning of the
story. The story proceeds casually. In spite of this, the vivid particulars full of subjective expression in depicting the lives of the
husband and wife betray the coroner's closeness to the events. The
wife's insistence that she will die immediately after childbirth is
constantly emphasized:

"Do whatever you wish - it is all the same to me. By summer
I will already be in the cemetery."
Her husband, of course, shrugs his shoulders and smiles.
"I am not joking at all", she says. "I declare in all seriousness
that I am going to die soon."
"And just how soon?"
"Right after childbirth. I will have the baby and die" (143).

The use of verb tenses and the temporal perspective of the narration
tend to bring together the husband who is the subject of the conversation and the coroner himself, who is the narrator.

Her husband did not place any weight on these words. He does not
believe in premonitions and in addition he knows full well that
women in an interesting condition tend to be capricious and are
generally given to gloomy thoughts (143).

There is yet another significant detail: the wife's expressiveness
of speech when she speaks of her approaching death ("just as soon
as I give birth, I will die immediately"):

She spoke in earnest, with an unpleasant smile, even with such a
hostile expression on her face as would not allow contradiction
(144).

The closeness of the narrator to the husband is revealed also in the
sudden utterance of the wife's name, Nataša, and in describing the
following episode:

Finally the husband got tired of this sort of thing. Once at dinner
he lost his temper and asked his wife:
"Listen, Nataša, when is this nonsense going to end?"
"It is not nonsense. I am speaking seriously."
"Rot! I would advise you to stop making such a fool of yourself,
so you won't feel ashamed of it later" (144).

In conclusion we find:

The coroner paused, sighed and then said:
"Can you tell me what she died of? I assure you on my word of
honor that this is not fiction but fact."

"The Coroner" was first published in Peterburgskaja Gazeta (1887,

No. 127, in the section "Flying Notes", p. 3); when he reworked the text for a collection of his works (1901, Vol. III), Čexov eliminated everything which, on one hand, could prematurely suggest or give a clue to the personal drama of the coroner as the <u>sujet</u> of his story. For example:

> . . . she avoided the company of old women, she was not afraid of the dark - in other words, I repeat, she was intelligent. I say this because <u>I knew her almost as well as I know myself</u>.

On the other hand, the description of the last will and testament is deleted, since the very style of the will - business-like, detailed, carefully considered, and sorrowful - could have been evidence for premeditated suicide.

> In her last will and testament she asked her husband not to remain a widower for long, but to remarry as soon as possible; she forgave him everything, willed all her belongings to her future child, and left all her dresses to various people by name. She did not even forget about her tortoise shell match box, which she asked be given in her memory to her brother-in-law, a high-school student.

Finally, Čexov makes the naturalistic expression more gentle in depicting the wife's state before her suicide and in the depiction of her husband's attitude towards it:

> The nanny and the cook, of course, were in tears because there is no woman in the world who is not glad to have an opportunity to break into tears. <u>But the wife drove no one to grief with her whining as much as she did her guests</u> . . . A guest at first would stare in wonder, and then burst into tears. It seemed to the husband that all this was a minor, temporary insanity, but he soon began to notice a definite change in his wife's actions and way of life. . . . To be sure, she loved him very much and was deeply insulted by that incident, but . . .

Later the doctor appears in the function of a detective uncovering the factual internal basis of the events, and the coroner himself takes the place of an actor in the drama - a role which first approaches and then merges into that of her husband.
Doctor:

> "But she died, for sure, not because she predicted it. <u>Most likely she took poison</u>."
> The inspector <u>turned his face quickly</u> to the doctor and narrowing his eyes asked:
> "What makes you conclude that she poisoned herself?" (145)

In this way the subtle description of the coroner's reactions to the

doctor's questions strengthens the conjecture that the poisoned
woman's husband is the coroner himself, the narrator of the puzzling story. "The coroner gazed intently at the doctor as if wishing
to find out why he had asked such a question." The anxious voice of
the suicide's husband rings out distinctly in the style of his answer,
in his recollections, and his expression of agreement which he
reaches after hesitation:

"Just a second", he answered after a short pause, "just a second,
let me recall." The coroner took off his hat and rubbed his forehead. "Yes, yes . . . she began to talk about her death right after
that incident. Yes, yes."
"Well, there you are . . . very likely it was at that time that she
had decided to poison herself, but since she probably did not want
to kill her child too, she postponed her suicide until after she gave
birth."
"Not likely, not likely . . . It is impossible. She forgave him at
that time."
"That she was so quick to forgive indicates that she was thinking
about something evil. Young wives do not forgive quickly."
The coroner gave a forced smile and, to hide his all too obvious
agitation, he started to light a cigarette.

Then in the response of the coroner - although this time only as a
slip of the tongue - a change from the third person to the first person takes place - from some other man to the "I" of the narrator
himself.

"Not likely, not likely . . ." he went on. "The notion of such a
possibility never entered my mind . . . And then . . . He was
not as guilty as might seem . . . He was unfaithful to her in a
curious fashion, without really wanting to . . ." (145)

It is evident that the expressive verbal means by which the coroner's
inner struggle, agitation, and hesitation, and his attitude to his wife's
suicide are expressed are now sharply and dynamically revealed in
the unexpected, contrasting, and individually-characteristic forms
of dialogue. The very style of the inspector's statements changes
sharply, and tends to be broken and hesitating. The dialogue's movement reflects complex expressive speech colourings - an inner
struggle, embarrassment and confusion ("And then . . . he was not
as guilty as might seem" . . . "He comes across a woman, devil
take her . . .").

"That is so, of course, but still . . . I cannot admit that she
poisoned herself. But it is strange that the possibility of such a
death never occurred to me . . . And really it is impossible that
she took poison! No!" (146)

Thus the dramatic quality of the dialogue is strengthened and inten-

sified. The coroner's style of speaking acquires a distinctly subjec-
tive-expressive colouring. In it the deep internal contradictions of
his feelings and thoughts, his struggle with himself and his previous
feelings and conclusions are vividly revealed. The narrator presents
the external expression of the protagonist's emotions objectively,
but now with more subtle detail.

> The coroner fell to thinking. Thoughts of the woman who died so
> strangely did not leave him even during the autopsy. While he was
> taking dictation from the doctor, he frowned gloomily and rubbed
> his forehead.
> On the way back the coroner looked exhausted; he bit his moustache
> nervously and spoke reluctantly.

During their walk which he himself had suggested, the coroner
quickly lost his strength,

> as if he was climbing up a high mountain. He stopped and looking
> at the doctor with strange, as if drunken eyes, he said:
> "Oh my God! If your hypothesis is correct, then it . . . it is cruel,
> inhuman! She poisoned herself to punish someone else!? . . ."

Then follows the inspector's final acknowledgement that the story
which he had told was about his wife and himself.

Thus, in analyzing the individual style of a story, novella, or short
novel, a critic's attention is concentrated not only on the unique features of the narrative style (of an author or narrator) but also on the
various forms of narration in their movements, interactions and
shifts, on the devices of construction and development of dialogue
used by the characters and on the structure of characters' speech.
It is also concentrated on the methods and rules of shifting the style
of the narrative or skaz (12) into a dialogue of persons, into dramatic
speech, as well as on the relationship of an author's narrative to the
colloquial speech of the characters, on the 'author's image', his relationship to events and to the utterances of his characters being depicted.

NOTES

(1) [From: V. V. Vinogradov, Stilistika. Teorija poètičeskoj reči.
Poètika (Moskva, Akademija Nauk, 1963), pp. 46-51; 56-61; 80-85.]
(2) [In this article speech is used in the sense of parole and language
in the sense of langue.]
(3) Literaturnyj arxiv, vol. I: A.P. Čexov (Moskva, 1947), p. 243.
(4) [Numerals in parentheses refer to the page number in Volume
VI of A.P. Čexov, Polnoe sobranie sočinenij i pisem (Moskva,
1944).]
(5) A.P. Čexov, Polnoe sobranie sočinenij i pisem, vol. VI (Moskva,
1946), pp. 226-230. Compare with the text of the first edition

(<u>Oskolki</u> (1887), no. 30, June 25, p. 4): "So as not to insult you, and in order for you to act in accordance with your conscience, it is best to come to an agreement as soon as possible. Any matter hinges on <u>internecine agreement</u> ...").

(6) [The speaker here confuses the Russian word for Hymen and the word for abbot. The word he uses is somewhere in between the two.]

(7) However, in the first version of the story there was the following scene at its very beginning:

"How much do you charge for your services?"

"I do not have an established rate for such a matter", said the matchmaker in embarrassment. "Whatever you will give."

"Please understand, Ljubov Grigor'evna", Styčkin said solemnly, "I am a practical man with character, and I like to have order in everything." (<u>Oskolki</u> (1887), no. 30, June 25, p. 4).

(8) In the first version of the story (<u>Oskolki</u> (1887), no. 30, p. 4), in place of "The matchmaker shed a few tears, smiled, and clinked glasses with Styčkin to show that she agreed", we find the following:

"In that case, allow me to go home to think it over."

This was the answer to the views of the conductor (omitted in the final version): "Instead of going far away, you could settle the problem right now, and if I ...." (Compare with what is found in the text of the <u>Sobranie sočineij</u>: "and, if you like me".)

(9) A.P. Čexov, <u>Polnoe sobranie sočinenij i pisem</u>, vol. VI, p. 494. "Variantv i kommentarii".

(10) A.P. Cexov, <u>Polnoe sobranie ...</u>, vol. VI, pp. 142-147. [The original title is "The Investigating Magistrate" which means a person who combines some functions of detective, coroner, and district attorney. However, in this story, the main character is shown fulfilling only the role of coroner.]

(11) It is significant to the structure of the doctor's image that the doctor's esthetic comments on the inspector's descriptions were removed from the original text of the story (cf. the text in <u>Peterburgskaja Gazeta</u> (1887), no. 127, May 11, p. 3):

"Her facial features were not classic, but were somewhat large and maybe a little heavy but they showed such youth and motion that one could not help being captivated by them.

" 'You certainly know how to describe things', said the doctor, smiling.

" 'Wait!' the inspector interrupted heatedly."

(12) [<u>Skaz</u> - a story told with elements of the speech of the narrator and reflecting his individuality as distinguished from the author's.]

X

THE ROLE OF ADVERSATIVE INTONATION IN ČEXOV'S PROSE (1)

A.V. ČIČERIN

"The style of Čexov's stories is clear, transparent, and simple; it is characterized by accuracy in every expression he uses." There is no need to give the source of this quotation. It can be found in special articles, in courses in the history of literature, and in text-books.

It is a commonplace.

But is it true? Is it completely true?

Čexov defended the idea that originality in a writer is a necessary characteristic of art. He said: "A writer's originality resides not just in style, but even in his mode of thought, in his convictions . . ." (2) It is probable that the secret of Čexov's style lies not in such general features as accuracy and transparency but in something which sets him further apart, in something inherent in his style. There is a well known statement by Čexov: "If you want to describe a poor girl, the thing not to say is 'a poor girl was walking down the street' etc., but rather you should hint that her raincoat was thread-bare or faded." (3) This and many similar comments make it clear that Čexov refrains from direct depiction. What could be simpler, clearer, more exact than the sentence which he rejected? Čexov defends the necessity not of direct, but rather of oblique expression of thought. Each sentence ought to allow the reader some internal freedom. From the details of dress or facial expression the reader himself ought to understand whether the girl is poor or rich, happy or sad. These details ought to express something greater, something more individual than these general words which spell every-thing out.

Čexov, like his great predecessors, came out from under Gogol''s "Overcoat" and absorbed much of Turgenev's delicate lyricism. The way in which he mixed it with the satiric causticness of Ščedrin was remarkable. Dostoevskij and Tolstoj passed through his soul like two raging storms. This was the fare which nourished Čexov.

But a new reality which determined his style, surrounded him. This style, so related in its spirit to its closest predecessors, was nevertheless essentially opposed to them.

In Čexov's prose there is neither the striking force in the application of a particular word when that word is hammered like a nail, nor is there the sharp specificity of expression which was all important in Dostoevskij's and Tolstoj's language.

It is just the opposite.

"I probably also loved him, although I cannot say it for certain . . ." Such is a Čexovian sentence in which an affirmation, presented

indecisively and conjecturally, immediately and abruptly comes to
an end and is refuted, although only in part. Consider the story
"Terror", published in 1892. It is constructed entirely along the
above-mentioned principle: "This was an intelligent, good, lively,
and sincere person, but . . ."; ". . . I liked his wife extremely.
I had not fallen in love with her, but . . ."; "By birth he belonged
to the privileged class, but . . . he himself spoke with a slight uncertainty about his privileged position, as if it were some sort of
myth"; "The fact, of course, is that I am a confused and incom-
petent sort of person, but . . ."; "Her words and her pale face were
angry, but . . ."; "For a long time I had not experienced such delights. But nevertheless far off, somewhere in the depths of my
soul, I felt a certain uneasiness and did not feel comfortable . . .
This was a great serious love, complete with tears and promises
to be faithful, but I had not wanted it to be serious . . ."

I hope that no one thinks I am criticizing Čexov for monotony.
Everything is 'but' upon 'but'. No, this stylistic leitmotif is carried
throughout the whole story in such a delicate thread that there is
no feeling of monotony.

However, 'adversative' intonation is found even more often than
adversative conjunctions. This is obvious even in some of the above
mentioned words: ". . . liked extremely . . . not fallen in love . . .
but" - here are two adversative intonations with a clear goal: to
depict an undecided feeling which, even for the hero himself, was
quite confused.

This adversative displacement exists in a multitude of indefinite
words, both in those which have already been mentioned, and those
which have not yet been. "As if it were some sort of myth", "a certain uneasiness", "there was something uncomfortable", "for some
reason or other it was pleasant to think", "I was happy for some
uncertain reason . . ." All these words and phrases, such as "a
certain", "something", "for some reason or another", "it seemed",
oppose the common idea about the definiteness of a person's feelings
and emotional states. This is an elimination of elementarily clear-
cut ideas such as "he loves her, but she does not love him". At the
same time, it is a search for nuances, which at the final tally are
exactly specified; it is a search for intersections of feelings which
are greatly confused but are more common and real than those which
are purely crystalized and clarified: " A hopeless love for a woman
who has already presented you with two children. Could this really
be understood and yet not be frightening? Is it not more terrible
than ghosts?" Adversative intonation is connected with the nature
of Čexov's prose, which is similar to that of a tragedy. Very deep
and very painful contradictions are amassed in this intonation -
especially the contradictions of an undecided, shallow feeling.

". . . She liked him, the wedding was already set for the seventh
of July, but she did not feel any happiness . . ." In this adversative
rift is presented the complication of the story "The Betrothed". And
further: "He had barely managed to graduate in the Department of
Agriculture, but . . ."; "She owned a row of commercial stalls at

the fair and an old house with columns and a garden, but . . . .;
"He graduated from the Department of Philology at the University,
but . . ."; ". . . Gradually she began to value this good, intelligent
man. But . . ."; "He joked all the time while they ate, but . . .";
"Remarkable people . . . but . . ."; "She understands, but . . .";
"She had never loved him, but . . ." All of these "buts" interrupt
thought. Life does not proceed in a straight line, but it meanders,
full of jolts and frustrations.

This rift enters into the speech of the personages and dualizes
their statements: "My mother certainly does have weaknesses, but
. . ."; "Your mother, in her own way, is a very good and sweet
woman, but . . ." The adversative conjunction gets in the center
of that unspecified colorless phraseology which sounds like satire:

"Perhaps then you believe in hypnotism?"
"I cannot, of course, affirm that I do believe in it", Nina Ivanovna
answered with a very serious, almost severe facial expression,
"but one must keep in mind that there is much in nature which is
mysterious and not understood."
"I am in complete agreement with you, although . . ."

And immediately afterwards the concrete yet vulgar image of the
"very fat turkey" eaten up by the fanciers of that which is "mysterious and not understood" serves as adversative intonation to this indefinite yet lofty conversation.

In the structure of "The Betrothed" the pictures of nature also
contain their own form of "buts":

. . . gentle May! She breathed deeply and wanted to think that
somewhere, not here, but under the sky, above the trees, far
beyond the city, in the fields and forests its own springtime life
has developed, flourished, secret, wonderful, rich, holy, and
innocent, inaccessible to the understanding of a weak, sinful person. And for some reason she wanted to cry.

And then - "Summer turned out to be damp and cold. . . ." Thus
the first picture contains a rift, and summer speaks its "but" to
spring.

These "buts" split the imaginary well-being of everyday existence
and lead Nadja to a crisis and moral purification.

But what does it mean when we read "for some reason she wanted
to cry"? To understand it better we will go to another story, "The
Beauties".

This is as realistic a work as any that Čexov wrote. In it there
are geographical designations such as "He went with Grandpa from
the village of Bolshaya Krepkaya in the Don Region", and mention
is made of the state of the weather: "It was a sultry August day",
as well as examples of the Čexovian modifiers as "languidly dreary".
So too is the caricatured appearance of the rich Armenian: "Imagine
a small shaven head with bushy eyebrows that hang down and a bird-

like nose . . .," and further: "Flies, flies, flies everywhere"; the
words "unpleasant, stuffy and dreary" become a leitmotif - no, it
is a background, and on this background rises a leitmotif of a completely different sort. The daughter of the bird-nosed Armenian appears - it is Maša, or, as her father calls her, Mašja. (4)

> "I caught sight of the fascinating features of the most beautiful
> of all the faces which I had met in my waking hours and had im-
> agined in my dreams. A beauty stood before me, and I recognized
> this at the first glance - in the same way that I recognize light-
> ning."

Two "buts" follow this:

> I am prepared to take an oath that Maša, or, as her father called
> her, Mašja, was a real beauty, but I don't know how to prove it."

And here, immediately following, is a fairy-tale picture in which
the glow of sunset spreads over a third of the sky:

> "Everyone looks at the sunset and all without exception find it ex-
> tremely beautiful, but no one knows or can say in what its beauty
> lies."

The purpose of these "buts" is to show something mysterious and
hidden in beauty, in its incomprehensible and powerful force. Nevertheless, the portrait of Maša is given subtly and in great detail. It
is a real portrait, a portrait which is full of meaning: something
yet undiscovered and not yet completely expressed by the author
shines through it. It begins to be uncovered through the impact of
her beauty: "You look (at Maša) and little by little the desire comes
to tell her something unusually pleasant, sincere, beautiful - as
beautiful as she herself is"; ". . . little by little I forgot myself
and gave myself up to the sensation of beauty. I was no longer aware
of the monotony of the steppe, the dust; I did not hear the buzzing
of the flies."
  Is there still an unspoken thought contained in the portrait of
Maša? Čexov expresses it in his own way, at first glance somewhat
confusedly, but actually quite clearly, and the entire set of negations,
of adversative conjunctions, and "somehows" and "for-some-reason-
or-others" and epithets which speak of nothing definite come into
play.

> "I felt strange about her beauty. Maša aroused in me neither de-
> sire nor delight nor pleasure, but a sadness which was heavy even
> though it was pleasant. This sadness was indefinite and vague as
> a night dream. For some reason I felt sorry for myself, for my
> grandfather, for the Armenian and even for the girl, and I had the
> feeling that all four of us had lost something important and necess-
> ary for life which we would never find again"; "I felt sorry for my-

self, and for her and for the Ukrainian . . ."

From this indefinite and vague feeling his own personal sadness is
singled out first: "I was a stranger to her", and then something less
personal: "Rare beauty is accidental . . . and short-lived." But it
is evident that this is not the crux of the matter, for why would one
then pity the Armenian, the grandfather, and the Ukrainian?

For Čexov, beauty is always a living reminder of how beautiful
all human life can and should be; one becomes sad for every person,
including as well someone marked by unusual beauty, because life
is terribly removed from that perfection which sometimes appears
and then hides without a trace. Nadja, the heroine of "The Betrothed",
"for some reason wanted to cry" on that wonderful spring day. Why?
Now the parentheses are opened. That indefinite word (5) is explained: because she, enmeshed in her narrow-mindedness, could
not live as nature did in the spring.

So the epithets "confused", "indefinite", all these "somethings",
"for-some-reasons", "somehows", "nots", "buts", "althoughs",
are connected with the revelation of a very delicate thought. But
this thought, contained in a living image, in a living feeling, is revealed clearly and completely at the final tally.

The style of Čexov's prose is by no means simple and is not at
all rectilinear. His logic is tenacious and flexible, penetrating into
the very labyrinths of being, and his clear thought explains that
which is confused and dim.

Čexov mainly depicted grey life and gloomy people, but with the
whole force of his immense talent he strove toward the beautiful,
to the authentically human, to that which he saw ahead. His work is
penetrated by a search for joy and beauty.

A deep dissatisfaction rings forth in each line he wrote - an angry
consciousness that the life surrounding him was far from beautiful.

NOTES

(1) [From:A. V. Čičerin, Idei i stil' (Moskva, 1968) (2nd ed.), pp.
314-320.]
(2) A.P. Čexov, Polnoe sobranie sočinenij i pisem (Moskva, Goslitizdat, 1948), vol. XIII, pp. 285-286.
(3) Russkie pisateli o jazyke (Leningrad, Sovetskij pisatel', 1954),
p. 666.
(4) [This peculiar pronunciation renders Armenian accent in Russian.]
(5) [In Russian the phrase "for some reason" is rendered by a single
word.]

SELECTED BIBLIOGRAPHY IN ENGLISH

A. ARTICLES

Chizhevsky, D., "Chekhov in the Development of Russian Literature", in Jackson, Robert L., Chekhov. A Collection of Critical Essays (Englewood Cliffs, Prentice Hall, 1967), pp. 49-61.

Conrad, Joseph L., "Čexov's 'The Man in a Shell'; Freedom and Responsibility", Slavic and East European Journal, vol. X, # 4 (1966), pp. 400-410.

_____, "Čexov's 'An Attack of Nerves' ", Slavic and East European Journal, vol. XIII, # 4 (1969), pp. 429-443.

_____, "Čexov's 'Veročka': A Polemical Parody", Slavic and East European Journal, vol. XIV, # 4 (1970), pp. 465-474.

_____, "Unresolved Tension in Čexov's Stories, 1886-1888", Slavic and East European Journal, vol. XVI, # 1 (1972), pp. 55-64.

Curtin, Constance, "Čexov's 'Sleepy': An Interpretation", Slavic and East European Journal, vol. IX, # 4 (1965), pp. 390-399.

Gotman, Sonia, "The Role of Irony in Čexov's Fiction", Slavic and East European Journal, vol. XVI, # 3 (1972), pp. 297-306.

Grossman, Leonid, "The Naturalism of Chekhov", in Jackson, Robert L., Chekhov. A Collection of Critical Essays (Englewood Cliffs, Prentice Hall, 1967), pp. 32-48.

Hagan, John, "The Tragic Sense in Chekhov's Earlier Stories", Criticism, VII, # 1 (Winter, 1965), pp. 52-80.

_____, "Chekhov's Fiction and the Ideal of Objectivity", PMLA, LXXXI # 5 (October, 1966), pp. 409-417.

Harrison, John W., "Symbolic Action in Chekhov's 'Peasants' and 'In the Ravine' ", Modern Fiction Studies, VII, # 4 (Winter, 1961-62), pp. 369-372.

Hoppe, Harry R., "Form in Chekhov's Short Stories", University of California Chronicle, XXXIV, # 1 (1932), pp. 62-67.

Karlinsky, Simon, "Nabokov and Chekhov: The Lesser Russian Tradition", Tri-Quarterly, 17 (Winter, 1970), pp. 7-16.

Lavrin, Janko, "Chekhov and Maupassant", The Slavonic Review, vol. V (June, 1926), pp. 1-24.

Lynd, Robert, "Tchehov. The Perfect Storyteller", in Old and New Masters, T. Fisher Unwin (London, 1919), pp. 171-177.

Mathewson, Rufus, "Afterword", in Anton Chekhov. Ward Six and Other Stories (New York, The New American Library, 1965).

_____, "Intimations of Immortality in Four Čexov Stories", in E. Harkins (ed.), American Contributions to the Sixth International

194

Congress of Slavists. Prague 1968, vol. II. Literary Contributions (The Hague, Mouton, 1968), pp. 261-283.

Matlaw, Ralph A., "Čexov and the Novel", in Eekman, J. (ed.), Anton Čechov, 1860-1960. Some Essays (Leiden, E.J. Brill, 1960), pp. 148-167.

McLean, Hugh, "Čexov's 'V ovrage': Six Antipodes", in E. Harkins (ed.), American Contributions to the Sixth International Congress of Slavists. Prague 1968, vol. II. Literary Contributions (The Hague, Mouton, 1968), pp. 285-305.

Mirsky, D.S., "Chekhov and the English", The Monthly Criterion (1927), # 6, pp. 292-304.

Reeve, F.D., "Tension in Prose: Chekhov's 'Three Years', Slavic and East European Journal, vol. XVI, # 2 (Summer, 1958), pp. 99-108.

Rosen, Nathan, "The Unconscious in Čexov's 'Van'ka' (with a Note on 'Sleepy')", Slavic and East European Journal, vol. XV, # 4 (Winter 1971), pp. 441-454.

Rossbacher, Peter, "Nature and the Quest for Meaning in Chekhov's Stories", Russian Review, XXIV, # 1 (Jan. 1965), pp. 387-392.

Schneider, Elisabeth, "Katherine Mansfield and Chekhov", Modern Language Notes, v. 50, # 6 (1935), pp. 394-397.

Shestov, Leon, "Anton Chekhov: Creation from the Void", in Anton Chekhov and Other Essays (Ann Arbor, The University of Michigan, Michigan, 1966), pp. 3-60.

Struve, Gleb, "Chekhov in Communist Censorship", The Slavonic and East European Review, vol. XXXIII (June, 1955), pp. 327-341.

_____, "On Chekhov's Craftsmanship: The Anatomy of a Story", Slavic Review, XX (October, 1961), pp. 467-476.

B. BOOKS

van der Eng, Jan, Meier, Jan M. and de Valk, Frans, Čexov's Narrative Technique (The Hague, Mouton, to appear).

Friedland, Louis (ed.), Letters on the Short Story, the Drama and other Literary Topics by Anton Chekhov (New York, Benjamin Blom, 1964).

Gerhardi, William, Anton Chekhov. A Critical Study (New York, Duffield and Co., 1923).

Hingley, Ronald, Chekhov: a Biographical and Critical Study (London, Allen and Unwin, 1966).

Kramer, Kark D., The Chameleon and the Dream. (The Image of Reality in Čexov's Stories) (The Hague, Mouton, 1970).

Magarshack, David, Chekhov. A Life (New York, Grove Press, 1952).

Muchnik, Helen, An Introduction to Russian Literature (New York, Dutton, 1964), pp. 192-215.

Nilsson, Nils Åke, Studies in Čexov's Narrative Technique ('The Steppe' and 'The Bishop'.) (= Stockholm Slavic Studies, # 2)

(Stockholm, Almquist and Wiksell, 1968).

Paggioli, Renato, The Phoenix and the Spider (Cambridge, Mass.,
Harvard University Press, 1957), pp. 109-131.

Simmons, Ernest J., Chekhov: A Biography (Boston, Little, Brown
and Co., 1962).

Slonim, Marc, From Chekhov to the Revolution. Cptr. 4 Chekhov
(New York, Oxford University Press, 1962), chapt. IV.

Speirs, Logan, Tolstoy and Chekhov (Cambridge, Cambridge University Press, 1971), pp. 137-182.

Winner, Thomas, Chekhov and his Prose (New York, Holt, Rinehart
and Winston, 1966).

STUDY QUESTIONS FOR STUDENTS

Introduction

1. Characterize briefly each period of XX century Russian literary criticism.
2. Which features are characteristic of the present trend of Soviet literary criticism?

Chapter I

1. What is meant by Čexov's requirement that his readers cooperate with him?
2. Summarize the advice which Čexov offered to novice writers.
3. How do the two versions of "The Fat Man and the Thin Man" differ, and what is the significance of the difference?
4. What did Čexov mean when he compared his readers to a jury?

Chapter II

1. According to Dobin, how does a "detail" differ from a "particular"?
2. What types of 'details' are employed by Čexov?
3. In what respect do Čexov's descriptions present an innovation?

Chapter III

1. What is the significance of the "green spot" in "To Sleep, Sleep ...!"?
2. How is the problem of human happiness related to "the gooseberries"?
3. How did Čexov create the sense of physical space in "The Steppe"?

Chapter IV

1. According to Lakšin, how are Čexov's artistic devices comparable to those of Tolstoj?

Chapter V

1. In what respect were Čexovian beginnings (complications) of his mature stories unusual?
2. How did Čexov use "signposts" in the development of plot?
3. What is particularly characteristic of the denouements in Čexov's mature stories?

Chapter VI

1. According to Pospelov, what is the link between ideological matter

and form in Čexov's short novels?

Chapter VII
1. Which structural elements are particularly significant in "The Man in a Case"?

Chapter VIII
1. What features are characteristic of Čexov's lyrico-dramatic stories?
2. What parallels are at the base of "The Flutterer"?
3. What elements were emphasized by the stylistic changes in the second version of "Anna Around the Neck"?
4. Explain the structure of "Anna Around the Neck".
5. Identify the two types of discourse in "On the Cart", and discuss their essential characteristics.

Chapter IX
1. How do linguistic devices participate functionally in the literary effects of Čexov's stories? Give examples.

Chapter X
1. What is "adversative intonation" and what role does it play in Čexov's style?

General
1. Compare the interpretations of "The Student" in the Introduction and in Chapter I.
2. Compare the treatment of 'details' in Chapters II, III, IV and in the Introduction.
3. Compare the treatment of Čexovian structure in Chapters II, IV, V, and VI.
4. Compare the interpretations of "The Fat Man and the Thin Man" as found in Chapters I and III.
5. Compare the interpretations of "Rothschild's Violin" in Chapters II and III.

AUTHOR-SUBJECT INDEX

INDEX OF CEXOV'S SHORT STORIES